NEPAL IN THE

SOAS Studies on South Asia

NEPAL IN THE NINETIES
Versions of the past, visions of the future

edited by
Michael Hutt

OXFORD
UNIVERSITY PRESS

OXFORD
UNIVERSITY PRESS

YMCA Library Building, Jai Singh Road, New Delhi 110 001

Oxford University Press is a department of the University of Oxford. It furthers the
University's objective of excellence in research, scholarship, and education
by publishing worldwide in

Oxford   New York

Athens   Auckland   Bangkok   Bogota   Buenos Aires   Cape Town
Chennai   Dar es Salaam   Delhi   Florence   Hong Kong   Istanbul   Karachi
Kolkata   Kuala Lumpur   Madrid   Melbourne   Mexico City   Mumbai
Nairobi   Paris   São Paulo   Shanghai   Singapore   Taipei   Tokyo   Toronto   Warsaw

with associated companies in   Berlin   Ibadan

Oxford is a registered trade mark of Oxford University Press
in the UK and in certain other countries

Published in India
By Oxford University Press, New Delhi

First published Oxford University Press 1994
Oxford India Paperbacks 2001

ISBN 019 565 8248

Printed by Pauls Press, New Delhi 110020
Published by Manzar Khan, Oxford University Press
YMCA Library Building, Jai Singh Road, New Delhi 110 001

Dedicated to the memory of
Martin Hoftun
(16. 1. 1964–31. 7. 1992)

CONTENTS

PREFACE TO THE PAPERBACK EDITION

I was surprised when I was informed by Oxford University Press that plans were being laid for a paperback edition of *Nepal in the Nineties*. It is gratifying to know that the book has been appreciated to the extent that it has, particularly in view of the fact that it addresses itself mainly to the events and conditions of the beginning of the decade, and not to the decade as a whole.

I had already submitted a new Preface to the publishers when King Birendra and all of his immediate family were killed in the palace massacre of 1 June 2001, and I have kindly been offered an opportunity to revise my original text taking that unforeseen development into account. However, at the time of writing, this appalling tragedy remains too recent for anyone to attempt an objective assessment even of its human meaning, let alone its broader political implications. With hindsight, it may come to be seen as a watershed; as a moment of catharsis; as the end of something old; as the beginning of something new: but only a fool would attempt to predict which, in the climate of distress and bewilderment that has prevailed to date.

Where did Nepal stand on the eve of this terrible event? What had the legacy been of the political changes of 1990–1? Two further general elections had taken place (one elected a shortlived minority Communist (UML) government and the other a Congress majority), and a range of other political and sociocultural changes had occurred. The potential for some of these—the growth of minority ethnic consciousness, for example—is hinted at in these pages. Other problems—the falling esteem in which the Nepali people would hold their politicians ten years later, for instance—were not really foreseen in the general spirit of optimism which informed our writings soon after the dismantling of the Panchayat system. The emergence of a strong extra-parliamentary Maoist movement and its waging of a 'People's War' against the government, first from 'base areas' in Nepal's western districts and then on many other fronts too, became a matter of increasingly serious concern as the decade drew to its close, particularly as the Nepali Congress government became progressively more dysfunctional. On the other hand, the public discussion of difficult issues in Nepal was more free and frank than it had ever been, and the quality of the Nepali media, in both English and Nepali, had improved dramatically.

Sadly, Martin Hoftun and Richard Burghart are no longer with us; all of us others whose work appears in these pages still take an active and engaged interest in Nepali affairs. To gain a more up-to-date understanding of Nepali politics and political culture since the Jan Andolan of 1990, the reader is directed to *People Politics and Ideology: democracy and social change in Nepal* by Martin Hoftun, William Raeper and John Whelpton (Mandala Book Point, Kathmandu, 1999), and to Louise Brown's *The Challenge to Democracy in Nepal: a political history* (Routledge, London, 1996). The growth of ethnic and identity politics in Nepal is described and analysed in detail in *Nationalism and Ethnicity in a Hindu Kingdom: the politics of culture in contemporary Nepal* edited by David N. Gellner, Joanna Pfaff-Czarnecka and John Whelpton (Harwood Academic, Amsterdam, 1997), and *Domestic Conflict and Crisis of Governability in Nepal*, a collection of papers edited by Dhruba Kumar (Centre of Nepal and Asian Studies, Kirtipur, 2000) is probably the most important analysis of recent political developments.

M. H.

PREFACE

The bloody massacre in Bangladesh quickly covered over the memory of the Russian invasion of Czechoslovakia, the assassination of Allende drowned out the groans of Bangladesh, the war in the Sinai desert made people forget Allende, the Cambodian massacre made people forget Sinai, and so on and so forth until ultimately everyone lets everything be forgotten. In times when history still moved slowly, events were few and far between and easily committed to memory.... Now, history moves at a brisk clip. A historical event, though soon forgotten, sparkles the morning after with the dew of novelty. (Milan Kundera: *The Book of Laughter and Forgetting*, 1978).

The historic events that took place in Nepal in spring 1990 no longer sparkle with the dew of novelty, but they have yet to be forgotten. A broad-based democracy movement succeeded in removing the 28-year-old Panchayat system after a campaign that lasted only six weeks. Seven months later a new constitution was promulgated and, just over a year after the ending of the agitation, the Nepali Congress party secured a majority in a general election. Briefly, before other events elsewhere nudged it out of the headlines, the political situation in Nepal was world news.

Western academic institutions contain a sprinkling of people from a variety of disciplinary backgrounds who take a profound interest in Nepal. In January 1991 a series of weekly talks and seminars, the 'Himalayan Forum', began at the School of Oriental and African Studies in London, as an attempt to strengthen links and promote discussion between the various members of this scattered academic community. During the early months of the Forum, the content of many of the papers that were presented was quite naturally influenced by what had happened in Nepal so recently. Five of the eight essays presented here have grown from Himalayan Forum seminars. Whelpton's analysis of the 1991 general election was specially commissioned for this collection, whereas Hutt's paper on the framing of the constitution was presented to the annual conference of the British Association of South Asian Studies in March 1991 and later published in *Asian Survey* XXXI, 11 (November 1991) and Macfarlane's paper first appeared in *Cambridge Anthropology* XXIV, 1 (1990). I am grateful to the editors of both journals for their permission to include the articles in this volume. I am confident that all the contributors to this book support Seddon's assertion that 'the role of outsiders— whether academics or aid agencies—must be to provide sharper and more critical analysis of the complex and changing situation'.

Prior to 1990, Nepal's international image was one of a traditional, politically unsophisticated, culturally exotic kingdom. Although a small proportion of the population was educated and to some extent politicised, it was generally assumed that this élite's muted dissatisfaction with the Panchayat system was of no great significance when viewed in the context of the nation as a whole. Nepal's Shangri-la image was compromised by the visible poverty of its people, and by political unrest in 1979, but Said's maxim that 'if the Orient could represent itself, it would; since it cannot, the representation does the job, for the West, and *faute de mieux,* for the poor Orient' *(Orientalism* 1978, 1985: 21) still held a measure of truth in relation to Nepal: hence the amazed tone of much media coverage of Nepali politics in 1990.

These eight essays quite naturally include some divergent views on the detail of the political, cultural and social processes at work in Nepal in the 1990s, but they reflect a broad unanimity of opinion based on a combined total of several decades of research. Burghart's analysis of the 'counterfeit reality' of the Panchayat system is echoed in every other essay—and particularly in my own summary of the literary background to the period. Burghart's description of Nepal after the 1980 referendum as having been 'transformed from a partyless democracy to a one-party state that was run by the partyless party' amply demonstrates the contradictions that made the changes of 1990 inevitable. The actual mechanics of the revolution are described by Martin Hoftun, who was present in Kathmandu throughout the spring of 1990. Hoftun's analysis was written quite soon after the events he describes, and his view of the government's essential weakness, and of the importance of the growth of an educated but discontented urban class, gains credence as the months go by.

The democracy movement had been made possible by an understanding between the Nepali Congress party and a coalition of leftist groups; once the movement's aims had been achieved, this understanding came under strain. Considerable uncertainty also surrounded the role of the palace, not least on the part of the palace itself. The mutual suspicion that existed between the three main forces (Congress, communists and palace), with the communists apprehensive that the Congress-dominated interim government would concede too much to royalist elements, was clearly apparent during the series of controversies and fiascoes that eventually produced a new constitution. Rishikesh Shaha's assessment of 'a good constitution that could be better' seems still to be appropriate. The tension between the elected Congress government and the communist-dominated opposition, which Seddon notes in a postscript, heightened during 1992, particularly in the debate over the Tanakpur barrage scheme which, the communists alleged, involved a violation of the constitution. The continued existence of a strong communist movement is one of the features of Nepali politics that puzzles many observers, and the ideological debates that have taken place within this much-splintered movement form a central part of Whelpton's analysis of the general elections of 1991.

Burghart describes the way in which the Panchayat system erected a facade of linguistic and cultural unity for Nepal, and a common theme in several of these essays is the extent to which this facade collapsed after 1990. Cracks first appeared during the drafting of the constitution, in a debate over the question of whether Nepal should remain a Hindu state, and they widened as ethnic, communal and regional interests and grievances were articulated by newly-formed organisations, despite the existence of constitutional safeguards against the splintering of the body politic along ethnic lines. The reassertion of separate ethnic and cultural identities within Nepal has led to a concerted attack on 'Brahmanism' *(bahunvad)* for which Bista's monograph, the basis for Macfarlane's essay, is now a controversial key text.

Despite the euphoria that surrounded the reintroduction of multi-party democracy, views on the political and economic future are mixed. One certainty is that the income generated in the hill regions by service in the Gurkha regiments of the British Army will decline as the century draws to a close. Collett examines these prospects from an authoritative position. More equivocal answers are given to the question of whether the changes are permanent, and whether they will bring tangible economic benefits to the people of Nepal. Hoftun's final statement, suggesting that a 'political comeback by the palace' remains a possibility, may startle some readers, but in my last conversation with him in summer 1992 he refused to rule this out. Macfarlane and Seddon present different analyses of Nepal's present economic plight: Macfarlane discusses Bista's view that many of the kingdom's problems proceed from cultural traits inherent in the dominant higher castes, while Seddon challenges the 'radical pessimism' of earlier analyses, including his own, and clearly sees scope for reform and progress. So our views of Nepal's future are less unanimous than our interpretations of its past—which is surely inevitable and appropriate, when the dew has only recently ceased to sparkle.

Michael Hutt

Chapter 1

THE POLITICAL CULTURE OF PANCHAYAT DEMOCRACY

Richard Burghart

On 16 December 1960 King Mahendra Bir Bikram Shah Deva assumed emergency powers and dismissed the Nepali Congress government that had been elected with a substantial majority only eighteen months earlier. Arguing that parliamentary democracy was alien to Nepalese tradition and fundamentally unsuited for the development of the country, Mahendra also arrested the prime minister, banned all political parties and suspended the constitution. On 8 May the following year a commission was appointed to draw up a draft constitution which was later discussed by the Council of Ministers and approved by the palace. On 16 December 1962 King Mahendra promulgated this new constitution, in which sovereignty was vested in the royal dynasty and powers of state were enjoyed by the king. The king, however, was to be aided and advised in his rule by a national assembly, or *panchayat,* some of whose members were appointed by the king but most of whom were elected indirectly by the people. The new constitution quickly became identified with the institutions of panchayat democracy .

The abolition of parliamentary rule, and the establishment of a national assembly possessing only advisory powers, created a political system in which the king was to lead his people in the development of the country and in which his relations with the citizenry were unmediated by rival interpretations of the popular will: especially those of organised political interests, the now banned political parties. One may interpret variously Mahendra's motives for constitutional change, but his aim to bring about a change in the political culture of the country by constitutional means is incontrovertible. By political culture I mean not the legally constituted body politic as analysed by political scientists, nor Nepalese culture as might be observed by anthropologists, but the sorts of agencies that work through a society, structuring and transforming it, and that are at the same time given in culture. Here one may discern a contradiction in Mahendra's constitutional policy. On the one hand, his argument against parliamentary democracy was that it was alien to the traditional political culture of Nepal. Mahendra's aim was to constitute political relations so that they were in harmony with the traditional order. On the other hand, the 1962 constitution had clearly modern intentions in its aim not to restore, but to create by legal means a Nepalese political culture. In the former case the state is the instrument through which the nation, as agent, expresses its genius and in the latter it is the agent that through legal means builds the nation. Not only is the state simultaneously both cause and means of political action, so also is the nation something that is both given and yet made. One might ask, though, why the traditional political culture had to be made if it already existed? The aim of this paper is to explore the effects of this contradiction and the popular awareness of it during the period of panchayat democracy (1962-1990).

'Nation-Building' Under Panchayat Democracy

The early 19th century European idea that a nation requires a state through which to express its will underlay the 20th century notion of self-determination to which so many third world freedom movements had recourse in delegitimating colonial rule. Many of these newly independent territories, however, were bounded without regard to cultural frontiers and this was felt to pose a problem for young regimes. In constituting a polity, the nation-state was taken as the norm. The nation was the source of legitimacy for a state; that is, it was the 'body' in which sovereignty was vested. Alternatively a nation could only express itself through the institutions of the modern state. With the establishment of numerous multi-ethnic regimes in Africa and Asia in the 1960s it was obvious that the state existed, but not yet the nation. The first task of the state, therefore, was to forge the nation.

The expression 'nation-building' dates from the late 1950s and early 1960s and was largely developed by political scientists and sociologists in America, such as Lucien Pye, Myron Wiener and Karl Deutsch. Nation-building was a process through which European nations had gone, but which now must be passed through quickly in third world regimes, if there was to be political stability in the post-colonial period. In an influential book Lucien Pye (1972) described six crises experienced by young states: the identity crisis (which, if not resolved, leads to ethnic conflict), the legitimation crisis (which, if unresolved, may result in coups d'état), the penetration crisis (whereby the state cannot change people's values and thereby forge the nation), the participation crisis (which, if unresolved, leads to resignation or to antagonism between rulers and national elites), the integration crisis (which culminates in the isolation of the people from the national mainstream) and the distribution crisis (which leads to popular disaffection in the state because it is not providing adequate goods, services and opportunities for the people).

The concept of nation-making, as found in North American academic discourse, quickly passed into Nepalese political discourse, being reworded by the apologists of panchayat democracy as *desa banaune*. Indeed, the concept of nation-building is so central to the 1962 constitution, and to its apologists, that one suspects the framers of the constitution to have already been familiar with it.[1] From Mahendra's proclamation promulgating the constitution of Nepal it is clear that the purported failure of parliamentary democracy was evaluated in terms of the crises of nation-building, crises that only panchayat democracy could resolve.

Whereas, the parliamentary system could not prove suitable on account of the lack of education and political consciousness to the desired extent and on account of its being out of step with the history and traditions of the country and wishes of the people;

Whereas, even the installation of the government elected by the people could not impart to the people a sense of participation in the administration...

Whereas, the country has experienced that the fulfillment of OUR aim, namely to conduct the administration of the country on the basis of popular consent and to achieve the real objective of democracy by associating the people to the maximum extent possible with the administrative system, which is possible only through the medium of the Panchayat system which has its roots in the soil of our country and is capable of growth and development in the climate prevailing in the country.[2]

What, though, was the country? The preoccupation with the national question dates from the Rana period, as do its two answers: that Nepal is the country of the Nepalese people and that Nepal is a Hindu kingdom. Questions of ethnic identity were first raised in the late 1920s. Prior to that time the 'Kingdom of Nepal' was an outsider's designation for what the so-called Nepalese people referred to as the Gorkha Government (*gorkha sarkar*). An attempt by Newars to have their language designated as Nepali (because it was the language of the Nepal valley) led the Gorkha government to rename their mother-tongue, which had previously been known as Parbatiya, Khas or Gorkhali, as Nepali. Furthermore the kingdom began to refer to itself officially as the Kingdom of Nepal, thereby bringing state and territory, people and language together as a single politico-cultural entity. The attempt to create a national religious identity is more difficult to date, but it presumably goes back to at least 1854 when Jang Bahadur Rana promulgated a law of the land, in which the caste systems of the various countries of Nepal (primarily the Tarai, the Hills and the Nepal valley) were brought together to form a single national caste system, thereby implying that Nepal itself was a country.

The ethnic and religious bases of national identity became a more compelling preoccupation in the 1950s when the polity was legally constituted as a democracy, such that issues of political authority were

---

[1] See, for example, Sharma, 1973.
[2] Neupane, 1969: xi.

legitimated with reference to claims about the source of authority in the national culture. Despite ambiguity and conflict over such claims, it was clear that policies had to be legitimated with reference to the will of the people, and this popular will was seen at times to be an ethnic consciousness and at times a religious one. The uniqueness of Nepalese political culture served to legitimate both the state's continuing autonomy in a world of nation-states as well as the appropriateness of the particular form of government in Nepal for national unity and development. In sum, the nation, defined ethnically and religiously, was the enduring particularising consciousness that legitimated the state.

Although there was considerable consensus among all varieties of political opinion for the notion of a Nepalese people, the enforcement of popular unity by the state seemed at times to belie its existence. Nowhere was the forced unity more in evidence than with respect to language policy. According to the 1961 census Nepali was the mother tongue of a bare majority of the population and the *lingua franca* for many non-native Nepali speaking groups in the hills. In the Tarai lowlands of Nepal that constitute 18 per cent of the ground surface and then contained 31 per cent of the population, various regional dialects of Hindi were mother-tongues, with Hindustani as *lingua franca*. Although there was broad agreement in the late 1950s for the perpetuation of Nepali as the official language of the kingdom, there was sharp debate on the role of regional languages in public life, especially in education and in mass communication. Both Congress and leftist parties favoured regional languages. Mahendra, however, favoured Nepali, and shortly after the abolition of parliamentary government he ensured that his views became policy. According to the 1962 Education Act the medium of instruction in all state schools was to be Nepali, and in 1965 Hindi and Newari news broadcasts were terminated on Radio Nepal.[3] The elimination of Hindi was sealed in the 1971 Census when the census commissioners listed the Tarai regional languages as Tharu, Awadhi, Bhojpuri and Maithili. These last three speech communities, which in the Indian census are classified as 'dialects' of Hindi and which therefore swell the number of Hindi speakers, are listed as 'languages' in the Nepalese census such that the number of persons returning Hindi as their mother-tongue became so low that in subsequent censuses Hindi did not need to be officially mentioned as a language spoken in Nepal. The idea 'to each speech community a country' served to legitimate the national autonomy of Nepal but it was a potentially subversive idea when applied within the country to minority languages. In official documents the provinces where minority languages were dominant were referred to as regions (*ksetra,* as in the *maithili ksetra*) rather than as countries (*desa*). By such statistical and rhetorical means Nepali became

---

[3] See Gaige, 1975: 124-5.

the sole language with official status and the people were made one.

Yet if the people were one, then it was in name only. Nepalese citizens from the Tarai were suspected of really being Indian. Despite the fact that migration from the hills to the Tarai dates only from the early 1950s with the eradication of malaria, and that some of the Tarai villages are from archaeological evidence at least a half millennium old, the Maithili, Bhojpuri and Awadhi speakers were suspected of being Indian immigrants. The second class status of Tarai residents was further evidenced in the prospects for government employment. Due to the Tarai's proximity to India the Tarai people count among the most highly educated in the kingdom and therefore among the most qualified for high-ranking posts. Nonetheless only 0.5 per cent of the senior army officers came from the Tarai[4] in 1967. In other branches of national security, such as the police service, the number of plains Hindus and Muslims was completely disproportionate to their percentage of the population. It is clear that Nepalese citizens from the Tarai were not to be entrusted with matters of national security. With other civil service appointments the picture brightens until one reaches higher administrative posts, where once again the Tarai citizens found themselves shut out. In sum, all persons are Nepali, but some are more so than others.

With regard to its religious identity the 1962 constitution defined Nepal as an 'independent, indivisible and sovereign monarchical Hindu state' (I.3.1) and vested sovereignty in the royal dynasty. The problem for the advocates of panchayat democracy was that in some sense the nation had also to be Hindu, if the kingship—as a Hindu kingship—was to have legitimacy. The Nepalese census recorded in 1961 that 88 per cent of the population was Hindu. The figure exaggerates somewhat the numbers, for Hinduised 'tribals' were often recorded as Hindu, rather than as members of their own tribal religion. What sort of Hindu religion this is, however, is not so easy to determine. Among soteriological paths one must speak of Vaishnavite, Shaivite and so on. The word Hindu here has no sense, for it corresponds to no deity with redemptive powers. The caste system is often recognised as being a fundamental Hindu organisation and castes do exist in Nepal. The democratic state, however, does not accord caste an official status. The Nepalese legal code no longer discriminates between castes in matters of employment, adjudication, etc. The state did, however, take upon itself the role of defender of local 'traditions' and prohibited any action that would disturb a citizen's observance of his tradition. In a roundabout way one returns to the caste system being upheld by the state, not as caste but as tradition. This, however, could not be directly stated. That Nepal is officially a Hindu kingdom has nothing to do with caste.

[4] Gaige, 1975: 167.

These few remarks are necessary to underscore the fact that the existence of Nepal as a Hindu kingdom does not gain very much purchase on Nepalese society as described by anthropologists. The importance of Nepal as a Hindu nation appears rather in the way in which the state tried to construct the nation. Hindu kingship was important as a way of constituting relations of intrinsic loyalty between a king and his subjects by virtue of their common religious bond. Furthermore, Hindu kingship enabled Nepal to claim a source of authority that was uniquely Nepalese. In the past there had been good reasons for the derivation of authority from imperial centres of the world: hence Prithvi Narayan Shah sought the title of *behadursam ser* from the Mughals and from the time of Jang Bahadur Rana the title of *chautariya* was reworded as *praim ministar*. After decolonisation, however, the world order was officially egalitarian. Nations derived their political authority from their own past, not from imperial centres of civilisation. One of the local effects of this change in world order was Sanskritisation of titles and offices. With panchayat democracy the *praim ministar* became *pradhan mantri*. Everyone talks about the Tourist Office, but the sign over the door reads *paryatan vibhag*. Mahendra meanwhile removed *behadursam ser* from his list of titles so that it contained nothing that would suggest alien legitimation of his rule.

Another reason for the construction of Nepal as a Hindu country is that it provided the basis for a vision of panchayat democracy as civil society. The notion of civil society took root in Europe in a complex of ideas and experiences. It spoke to the emergent bourgeois life in urban areas and came to serve as a source of authority independent of the monarch. It also set itself up as a solution to the religious wars by making religion a private matter between citizen and god, thereby removing religion from public life. Unlike European democracy, where public order stems from the counterbalancing of conflicting but overlapping private interests, in Nepal public order was defined in terms of unity and represented by the kingship. This Nepalese model of democracy required a particular type of citizen who, according to the government, was none other than the Nepalese person in his cultural character. Krishnamurti, a panegyrist for the panchayat democracy of King Mahendra, wrote:

Does Nepal present two faces, the Hindu and the Buddhist? It is true the people are massively confronted with a choice. But they do not surrender to the inverted ethics of conversion. Philosophy with synthesis fascinates them.[5]

Like good Hindus, the Nepalese people know the higher truth that all is one. Furthermore they put this truth into practice. It is because the

[5] Krishnamurti, 1965: 11

Nepalese are *really* Hindu that there is no ugly communalism in Nepal:

The Hindu and the Buddhist play the perfect gentleman. One can see the heart-warming scene of the Buddhist watching *arati* at Pashupatinath and the Hindu kneeling at Swayambhu. While the din of clichés is heard in the Indo-Gangetic plain, till now Nepal has produced no professional brainwasher.[6]

The location of communalism is appropriate, for India is a secular state in which, for the Nepalese palace, democracy means the unbridled expression of private gain without any thought being given to the public good or to a higher truth. For the Nepalese government secularism promotes pseudo-tolerance, for it is not based on a higher truth. Secular tolerance contrasts with the Hindu form found in Nepal. The Nepalese discussion on communalism situated Hindu tolerance in Nepalese personhood. The Nepalese vision of civil society was seen to derive from the specific ethnic or religious characteristics of the Nepalese nation, which in turn determined the form of the state.

Public and Private Life Under Panchayat Democracy
The constitution guaranteed fundamental *duties and* rights so as to safe-guard a Nepalese vision of civil society. What were the legal structures of public life that served to constitute civil society? The most commonly used term in Nepal, corresponding to the European word public, is *sarkari*. During the period of panchayat democracy the term figures in three different socio-legal contexts: it referred to something belonging to the person of the ruler (his Mercedes), something pertaining to the state (*sarkari* land as state property) and something to which all people had right of access (a *sarkari* tubewell). The legal coherence of the 'personal', the 'state' and the 'common' made sense in a lordly political culture, in which the public domain was personally represented by the sovereign, whose will was executed by his state agents for the common good of an indivisible body politic.

His Majesty's Government legally and ritually represented the body politic. Public order was understood to exist in unity. It follows that private is something that does not speak for the collectivity and can only be countenanced in the public arena when permission has been granted by the government. In common parlance the private was characterised by self-interest *(swarth)*. In European society personal interests are openly expressed in public places, either individually or collectively by political parties and voluntary organisations. Public order is maintained by the counter-balancing of interests. In Nepal, though, public order was defined in terms of unity. Antagonism and conflict of interest could not, therefore, be openly expressed in the king's body politic.

The absence of any expression of disunity in the body politic showed itself in the Nepalese class system, as depicted by the govern-

[6] Ibid.

ment. The class system (which possessed many similarities with the class system in the abortive Rana constitution of 1948), presented the body politic as being made up of five social classes. Each class is made up of those persons who by virtue of their common status or livelihood are thought to share common interests. The five classes were the peasantry, youth, women, workers and ex-servicemen. The constitution made provision for national and local class organisations so that the members of each class could legitimately express their interests. The organisations were supported by government funds, and their national activities were reported in the government press. Particular groups of workers, such as rickshawwalas, or peasants of a particular political persuasion, such as the Maoists, remained from the point of view of the state 'private-interest groups'. This meant that, despite the public claims advanced by these groups, their motivations were deemed by the government to be founded in self-interest. Hence they remained private groups. Since the official classes in Nepal were non-antagonistic, there was no question of the peasants, workers, women and students going on strike.

In a similar vein the underground political parties expressed the self-interest of their leaders, if not the collective self-interest of their followers. Opinion was publicly expressed in newspapers, of which each party, or major faction within a party, had one. These newspapers were considered by the government to be private and because they entered public space they were subject to censorship. By contrast, the public newspapers, *Gorkhapatra* and *The Rising Nepal*, merely announced the sort of information that was appropriate for a state which defined public order in terms of unity. They were read primarily for announcements of jobs, government tenders and the like. For news, the intelligentsia read one or more private newspapers.

As for other 'private' institutions (literary societies, businessmen's clubs, and so on), they were allowed to enter public space only with the prior authorisation of the state. Every local meeting, publication and procession that was not sponsored by a state organisation required government approval. The censorship was often severe, but it must be stressed that state repression aimed not at the control of private minds but at the public expression of the private. During periods of social unrest, democratic activists were rarely arrested by local police so long as they remained in their homes; rather they were arrested as soon as they entered the public space of the market.

In concluding this section, one might mention one of the more remarkable aspects of panchayat democracy: namely, the role of the state in serving the public. It is commonplace in the sociological literature to maintain that the modern state claims a monopoly in the legitimate use of force, but in Nepal the state also claimed a monopoly in the legitimate expression of public service. Hardly a day would go by without some member of the royal family or some cabinet minister being depicted in the government press opening a bridge, dam, school, hospital, seminar on national development, etc. Political parties would try to contend this very point with the government forces. For example, the student union at one of the campuses of Tribhuvan University, being run by one of the underground parties, would organise a clean-up of the town. The students would meet inside the campus and go on procession throughout the town cleaning up rubbish from the roadside. The local police would then be in a quandary. Should they arrest the students, in which case they would say that the government is so opposed to public health that when a group of students decide to clean up the town they are arrested. Or should they not arrest the students, in which case the students would then say that the government is so negligent in its responsibility to maintain public health that honest citizens like themselves have to do the work instead. Interestingly in such cases the police invariably arrested the students. The state preserved its privilege to serve the public. This service was carried out by the king, or persons acting in the name or with the authority of the king.

Public Life as Counterfeit Reality

A constitution enables persons to act in a political system by defining the criteria for their participation and the rules for decision-making. These criteria and rules are constitutive in the sense of the word as found in speech act theory[7]. Constitutive rules determine the very behaviour that they regulate. That is, they define the behavioural forms and describe what will be recognised as a particular type of behaviour. Games, such as chess, are constituted by such rules: e.g. the king moves one step at a time in any direction, 'check' is when the king's movement in a direction is prevented by an opposing piece, 'checkmate' is when all the king's potential movements are in check, 'checkmate' means loss of game and end of play. A constitution also contains regulative rules, that is rules that regulate behaviour that is independent from the rule. As a speech act, the rules of etiquette take the form of regulative rules.

Constitutions are normally composed of laws, some of which are constitutive and others regulative. For example, those provisions that define who is a citizen (II.7) and who may become a citizen (II.8) are constitutive in character; those provisions that define the fundamental duties and rights of citizens are regulative (III.9-16). Both constitutive and regulative rules define areas of legitimate political action, but they create different sorts of relationships between state and society. Regulative rules regulate behaviour that exists independently of the state; constitutive rules regulate behaviour that is determined by the

[7] Searle, 1969: 33-42.

constitution and enforced by the state. In both cases the aim of the constitution is to create a certain political culture, both in constituting a
person as a citizen and in protecting the citizen in the exercise of his
rights.

It is in the character of the modern state to have something fictional
about it, for constitutive rules create legal fictions that entitle persons
to act within the polity. A society does not necessarily work by constitutive rules, but it must do if it is to work with the modern state. There
is, however, in all rule-governed systems an inevitable gap between the
system and how the system 'really' works. In Nepal the fiction began
with the referendum. After the 1979 public disturbances, in which university students played a prominent role, King Birendra agreed to hold
in the following year a referendum on the 1962 constitution. This was
won by the panchayat side, but only by 2.4 to 2 million votes, and
with all major towns in the opposition camp. Nonetheless Birendra was
able to claim popular legitimacy for panchayat democracy. The 1962
constitution was retained, but in line with an announcement made in
the run-up to the referendum, the system was modified to allow direct
elections by universal suffrage to the National Assembly and to make
ministers responsible to the assembly rather than to the king. Direct
elections made it easier for groups within the legislature to appeal for
support in the country at large, and the factionalism among panchas
which had occurred even under the unreformed system was intensified.
Moreover, the fact that the political parties were able to mobilise the
electorate for the multi-party vote in the referendum meant that,
although being 'illegal', they were nonetheless tolerated within limits
by the state. Both the factionalism among the panchas and the tolerance
by the state of the political underground created a half-real political
world where things were not what they seemed.

By having to fight against political parties to win the referendum,
the 'Panchas'—that is to say, the local leaders who were reputedly
above party politics—had to fully immerse themselves in it. By fighting against the collectively organised parties, the Panchas became effectively a political party of partyless people and Nepal was transformed
from a partyless democracy to a one-party state that was run by the
partyless party. Meanwhile, despite their illegal status, Congress and
various leftist groups were able to operate fairly openly within the
country. Congress boycotted the 1981 and 1986 general elections,
objecting to the requirement that all candidates be members of one of
the 'class organisations' set up under the panchayat system and to the
ban on standing avowedly as the representative of a party. It did,
however, field candidates (as partyless individuals) in the 1987 local
elections and won a number of seats, including the mayorship of
Kathmandu. The duly elected party members, however, were later
removed from office by the government upon their refusal to take part

in public processions on 16 December. This was the day when, from the government's point of view Mahendra gave (panchayat) democracy to the people, and when, from the parties' point of view the government took (parliamentary) democracy away. Meanwhile, some leftist groups campaigned in the national elections, and managed to return candidates in a few cases where their network of activists was particularly strong, as in the Bhaktapur constituency in 1981 and 1986 and Chitwan in 1986. In the minds of the Nepalese intelligentsia the work of the political parties had become an 'open secret' and the hidden work of the state revealed that public life was a 'counterfeit reality'.

The fiction became morally bankrupt in the 1980s when corruption scandals caused growing discontent even among liberal supporters of the panchayat system and the private newspapers took on the self-appointed task of exposing the 'real' workings of the panchayat system. The exposures of the private newspaper *Saptahik Bimarsha* that the consti—tutional process was being manipulated behind the scenes by an 'underground gang' with palace connections gained considerable plausi-bility after an assassination attempt on its editor. The politics of expo-sure inverted public/private relations, as defined by the state, by playing on the distinction between the inner and the outer in the body politic. The 'private' newspapers revealed the inner workings of the government, the 'cover-ups' that the government wanted to keep from public knowledge. In so doing, these newspapers hoped to deprive the government of its moral authority to rule. Their criticism could be directed at all government personnel up to the office of Minister. The royal family, however, could not be criticised, for in this lordly political culture the law of treason did not distinguish between treason against the state and personal criticism of the king. In sum, the private newspapers censured the government by exteriorising (making public, as it were) their knowledge of the inner workings of the system. Meanwhile the government, acting in defence of public unity, censored the private press. The journalists, however, were often courageous and enterprising. It happened not infrequently that editors were arrested because of critical reports and that the same editors, after they had been released, published their paper under a different name, which they had already registered before their arrest as a precautionary measure.

The activities of the private press, in exposing the 'real' workings of the panchayat system, became critical in the 1980s, for throughout the latter decade the panchayat system itself became more and more a coun-terfeit reality. By this is not meant that it lacked popular legitimacy (for it obviously had supporters) or that it was ineffective (or, at least, any more so than parliamentary democracy), but rather that the inevitable disjunction between the rules that govern a system and the way in which the system actually works had become so great that the structures of panchayat democracy began to acquire a fictional character. These

structures set up institutions of representation whereby public opinion
could be expressed and brought to bear upon official decision-making.
Politically active people, however, had their expression of opinion constantly subverted by institutions of control. In 1985 during the
Congress *satyagraha* campaign the prisons of Nepal literally overflowed
with prisoners of conscience. Meanwhile the judgement of the people,
to whom both panchayat members and the political parties appealed,
was constantly corrupted or subverted by electoral shenanigans, such as
the purchase of votes and booth capture.

In 1989 the dramatic changes in eastern Europe not only encouraged
hopes among Nepalese political activists generally, but also led some
of the Nepalese communist factions to reassess their view of 'bourgeois
democracy' and to consider cooperation with the Congress party. At a
Nepali Congress conference in Kathmandu in January 1990, plans were
announced for a Movement for the Restoration of Multi-Party
Democracy to be launched on 18 February, the anniversary of the 1951
establishment of the interim government after the overthrow of the
Rana regime. The United Left Front (ULF), an alliance of seven
communist groups established early in the month, joined with
Congress in organising the campaign. The rest, as they say, is history.

Conclusion

Scholars and opposition politicians refer to the events of 16
December 1960 as the 'royal coup', but those events were in
themselves true to the original sense, that is the pre-modern sense, of
the word revolution. The Glorious Revolution referred not to the
beheading of Charles I nor to the establishment of parliamentary
sovereignty, but to the accession of Charles II to the throne and the
restoration of kingship. Revolution meant the restoration of the old,
everpresent order. Mahendra's 'royal coup' was truly a revolution in this
original sense of the term, for it saw itself as restoring two fundamental
institutions of Nepalese polity, without which there was neither unity
nor growth: the kingship and the panchayats. As for unity, however—
both national unity and the unity of public opinion—these were
constructed and enforced by the state. And as for growth, throughout
this period Nepal's position among the least developed nations remained
unchanged.

A contradiction lay at the heart of the 1962 constitution. The constitution was portrayed by Mahendra as a 'gift' to the Nepalese people, but
with the unlikely proviso that the king could resume the gift or make
amendments to it from time to time. The one thing that makes a trans-
action a gift is, of course, that it cannot be reclaimed; and in this very
'it is but it isn't' lies the contradiction that lay at the heart of panchayat
democracy. On the one hand, the people received a gift which enabled
them to act, to enter into action with the king in determining political

decisions in a form of democracy whose structures were democratic, even though the balance of power was weighted in favour of the palace. On the other hand, the king could revoke everything. Behind the system of democratic representation lay a system of control by the palace. The fate of such regimes, as in the case of Gorbachev's rule in the former Soviet Union, is often short-lived, usually reverting to either a system of control or of representation. In the case of Nepal twenty-eight years went by before multi-party democracy was restored.

REFERENCES

Census of Nepal, 1961. Kathmandu, His Majesty's Government.

Census of Nepal, 1971. Kathmandu, His Majesty's Government.

Gaborieau, Marc, 'Les rapports de classe dans l'idéologie officielle du Népal.' In Jacques Pouchepadass (ed.) *Caste et Classe en Asie du Sud,* (Collection Purusartha, 6) Paris, 1982.

Gaige, Frederick H., *Regionalism and National Unity in Nepal.* Berkeley and Los Angeles, 1975.

Neupane, P., *The Constitution and Constitutions of Nepal.* Kathmandu, 1969.

Proclamations, Speeches and Messages of His Majesty King Birendra. 2nd ed. Kathmandu, 1977.

Pye, Lucien, *Aspects of Political Development.* Boston, 1966.

Searle, John R., *Speech Acts: an Essay in the Philosophy of Language.* Cambridge, 1969.

Sharma, Khagendra Nath, *The Panchayat System in Nepal.* Kathmandu, 1973.

Chapter 2

THE DYNAMICS AND CHRONOLOGY OF THE 1990 REVOLUTION

Martin Hoftun

The title of this article suggests an in-depth analysis of political events in Nepal during the spring of 1990 but, because these events are still so recent, it is difficult to obtain the distance from the material required for such an analysis. Many important sources will only be available at a later stage. Therefore, this is not an historical treatise. It is largely a description of political events seen through the eyes of one witness. To a lesser degree it is a preliminary attempt to analyse material about these events based on interviews and newspaper reports. It is perhaps necessary to emphasise that the perspective is largely limited to Kathmandu. I shall begin with a blow-by-blow account of the actual events. I will then try to answer two main questions: what actually happened? and why did it happen? In my conclusion, I will try to place what happened in Nepal into the international context of political change and democratic revolutions. The period covered is from January to December 1990. Though the revolution itself took place between 18 February and 9 April, the periods before and after these dates are crucial for an understanding of the forces behind the events.

The Panchayat System
Since the late King Mahendra toppled Nepal's first elected government in December 1960, the centre of political power in the country has been in the palace. The absolute monarchic nature of this rule, however, was never officially acknowledged. Two years after the royal coup, when King Mahendra introduced the Panchayat system, the concept of guided democracy figured prominently in many 'third world' countries. The Panchayat system was said to be based on 'grassroots'or village democracy, and the idea was one of a gradual development towards fully-fledged democracy at the national level.

When King Mahendra overthrew the Congress government in 1960, he promised that he would 'introduce a democracy more suited to the conditions of Nepal'. In practice, the Panchayat system functioned mainly as a tool by which power could be exercised from above. A characteristic of the Panchayat system was its fragmentation of power into several parallel governmental structures. The parliament, including the cabinet, was one of these structures. Another was represented by half a dozen class organisations based on the idea of corporate political

power. A third structure was the palace secretariat and the other bodies
functioning inside the royal palace. In addition there came institutions
established by the king at a later stage and legalised through constitutional amendments. These included the Back to the Village National
Campaign and the Panchayat Policy and Evaluation Committee. The
Back to the Village National Campaign was introduced in the mid-six-
ties, became a part of the constitution in 1975, and was abolished in
1980. Inspired by the Chinese cultural revolution, it was set up to
strengthen involvement in politics at grassroots level. In practice, however, it strengthened palace control over the electorate and became popularly known as Nepal's politbureau. The Panchayat Policy and
Evaluation Committee was set up after the national referendum in
1980, to implement the political reforms promised by the king. In
practice this merely replaced the Back to the Village National
Campaign, and became equally unpopular.

The word *panchayat* refers to the village council which was, in principle, the backbone of the system. In reality the system was a mixture
of bits and pieces from very different settings. One of these was the
vague idea of a Hindu kingdom. Another principle which more than
anything else characterised the panchayat philosophy was that of a non-
party system, expressed through a constitutional ban on all political
parties. The lifting of this ban was the main objective of the political
opposition throughout the panchayat period, and was also the basic goal
of the 1990 democracy movement. This movement was not directed
primarily against the king, but against the Panchayat system which
institutionalised the king's absolute power. To the opposition, the
system symbolised the misrule and corruption of the old regime. It was
therefore a conscious strategy among the opposition leaders to attack
the political system rather than the monarchy. They wanted to take
away the king's political power without harming him as a symbol of
national unity.

The Political Context
To understand what happened in Nepal during the first months of 1990
one needs to know the general situation in the country at the end of
1989. The leaders of both the Nepali Congress party and the communist
parties seemed fairly confident that this was the time to launch a new
movement which would be successful. The unsuccessful *satyagraha*
movement of civil disobedience, which came to an abrupt end with the
explosion of four bombs at various places in the country on 20 June
1985, was still fresh in their memories. The scenery had changed very
much during the four and a half years which had passed since then. For
the first time the communists and the Congress showed a willingness
to join hands in a united struggle. Since 1980 a new group of
intellectuals had come to the political forefront in Kathmandu and other

cities. The appearance of this new intelligentsia was most evident in the
formation and rapid growth of several human rights organisations. The
membership of these organisations consisted to a large degree of young
professionals with no previous affiliation to the banned political
parties. In the Kathmandu valley the existence of this new political
force was evident in the strong support given to Padma Ratna Tuladhar.
Elected to the Rashtriya Panchayat (National Assembly) from the
Kathmandu constituency, he was continuously using his post to criticise the system. As a populist leader, he represented and symbolised
this new group of politicised intellectuals. A writer and editor belonging to the Newar community of the Kathmandu valley, Tuladhar defined
himself as an independent leftist.

Late 1989 was also characterised by economic hardship caused by the
trade embargo which India had imposed on Nepal on 23 March. During
the first few months of the embargo, the Nepali people had accepted the
difficulties brought upon them by this crisis with remarkable patience.
But discontent grew as the crisis lingered on, and as prices rose. This
may have been the main reason for the opposition leaders to decide that
the time was ripe to launch a movement against the government. They
actively played this card throughout their struggle, heavily criticising
the government for its inability to solve the problem. At the same time
they expected that the general discontent would work in their favour
when they launched their movement.

Toward the end of the year the official media clearly reflected the
government's concern about the situation. The government newspapers
The Rising Nepal and *Gorkhapatra* were full of articles defending the
ruling political ideology, and government rallies in support of the ruling system were organised every week in various parts of the country.
At the same time, prominent members of the governing elite openly
criticised the government in a manner never heard before. A high degree
of defeatism and internal dissent was evident in the old regime. As a
final factor there came the revolutions in eastern Europe, fully displayed
on TV screens in the homes of Kathmandu citizens. Events in Romania
made a particularly strong impression, and the fall of Ceausescu very
soon became a major part of the rhetoric of Nepali opposition leaders.

The Build-Up to the Revolution
Between 1 January and 18 February 1990, tension grew in the
Kathmandu valley. The opposition displayed its new-found unity on 10
January when it announced the formation of a United Left Front uniting
seven communist factions, and joined the Nepali Congress party in the
Movement for the Restoration of Democracy. On 18 January the still
banned Nepali Congress held its first public party convention in ten
years, gathering a big crowd (which included several prominent Indian
politicians) in the centre of Kathmandu. This was the first real show of

opposition muscle. To general amazement, the police did not intervene, and the leaders could openly present their plans for a movement which would start on Nepal's official 'Democracy Day', 18 February. Activity also increased on the government side. A major government rally was organised in Kathmandu on 28 January and the number of arrests increased. In the morning of 14 February all the main leaders of the opposition were either imprisoned or put under house arrest, and telephone lines in the capital were disconnected.

From the day the movement began up until 30 March was a period of steady struggle. A series of demonstrations and strikes was organised in Kathmandu and other urban areas. Several times these resulted in confrontations between police and demonstrators, and on some occasions people were injured and killed. As government suppression increased, the populations of the cities showed a more stubborn defiance, displaying new forms of protest, such as voluntary blackouts at certain times in the evenings, silent marches, and the public burning of various symbols of the regime. There was a steady increase in the involvement of various professional associations such as the Medical Association, the Bar Association, teachers' associations etc. Apart from the revolt in Bhaktapur, which had already begun on 19 February, one could not describe the political conflict in Nepal at this stage as a mass uprising, though the open, broad-based opposition to the government was unique in the history of Nepal and focused the world's attention on Nepali politics. Nevertheless, the general impression was that the struggle could last for a long time. On 30 March the situation changed dramatically when the unrest in Bhaktapur spread to Patan. Police opened fire against demonstrators and several were killed. This display of violence just a few miles from the centre of the capital was probably the main reason for the struggle turning into a mass uprising in the Kathmandu valley. Within a couple of days the populations of Kirtipur and Patan had seized control of their city centres. The police kept safely outside the trenches and barricades which blocked the entrances to both towns. Behind the barricades a celebratory mood existed among the largely Newar population. In the following days the remaining professional associations, including civil servants and employees of Royal Nepal Airlines, organised strikes in support of the movement. The general strike in Kathmandu on 2 April was a considerable success.

The Climax

At the same time the top level of government showed the first signs of wavering. The foreign minister, Shailendra Kumar Upadhyaya, resigned in protest at government repression, and on 1 April there was a major reshuffle of the cabinet, though the prime minister still retained his position. However, it was only a matter of days before he too had to leave. On the morning of 6 April, the king announced the formation of a new cabinet under the leadership of Lokendra Bahadur Chand, due to the Shrestha ministry's failure to maintain law and order. The king also announced that the new cabinet was to start talks with leaders of the political parties, and form an investigation committee to study the recent incidents of violence. With this, the king had finally broken his long silence, but the main question that morning was whether the royal proclamation had come too late. The events of this day, 6 April, were remarkable, though further research is necessary to establish what actually happened, and how crucial these events were to the outcome of the whole revolution.

After the royal proclamation on Radio Nepal the populations of Patan and Kirtipur marched on the capital and joined with a huge crowd of Kathmandu citizens. During the first hours of the day the general mood of the demonstrators seems to have been joyous, and the meeting in the open air theatre on Tundikhel, the parade ground in the centre of Kathmandu, took the form of a celebration of an already obtained victory. But at a certain point the behaviour of the masses changed. Their joyous mood turned into anger against the government and slogans were now directed personally against the king and queen. From the parade grounds a part of the crowd moved towards the palace where the police and the military finally took action and killed more people than on any previous day during the movement. Most of the questions connected with the events of 6 April are still unanswered. Why did the mood of the masses change, and what made them decide to move towards the palace, a move that would obviously end in a disaster? Did they react to police provocation, or did they follow a call given by the extreme leftist Mashal party, who were the organisers of this rally?

A curfew was imposed in the Kathmandu valley the next morning. Had this not happened, control of the movement might have gone out of the hands even of the party leaders. After two days of uncertainty and tension, the population was probably more inclined to celebrate than to continue its struggle when the news of the lifting of the ban on political parties was announced in the late evening of 8 April . During these two days a truce had been reached between the party leaders and the king. Future historians may ask whether this came about as a result of an acceptance of common interest by the two parties, both of whom feared that they would lose control.

The Aftermath

The next period began with celebrations of the newly-found freedom on 9 April, and ended when the king dissolved the remaining structures of the Panchayat system on the recommendation of the new prime minister. This was a period of consolidation of power for the leaders of the Nepali Congress and the United Left Front. The only concession the king had given on 9 April was to delete a small paragraph from the panchayat constitution. By 7 May a new interim government had been formed which exercised, at least in principle, more power than any government in Nepal since Jang Bahadur Rana in the middle of the last century. But the main challenge to the new leaders during this period was not to obtain concessions from the king. Immediately after the new interim government had been installed a series of violent incidents occurred in the capital. This crisis in law and order was eventually surmounted, but at one point it was far from certain that the new leaders would be able to survive.

The interim cabinet under the leadership of Krishna Prasad Bhattarai may have been the most powerful government for over one hundred years, but it did not seem to exercise these powers. In the months which followed the revolution a wave of strikes swept over the country. Employees of all sectors, including those working for the government, put forward both reasonable and unreasonable demands. Relay hunger-strikes, the occupation of government offices, and *gheraus,* (encircling a person and thus publicly humiliating him), became daily events. Though the government had been able to curb the disturbances in Kathmandu, it was not able to enforce law and order in the rest of the country. There were repeated reports of violence from outlying districts, and to many villagers the word for democracy, *prajatantra*, became synonymous with crime.

The strikes and unrest did not come as a total surprise to the new government. More unexpected than these was the religious conflict which came to the forefront just after the revolution. The main political controversy during the first three months after the revolution centred on the question of religion in the new constitution, and on whether Nepal should be declared a secular state or continue to be a Hindu kingdom. The biggest demonstration between the actual revolution and the constitutional crisis in late October was organised by the Nepal Buddhist Association on 30 June to demand a secular state. This period also saw the birth of several political parties of a regional and ethnic character. All these trends flourished in the power vacuum which existed immediately after the revolution, but the general state of unrest continued and even increased throughout the autumn months.

Despite the fluid situation the Nepali Congress steadily strengthened its position at the centre of the Nepali power structure. The period from August to November was characterised by a quest for normalisation by the Nepali Congress. The promulgation of the new constitution on 9 November was the final proof of prime minister Krishna Prasad Bhattarai's success in establishing good relations with the king. The Nepali Congress moved slowly towards the old centres of power, and the steady flow of former *panchas* (members of the old regime) into the party resulted in the Congress old guard gradually being outnumbered.

Underlying Causes of the Revolution
This account reflects how the revolution and the period immediately
after were experienced by one witness. Obviously, many factors have
not been included, and the description might be biased, or even incorrect
in places due to the lack of precise information. It will only be possible
to measure the importance of all these incidents in retrospect, and there
are more questions than answers concerning what actually happened in
the spring of 1990. Countless answers are found to the most simple
questions. How many were killed? Who killed them? What happened on
which day? It is almost impossible to come up with answers to more
difficult questions, such as who actually exercised power in the old
regime and even in the new; or about the precise role of India in the
revolution; or the level of mass support the democracy movement
actually enjoyed.

To answer the question of what actually happened, only a few very
general points can be made in a definite manner. These are: (1) The
revolution was not caused by only one major factor, but by the interplay of several important elements. (2) One of these combinations was
that of a planned movement and an unexpected mass uprising in the
Kathmandu valley. (3) There was a favourable environment for such a
movement both externally and internally. Local discontent caused by
the Indian trade embargo coincided with the international wind of
democracy caused by the East European revolutions only a few months
earlier. Despite the difficulty of obtaining precise and reliable information about the revolution, I will try to analyse some of the events.
Having summarised the main events of the revolution, and its immediate background, I will now turn to the more general political, historical,
and cultural setting and try to explore some of the underlying causes.
The main question I would like to answer is: why did the revolution
take place at this point in time, and in this manner?

Government Weakness
Several perspectives may be helpful in answering this. First, I will
focus my attention on the role played by the old regime. In his description of the eastern European revolution Timothy Garton Ash[1] distin-
guishes between what he calls the 'pull' and the 'push' effects. He
writes that the recent political changes in Hungary may best be
described as a 'refolution'. By this he means that what really caused the
changes in Hungary was the fact that the 'old regime' on its own initiative pulled back from positions of power, not that the popular push
increased to such an extent that the government could no longer hold
back. Narrowly applied to Nepal, this was not the case. The push of the
opposition was certainly the driving force in the democracy movement.
But even so, there is a strong case for pointing out the importance of a

[1] Timothy Garton Ash, *We the People*. Cambridge, 1990.

weak government. The outcome of the movement might have been very different had there been a strong and determined government led by a central panchayat figure of a certain stature and strength. The prime minister at this time, Marich Man Singh Shrestha, had been installed in 1986 through the direct intervention of the palace. The main objective seemed to be to appoint a new prime minister who could be trusted, someone totally loyal to the rule of the palace. There are strong indications that the prime minister sought advice and blessings from the palace throughout his premiership, even for minor decisions.

Just before the democracy movement began, the king left the capital for his annual tour of the country's development regions, this time making Pokhara in western Nepal his base. He did not return until the very last stages of the revolution. To inaugurate the new airport building in Kathmandu on the first day of the movement, 18 February, he flew directly from Pokhara, to which he returned, without even going into Kathmandu town. There are therefore certain indications of a conscious strategy on the part of the palace to leave the prime minister on his own when he most needed support and advice in his dealings with the democracy movement. From this perspective it is easy to understand that the prime minister and his colleagues lost their nerve. The violent suppression of the democracy movement might also be seen in a different light, more as a sign of government weakness than as proof of its strength. The 'atrophy of the old regime', however, was evident much earlier on. In November 1989 the government, threatened both by internal dissent and external opposition, started a major propaganda campaign. Every day the headlines of the government newspaper, *Gorkhapatra,* carried some reference to the attributes of the political system, such as: 'The Panchayat system—true democracy' and 'Nationalism, democracy, and unity—the pillars of panchayat polity'. This had never happened before, not even in 1962, when the system was first introduced. Vocabulary which had previously been reserved for special occasions, such as speeches in connection with the celebration of Democracy Day or other national holidays, was now in daily use.

Subsequently, the outward signs of flaws in the government's self-confidence probably boosted the confidence of the opposition, and made it even more determined to launch its movement. Therefore, though there was no conscious pulling-back from positions of power, the government's behaviour did indirectly facilitate and accelerate the movement of the opposition.

The Problem of Information

While dealing with the role of the government in connection with the revolution in Nepal there is one level where the question of information is crucial: an aspect not usually thought of. There is a point at which a policy of controlled information backfires. From a general perspective this might be called the information problem of a dictator in a censored society. Everyone was aware that all information was censored and distorted before reaching the masses. But it still remains an open question how much information reached the ruler, in this instance the king. How much did the king actually know?

From the events of 1979, the last period of major political unrest in Nepal, we know that the king only intervened directly when the masses had reached the Durbar Marg, the street in front of the palace. After seeing with his own eyes the discontent of the masses he acted immediately and announced a national referendum: a very radical measure. Finding parallels from the Rana period, several political commentators in Nepal have described the position of the king as that of a prisoner, the prison walls being the group of people surrounding His Majesty and constantly feeding him with coloured, biased, and sometimes totally false information. But this information problem alone cannot explain the silence of the king during the period of the democracy movement. There are indications that the king actually was aware of what happened, and that his silence was a conscious political act. Even so, the king probably did not realise the seriousness of the crisis. It remains an open question whether the king himself or other figures inside the walls of the palace were responsible for the long silence, and whether an announcement of political reform could have turned the events into what Burk calls a 'revolution prevented'.

Internal Factors
Now, turning from the role played by the government, I will look more closely at the ingredients of the political movement itself, and at what made it successful. In contrast to previous campaigns led by the banned political parties, what was it that enabled this particular political movement to topple the government? The political events of 1990 may be seen as the coming together of several completely different forces. In this perspective it might be more correct to talk about several movements and not only one, or rather, one actual revolution and several potential revolutions. What happened in 1990 was the coming together of three different dimensions. First of all we have the core of the democracy movement, which I will call 'the quest for political participation'. A fatal combination of economic and educational development on the one hand with a lack of political reform on the other, erupted into open revolt. Only in 1990 did the social effects of development reach such a level that society was ready for a revolt. It was no longer possible for the bureaucracy to absorb all the newly-educated people, the main method used thus far by the government to neutralise political discontent. The educated sector of the population with economic and political aspirations had grown big enough to become a threat to the regime.

External Factors
Second comes the external aspect: Nepal's relations with India and
China, which have always been decisive factors for the outcome of
political movements inside the country. Since the royal takeover in
1960, the main principle of Nepal's foreign relations had been to
exploit the enmity between China and India, and (at least on paper) to
retain an equally friendly relationship with both neighbours. This
policy guaranteed a certain freedom of action inside the country. The
Panchayat system was, therefore, dependent on maintaining this
external equilibrium. With the slow normalisation in Sino-Indian
relations during 1988-89 this Nepali equilibrium became weaker, and it
finally broke down with the Indian trade embargo against Nepal in
March 1989. It is from this perspective that one must view India's role
in the democracy movement. It is too early to determine the importance
of Indian involvement, but I believe this was more crucial than it at
first appeared. Some political leaders in India declared their support for
the Nepali democracy movement at an early stage. Most remarkable was
the presence of Chandra Shekhar (then Janata Dal leader) at the Nepali
Congress convention in Kathmandu on 18 January. Of course, the
Nepali government tried to exploit his presence for its own benefit and
tried unsuccessfully to turn popular anti-Indian sentiment against the
democracy movement.

Throughout the revolution Indian politicians seemed to be divided
over how to deal with the political situation in Nepal. The V.P. Singh
government officially supported the democracy movement only at a
very late stage. There are strong indications that the Indian government
tried to make use of the weak position of the Nepali government to
impose a new trade treaty on Nepal which was more favourable to India.
There are even those who believe that the split among Indian politicians
did not reflect a real disagreement, but was rather a conscious strategy to
exploit the volatile political situation in Nepal. In an interview, the
former prime minister Marich Man Singh Shrestha said: 'The Indian
government is not interested in political stability in Nepal'. An extreme
view among certain politicians in Nepal is that the whole democracy
movement was staged by India and should have been dealt with simply
as an act of Indian interference.

Communalism
A third dimension of the revolution was one of ethnic and religious
conflict. Though it only came into the open after the revolution, I
believe that it was fundamental to the success of the democracy movement. What happened during the last stage of the uprising and in the
period after the revolution reflected a gradual growth of religious and
ethnic consciousness during the last years of the Panchayat regime, and
growing opposition to the ideology of a Hindu state. The uprisings in

Patan and Bhaktapur during the last days of the revolution were not only a result of a high level of political consciousness in these areas: they also reflected a strong sense of Newar identity. This can be seen in the political ideas of two central leaders, the populist leader in Bhaktapur, Narayan Man Bijukche, and the communist leader from Patan, Tulsi Lal Amatya: 'communist ideas of equality go hand in hand with a Buddhist concept of compassion and of the righteous Newar king'.

However, events in Patan and Bhaktapur during the last stage of the revolution did not take the form of a communal uprising. The political goals were solely of a general and national character. Movements of a more clearly ethnic and communal character emerged just after the revolution. The *madeshis,* the people of the Tarai, were the first communal grouping to form a political party. This was followed by the formation of several political parties representing the interests of the Tibeto-Burmese population. Parties were even formed to fight for the least privileged groups in Nepali society such as the Tharus, the Tamangs, and the Hindu artisan castes. Only the movement of the Tarai people had historical traditions: all the others were new features in Nepali politics. This ethnic dimension is the unintended irony of the revolution, most evident in the Newar uprising in the Kathmandu valley. The high-caste leaders of the democracy movement were totally dependent on the masses to succeed, but mass support took the form of an ethnic uprising. This interplay between high-caste leadership and a minority ethnic response became an internal contradiction of the democracy movement. The Brahman and Chhetri leaders of the Congress and the communist parties wanted democracy, but by their mere leadership they upheld the political dominance of an elite.

Historical Comparisons

Historically, it is of interest to compare the 1990 revolution with that of 1951. The parallels are obvious: connections between internal and external factors are evident in both events. The 1951 revolution happened in an international era of decolonisation, Indian independence preceding it by only three years. The 1990 revolution happened in an era of democratisation, preceded by democratic revolutions in eastern Europe in late 1989.

The role of India was crucial in both revolutions, though probably more important in that of 1951. Many of the main leaders of the 1951 revolution were also leaders of, or actively involved in, the 1990 democracy movement. But the most important similarity between these two events is the power vacuum which followed immediately after the upheaval, leading to similar forms of unrest. How far one wants to draw these parallels is also a question of choice. Does one want to emphasise the uniqueness of Nepali politics, or is the question of modernisation and development more important? Writers on Nepali politics often seem to choose only one of these options. On one side are those who stress points of continuity and uniqueness: Nepali politics are described as something fundamentally different from political life in the West, and history is seen to be repeating itself. On the other side are those who emphasise change and development: Nepali political life is seen in an international context where events inside the country are compared with similar developments abroad. From this perspective, history is seen as a process of development towards a distant goal of political emancipation.

So far I have used the word 'revolution'. One may of course discuss whether this word is appropriate to describe the political events of 1990 in Nepal and, even more so, to describe what happened in 1951. Usually the word 'revolution'implies a major, violent, popular uprising which fundamentally changes the whole political order of the day. Violence was certainly present during the democracy movement in Nepal in 1990, and to a lesser degree it was also part of the 1951 events. However, it may be argued that the political changes were not of a fundamental character in 1951 or in 1990, because the political dominance of one cultural and social elite survived both events.

What does make the revolution of 1990 significantly different from that of 1951, however, is the mass support it received. While the 1951 event may rightly be called a palace revolution, there is no doubt that the revolution of 1990 had the form of a mass uprising, at least in the Kathmandu valley. From this perspective I believe that what happened qualifies to be called a revolution. The impossible happened, and even the leaders of the democracy movement were taken by surprise. In an interview just after the revolution, the supreme leader of the Nepali Congress, Ganesh Man Singh, said, 'We did expect mass support but never to this degree'. This is what makes events in Nepal comparable to revolutions elsewhere, including those in eastern Europe in late 1989. The general state of confusion both during the revolution and in its immediate aftermath seems to be a feature common to all these events. In all countries the period after the revolution has raised more questions than answers about what actually happened. An upsurge of ethnic and regional politics following in the wake of the revolution is common to most of eastern Europe, as well as to Nepal.

Conclusion
It is still too early to draw far-fetched general lessons from what happened in Nepal in 1990. However, looking at the revolution in retrospect, events seem to have progressed through three major stages. These may be summed up as: (1) The 'build-up'. This consists of two aspects: the development of circumstances favourable to the success of a movement, and the planning of the movement itself. In Nepal this covers the period before 18 February, as well as the first part of the

actual struggle up to 30 March. This is followed by (2) the 'climax'. This stage starts with an eruption, when the masses come out and take over. This is what the leaders dream and hope for, and also what they rely on for their movement to succeed, but at the same time this is when the leaders lose control. Events get out of hand, and take on a life and momentum of their own. Inevitably the leaders, the former dissidents, are taken by surprise. The main actors at this stage are not individuals. The masses have taken over, this undefinable and uncontrollable entity which most of the time lies dormant and passive. The third and last stage (3) may be called the 'step back'. In order to regain control the leaders go in and try to stop the mass movement. The political aspirations of the masses are arrested at a certain level. In Nepal this third stage began when leaders of the Nepali Congress and the communists called off the movement on 9 April after the king had lifted the ban on political parties. Whether the leaders had actually succeeded at this point is still an open question. The next day the extreme leftist party, the Mashal group, appealed to the masses to disobey their leaders saying that they had betrayed the movement. By aligning themselves with elements from the old regime—the king and the armed forces—the moderates, in this case the Nepali Congress, succeeded in stabilising the situation.

From several comparative studies of the English, American, French, and Russian revolutions it seems likely that what I have called the third stage will inevitably be followed by a fourth. According to this scenario, the moderates who come to power through the revolution are unable to combine the running of government with the making of a new constitution. This leads eventually to the victory of a radical minority who believe more strongly in their convictions than the moderates. So far, such a theory seems not to apply to the events of 1989-90. In the democratic revolution of 1990 in Nepal, as well as in those of eastern Europe half a year earlier, the original leaders of the movement and their political goals seem to have survived. With the formation of a democratically-elected government in Nepal in May 1991 democracy has been secured, at least in the short term. What happens in the long run is still too early to say. The events of 1959-60, when King Mahendra dismissed the first elected government in Nepal after less than eighteen months in office, are still fresh in many people's minds.

In his recent book on the revolution in eastern Europe, Ralf Dahrendorf writes that a revolution cancels out the normal functioning of society.[2] Constitutional politics take over from normal politics. To a certain extent this description still fits the political situation in Nepal.

[2] Ralf Dahrendorf, *Reflections on the Revolution in Europe*. London, 1990.

Despite the elections and the Nepali Congress's bid for normalisation there is still a long way to go to create strong democratic institutions and traditions. Until that goal is reached the movement which started in the spring of 1990 might develop in any direction, including a political come-back by the palace.

Chapter 3

DRAFTING THE 1990 CONSTITUTION

Michael Hutt

On 9 November 1990, His Majesty King Birendra Bir Bikram Shah
Deva promulgated a new constitution for the kingdom of Nepal,
enshrining several basic concepts which the country's banned political
parties had demanded ever since King Mahendra's 'royal coup' of
December 1960.[1] The constitution has so far proved generally acceptable to the principal political parties in Nepal: it is the main achieve-
ment of the Movement for the Restoration of Democracy which was
launched on 8 February and called off on 9 April 1990, and the latest
product of the long search for appropriate political institutions and processes in Nepal which began soon after the departure of the British from
India and the subsequent collapse of the Rana regime in 1950-51.

The 1990 constitution is Nepal's fifth. The first was promulgated in
1948, and was an attempt by the Rana ruler of the time, Padma
Shamsher, to shore up the fast-crumbling Rana regime. After this
regime had collapsed, an Interim Government Act came into force in
1951, and was not replaced until 1959, the year of Nepal's first general
election. In 1960, King Mahendra revoked this 'democratic' constitution, using the emergency powers it granted him, and re-assumed all
powers of government. Though amended three times, the constitution
for 'partyless panchayat democracy' first promulgated in 1962 remained
in force until 1990. The 1962 constitution banned political parties,
vested sovereignty in the king, and made him the source of all legislative, executive and judicial power. It has therefore always been controversial, not to say notorious. [2]

The following chronological account of the struggles, debates and
controversies which surrounded the framing of the constitution between
the unbanning of political parties on 9 April and promulgation on 9

[1] The research for this essay was funded by a grant from the British
Academy, to whom I must express my gratitude. My thanks also to Leo Rose
and Dhrubahari Adhikari for their comments on earlier drafts.
[2] For an in-depth analysis of Nepali politics between 1950 and 1964, see
Joshi and Rose, 1966. See also Agrawal, 1980. For English translations of
earlier constitutions, see *The Constitution of the Kingdom of Nepal* (New
Delhi, 1959) and *The Constitution of Nepal, with First, Second and Third
Amendments* (HMG Nepal), 4th edn., 1983. Agrawal (1980: 8-21, 22-31)
summarises the Rana constitution of 1948 and the interim constitution of
1951.

November demonstrates the extent to which uncertainty persisted in
Nepal about the direction in which political development should proceed, about the role the monarch should play in this development, and
the uncertainty of the palace itself about the extent of the power it
would wield in the future. There was also evidence of a significant dis-
parity between popular priorities for change, and those of the national
leadership.

On the morning of 6 April 1990, King Birendra broadcast a proclamation on Radio Nepal which was remarkable for the concessions it
made to the democracy movement, especially in view of the administration's intransigence up until this point. Charging the council of
ministers with having failed to understand the 'tradition of public consent' and having caused loss of life and property, the king announced
the formation of a new council (under National Panchayat member
Lokendra Bahadur Chand) which would hold talks with 'people holding
different political views'. The king invoked Article 81(1), 'Formation
of the Council of Ministers in Extraordinary Circumstances' of the
1962 constitution, and he also promised to form two committees: one
for constitution reform suggestions, the other to investigate the recent
violence.

The democratic movement was launched by an alliance between the
Nepali Congress Party and the newly-formed United Left Front
(Sanyukta Bam Morcha, the ULF) on 18 February , and had reached its
climax by early April, resulting in massive civil disorder throughout
the kingdom. When security forces shot several dozen unarmed demonstrators in the streets outside the royal palace on 6 April, despite the
king's concessions that very morning, the situation had clearly deterio-
rated to such an extent that even the movement's leaders were only
nominally in control. Factions within the movement were escalating
their demands, calling not for a constitutional monarchy but for the
abolition of the monarchy itself.[3] To restore public order, a 22-hour
curfew was declared in Kathmandu and Lalitpur from 7 April, and in
Bhaktapur from 8 April .

Legalisation
The king made a further, fundamental concession two days later by lifting the 30-year-old ban on political parties and deleting the term
'partyless' from the 1962 constitution. After an audience with the king,

---

[3] Interpretations of the events of 6 April are varied. In this volume,
Martin Hoftun claims that the mood in the Kathmandu Valley after the royal
proclamation that morning was one of joyous celebration, and that this
mood changed dramatically during a mass meeting on the Tundikhel parade
ground during the afternoon. Other eye-witnesses have suggested, however,
that the people of the Kathmandu Valley towns were dissatisfied with the
king's concessions from the outset.

the four main leaders of the movement (Krishna Prasad Bhattarai and Girija Prasad Koirala of the Nepali Congress, Sahana Pradhan and Radha Krishna Mainali of the United Left Front) announced that the movement had been called off, since their two main demands had been granted. During the struggle that followed in subsequent months between the palace and political parties, the movement's leaders were regularly criticised for having taken this decision too soon. Many activists argued that their demands should have included the abrogation of the 1962 constitution, the promulgation of an Interim Act and the election of a constituent assembly to draft the new constitution. These complaints came from elements within the United Left Front, as well as from parties not represented in it, and were levelled principally at the leaders of the Nepali Congress, whose response was that, since these demands were not made before 8 April, it was not appropriate to make them now.

On 12 April, a joint meeting of the Nepali Congress and the United Left Front made demands which included the dissolution of the National Panchayat and council of ministers; the repeal of all provisions of the 1962 constitution that conflicted with the multi-party system; the dissolution of panchayat units from village to district level; and the formation of a constitution commission with 'adequate representation' of the Congress and the United Left Front. In a New Year message to the nation on 14 April, the king affirmed, 'Politics in Nepal has now taken a new turn. We have upheld the tradition of respecting the popular will and fulfilling the people's aspirations. The Constitution Reforms Commission in the process of being set up in the near future will consult elements of society professing different political views in the course of preparing its report'.[4] The palace view at this early stage was clearly that it was at liberty to form a body which would submit suggestions to the king for reforms of the 1962 constitution. It soon became clear that this view did not accord with that of the democratic movement.

The Formation of an Interim Government

Events moved rapidly after the Hindu New Year had been ushered in. On 15 April, five government ministers and five representatives of the Nepali Congress and the ULF sat down in the Royal Nepal Academy to begin negotiations. Outside, several thousand demonstrators surrounded the building, demanding the dissolution of all panchayat institutions and the formation of an interim government. The participants in this meeting were effectively besieged: when the newly-appointed prime minister, Lokendra Bahadur Chand, attempted to leave, his car was wrecked by the crowd. Clearly the more radical elements feared betrayal. Nevertheless, the negotiators escaped from the Academy after 14 hours

[4] *Nepal Press Digest*, 34, 16; 16 April, 1990.

of talks and the next day a royal proclamation announced the resignation of the hapless Chand ministry after only ten days in office, the dissolution of the National Panchayat, the Panchayat Policy and Evaluation Committee and the Class Organisations.[5] Clause (2) of Article 81 of the 1962 constitution, which empowered the king in extraordinary circumstances to suspend articles 25 to 29 on the formation and functioning of the council of ministers and dissolve the National Panchayat, was invoked to do just that. Articles 41B and 67A, which provided for the Panchayat Policy and Evaluation Committee and the Class Organisations respectively, were suspended, as was clause 2A of Article 11 which prescribed that 'no political party or any other organisation, union or association motivated by party politics shall be formed or be caused to be formed or run'.

Later the same day (16 April) the king asked Ganesh Man Singh, the supreme leader of the Nepali Congress, to form an interim government, but Singh declined on grounds of ill-health and asked the king to head the government himself. This the king declined to do, and eventually Krishna Prasad Bhattarai, the party chairman, was selected, with the ULF's agreement. Portfolios were allocated on 18 April, and the new prime minister was sworn in the following day. The new council of ministers was made up of eleven ministers: four members of the Congress, three of the ULF, two independents with records of work in human rights organisation, and two palace nominees.[6]

On the left of the political spectrum, few groups were willing to trust the palace to make the concessions to democracy that it had promised. The editorial of the *Drishti* newspaper on 18 April declared, 'the king cannot be a leader. No one can be above the constitution. The king must stay in his palace... if the Crown tries to support dictatorial ideals, a movement will be launched which will abolish the monarchy itself'.[7] The ULF parties had probably reconciled themselves to the retention of a constitutional monarchy in order to achieve a working

[5] Article 67A of the amended 1962 constitution provided for the formation of 6 Class Organisations of Women, Peasants, Youths, Elders, Labourers and Ex-Servicemen. (The original text had provided for five.) These were formed 'with a view to integrate and utilise the united strength of the various classes.' Membership of one of these Class Organisations was made 'compulsory for any person contesting as a candidate in the election of any level of Panchayat'. (Government of Nepal, 1983.)

[6] The new council of ministers *(mantri-parishad)* was: Krishna Prasad Bhattarai, Mahendra Narayan Nidhi, Yoga Prasad Upadhyaya, and Marshal Julum Shakya, (Congress), Sahana Pradhan (NCP (Marxist)), Nilambar Acharya (NCP (Manandhar)), Jhal Nath Khanal (NCP (Marxist-Leninist)), Keshar Jang Rayamajhi and Achyut Raj Regmi (royal nominees) and Devendra Raj Pandey and Mathura Prasad Shreshtha (independents).

[7] *Nepal Press Digest*, 34, 17; 23 April, 1990.

compromise with the Nepali Congress, but leftist groups outside the
Front, such as Mashal, considered this a temporary measure—a step on
the way to a totally republican state.[8] Thus, they orchestrated a hue and
cry each time the king appeared to take decisions without what they
considered sufficient consultation.

From this time onward, various groups began to make their own
demands regarding the new constitution. The Movement for the
Restoration of Democracy had not been a constitutional movement as
such: its demands were not couched in constitutional intricacies, but
were simply for the unbanning of parties, a constitutional monarchy
and respect for human rights. Once the movement was called off, a large
number of new parties emerged, many of which represented ethnic, religious and regional concerns.

On 23 April the situation in the Valley towns approached anarchy
when six policemen were beaten to death and subsequent police firing
killed about a dozen demonstrators. Later, anti-government demonstrations were organised by the police, and the office of the commissioner
for Bagmati zone was destroyed by arsonists. Night curfews were
imposed throughout the Valley by 26 April . The widespread rumour of
an imminent palace-led coup was eventually squashed on 25 April when
the palace issued a press release in which the king urged the nation to
support the interim government: 'the interests of the country and the
people lie in the development and strengthening of multi-party democracy. The government headed by Krishna Prasad Bhattarai should be
fully supported....'[9]

On 24 April the Nepali Congress and the United Left Front issued a
joint directive to the interim government: it made the following points
about the new constitution:

The new constitution must be fully democratic; the king must become a
constitutional monarch; the king must act only on the advice of the council
of ministers. All institutions and laws not conducive to democraticisation
must be repealed. Democratic rights must be ensured for all citizens.
Institutions and processes must be developed for the protection of democracy. A free election must be held as soon as possible, and an independent
election commission must be formed for this purpose. There should be press
and academic freedom, and equal rights for women. [10]

The Constitution Commission
The questions of who should frame the new constitution, and who

[8] Led by 'Prachand', the Mashal faction of the NCP remains committed to
Maoist revolution and denounces the Marxist-Leninists for their
revisionism. Not to be confused with the Masal faction, led by Mohan
Bikram Singh, from which it split in 1981.
[9] *Nepal Press Digest*, 34, 18; 30 April, 1990.
[10] Ibid.

should approve it, were debated fiercely for weeks, and the eventual solution to the problem did not find favour in all quarters. Most of the leftist parties outside the United Left Front demanded the promulgation of an interim constitution and direct elections on a party political basis to a constituent assembly. Several groups—notably the Nepal Communist Party (4th Convention), the United Nepal People's Movement and the Masal and Mashal factions—continued to make these demands throughout the year, and when the new constitution was finally promulgated they refused to recognise it. The leaders of the Nepali Congress resisted very vigorously. On 4 May Mathbar Singh Basnet, one of the four official spokesmen for the party, dismissed the idea of a constituent assembly as an 'intellectual luxury', on the grounds that all parties, including the Congress and the communists, had contested the 1959 general election under a constitution promulgated by King Mahendra.[11] It may be that the Congress felt, as supreme leader Ganesh Man Singh later stated, that the king could not be pushed too far too fast, and that the notion of a constitution which derived from the people and not from the king would provoke a reaction from the palace. It is also clear that the policy of 'national reconciliation' between palace and people pursued by B.P. Koirala continues to be a part of Nepali Congress philosophy. [12] On 6 July, Ganesh Man Singh quoted B.P. Koirala as saying, 'In a tussle between the Nepali Congress and the king, democracy would be the only casualty'. [13] The official line pursued by many Congress spokesmen, however, was that an Interim Act and the election of a constituent assembly would delay the general election, and that this was the communists' real objective in making such demands.

Soon, however, it seemed that the Congress's trust in the palace to conform with democratic norms had been misplaced, or else that the two sides had not fully understood one another's aims. On 11 May, without consulting the interim government, King Birendra formed a seven-man Constitution Reforms Recommendation Commission, and directed it to submit recommendations to him within three months for changes to the 1962 constitution. This was in direct contradiction to the ULF's demand for a commission including representatives of both political parties within the interim government. The prime minister, Krishna Prasad Bhattarai, shamefacedly admitted that he had not been consulted by the king before the formation of the commission. Demonstrating what appeared to be genuine political naïveté, he said that there were no real grounds for discontent, since the king had advised him that the government would be free to reject the new constitution.

[11] *Nepal Press Digest*, 34, 19; 7 May, 1990.
[12] See Mishra, 1985. Also Koirala, 1982.
[13] *Nepal Press Digest*, 34, 30; 23 July, 1990.

'The king told me', he said, 'he was not aware of the fact that there is a party behind me which has to be satisfied because there have been no political parties functioning in the country for a long time. He also did not consider such matters as the fact that there was a coalition government. So it has happened'.[14]

Predictably, few leaders were as sanguine as Bhattarai about this attempt by the palace to capture the constitution-drafting process. Girija Prasad Koirala, the General Secretary of the Congress, described it as 'a great insult to the people of Nepal'. He rejected the idea of reforming the 1962 constitution, and demanded a completely new dispensation. The commission should be dissolved immediately, he said, and in this he received the support of most leftist leaders. The ULF described the formation of the commission as 'un-democratic and disgraceful' and the Congress called for its dissolution and re-constitution in consultation with the interim government. This incident was the first of several palace attempts to regain, as it were, the high ground during the drafting of the new constitution. On each occasion, a hostile reaction from the press, the public and political parties forced a retreat, but such incidents demonstrated either that the king and his palace secretariat were not sincerely committed to the direction of political change upon which Nepal had embarked (the leftist view, perhaps); or that the king, inexperienced in dealings with free and active political parties, was adjusting only slowly to the changed circumstances (the public view of some in the Congress).

In any event, the palace ploy was a damp squib. The commission's chairman, Justice Bishwanath Upadhyaya, resigned and three of the six other members refused to join at all. The commission was dissolved after only four days. Unprecedented criticisms had been levelled at the king. Man Mohan Adhikan of the Nepal Communist Party (Marxist) had already said, 'The king should no longer be considered an incarnation of Vishnu. He too is a man, and a man can make mistakes'. The *Drishti* weekly of 16 May exclaimed, 'The nation has been stunned by what His Majesty did on 11 May. That step...was clearly aimed at turning the monarchy once again toward the tendencies of the panchayat period, and reinstating the despotism of the palace in every vital sphere'.[15] This incident revived the demand for an interim constitution that vested sovereignty in the Nepali people, a demand that was taken up even by some senior Congress officials. Bhattarai was instructed to consult the council of ministers, and other parties, to nominate persons for a new commission. Man Mohan Adhikari, filled with righteous indignation, demanded that the new body should not include anyone who had connections with the palace, the administration, or the 'black

[14] *Nepal Press Digest*, 34, 20; 14 May, 1990.
[15] Ibid.

history' of the previous thirty years.[16]

On 22 May, the king vested the legislative and executive powers of the dissolved National Panchayat in the interim government, under Article 81(2) (b) of the 1962 constitution. Despite this, Ganesh Man Singh complained on 1 June that the government was still hindered by a lack of judicial power, which had not yet been granted to it. Critics of the government said that it was still operating under the 1962 constitution, minus the word 'partyless', and that it therefore still sought palace approval for every move it made. Policy guidelines issued for the interim government on 4 June, began 'The main tasks of the interim government will be to maintain law and order, develop a multi-party system on the basis of constitutional monarchy, draft a new constitution, and hold general elections'.[17]

A new Constitution Recommendations Commission, its members nominated by Krishna Prasad Bhattarai, was inaugurated by the king at the end of May. The nine-member commission was again chaired by Justice Bishwanath Upadhyaya of the Supreme Court. The main political parties accorded the commission a cautious welcome. Man Mohan Adhikari objected to the inclusion of the word 'recommendations' in its title, while leaders of the Marxist-Leninist faction of the Nepal Communist Party demanded that it should form a *new* constitution, which should be presented to the interim government for final approval, not to the king. Soon after the formation of the commission, Justice Upadhyaya explained that each of its members had been assigned specific topics, on which they would collect suggestions from political parties and the general public, and report back to the commission. A deadline of 4 July was set for the submission of suggestions. Later in the month, six members of the commission were sent out to tour various zones of the country to canvas opinions, and the Congress lawyer Daman Dhungana was sent to Britain to study constitutional issues, especially relations between the elected government and the Crown.

Bishwanath Upadhyaya later expressed dismay over the fact that the vast majority of suggestions submitted to the commission concerned linguistic, religious, ethnic and regional issues. Since the 'unification' of Nepal in the late 18th century, political power has been monopolised by the 'twice-born' Brahman and Chhetri castes and the language and culture promoted by the government have been those of the Hindu populations of the hill regions. 'Tribal' hillpeoples who speak Tibeto-Burman languages, such as the Rai, Limbu, Tamang and Gurung, are under-represented at all levels of government, while the Tarai population—many of whom are of more recent Indian origin—suffer discrimination at the hands of the state bureaucracy. The demands made

[16] Ibid.
[17] *Nepal Press Digest*, 34, 24; 11 June, 1990.

to the Constitution Recommendations Commission for recognition of languages other than Nepali and religions other than Hinduism, and for the proportional representation of minority groups in the legislature, reflect the growth of communal grievances among minority and regional groupings in Nepal which are based on socioeconomic realities. Rather than attempting to accommodate these grievances, the commission and the interim government simply perceived them as a threat to national unity, and virtually dismissed them out of hand. Thus, Justice Bishwanath Upadhyaya said it was 'unfortunate' that most suggestions had been about 'peripheral' issues, and he called upon all political parties to educate the people on basic constitutional subjects.[18]

In an interview on 9 July, Upadhyaya confirmed that most political parties had made identical suggestions for a constitutional monarchy, a multi-party democracy, adult franchise, a bi-cameral legislature and the sovereignty of the people. But he expressed some concern over the procedure to be adopted for the promulgation of the new constitution: 'The individual or institution who gives the constitution is sovereign. The people will be sovereign if there is a constituent assembly, but we have not followed that path. If the constitution is granted by the king, under what power should he do so?'[19] The Nepal Communist Party (Masal) concurred with this view: 'We do not believe that the king will give up his powers and hand over sovereignty to the people. After all, even the new constitution will be a gift from the king. How can a mango tree bear oranges?'[20]

Suggestions Made to the Constitution Recommendations Committee
Most political parties agreed on the basic features of the new constitution. Other than these, the main points of controversy were: religious freedom; the status of Nepali and the other languages of Nepal; control of the army; the rights and representation in the administration of ethnic minorities, depressed castes and classes, the Tarai peoples and women.

Religious Freedom. Two articles of the 1962 constitution which concerned religion aroused controversy. Article 3(1) stated 'Nepal is an independent, indivisible and sovereign monarchical Hindu kingdom', while Article 14 on 'Right to Religion' (identical to Article 5 in the 1959 constitution) stated 'Every person may profess his own religion as handed down from ancient times and may practise it having regard to tradition. Provided that no person shall be entitled to convert another person from one religion to another'. Under this article, a number of people had received prison sentences for allegedly converting Nepali

[18] *Nepal Press Digest,* 34, 27; 2 July, 1990.
[19] *Nepal Press Digest,* 34, 29; 16 July, 1990.
[20] *Nepal Press Digest,* 34, 30; 23 July, 1990.

citizens to Christianity. The debate on these issues quickly became an impassioned argument between proponents of a secular state and proponents of a Hindu state. Those demanding a secular state included Buddhist, Muslim and Christian associations, ethnic organisations representing the predominantly non-Hindu Tibeto-Burman tribes, and leftist, liberal and republican elements. An enormous demonstration organised by the Nepal Buddhist Association to demand a secular state brought some 10,000 marchers out onto the streets of the capital on 30 June.

These demands were strongly opposed by traditionalist Hindu organisations, particularly by the Sanatan Dharma Seva Samiti and the Nepal committee of the Vishwa Hindu Parishad. The interim government's minister for housing, Achyut Raj Regmi, caused uproar when he threatened a hunger-strike if the constitution made Nepal a secular state. And when twelve 'religious prisoners' had their sentences remitted on 15 June, the *Saptahik Bimarsha* claimed that the state had already become secular, even before the constitution had been drafted.[21] The traditionalist Hindu stand reflected concern that the declaration of Nepal as a secular state would open its borders to a flood of Christian missionaries, who might have political as well as religious patronage and motives. This paranoia became evident during June, when several newspapers carried reports of mass conversions to Christianity in outlying districts.[22]

Language. The demands of communal groups ranged from suggestions that, although Nepali should continue to be the national language, other languages should be given some kind of constitutional status, to demands that Nepali's status as national language be abolished and that Nepal should become a federal state, each autonomous region having its own official language. There were strident calls from groups such as the Tarai-based Nepal Goodwill Council for the recognition of Hindi as a second national language.[23]

Human Rights. HURON (Human Rights Organisation of Nepal), FOPHUR (Forum for the Protection of Human Rights) and Amnesty

---

[21] *Nepal Press Digest,* 34, 26; 25 June, 1990.

[22] The Vishwa Hindu Parishad sent a 108-member delegation to Upadhyaya on 6 June, claiming that 30,000 Nepalis had been converted to Christianity since April (*Nepal Press Digest,* 34, 24; 11 June, 1990). The *Jana Jagriti* newspaper of 2 July reported that 48,000 had been converted in one day in Dhading district, 'due to financial allurements' (*Nepal Press Digest,* 34, 28; 9 July, 1990).

[23] These demands were not new: they were advanced vigorously during the 1950s and early 1960s, before King Mahendra's 'Royal Coup' stifled debate. See Gaige, 1975. On the other hand, the demands made by speakers of Tibeto-Burman languages other than Newari were quite without precedent.

International all called for the abolition of the death penalty, and for the endorsement by the government of international human rights conventions.[24]

Control of the Army. On 23 June a controversial circular was sent to all units of the Royal Nepalese Army directing them to submit the following suggestions to the Constitution Recommendations Commission: the king must continue to be the Supreme Commander-in-Chief and Field-Marshal of the Army; the king should appoint the Commander-in-Chief, who should have constitutional status, and sovereignty should be vested in the king. Nepal should also remain a Hindu state. [25]

Nirmal Lama, leader of the Nepal Communist Party (4th Convention) threatened to resign from the Constitution Recommendations Commission on 27 June. He expressed strong doubts that the king would approve the new constitution without extensive amendments. The suspicion was growing that events were moving in the same direction as they had under King Mahendra in 1959-60: in that instance, the demand for a constituent assembly had also failed, the king had promulgated the constitution at the very last minute, and had revoked it and banned parties 18 months later. These suspicions were subsequently fuelled by the king's appointment of ambassadors without consultation with the interim government. On 8 August posters appeared in Kathmandu in the name of Nirmal Lama's party, claiming that a palace conspiracy was underway. The posters claimed that the Constitution Recommendations Committee was being manipulated by the palace, and being forced to adopt provisions such as prohibiting debate of the king's conduct in the legislature. The posters were quickly removed and arrests were made, but even in January 1991 there were still slogans painted by the 4th Convention on Kathmandu streets. Mysteriously, however, Nirmal Lama did not resign. By late August, he was promising that the new constitution would be even more democratic than the one promulgated in 1959. For instance, the king would not possess the power to declare an emergency as he had under Article 55 of the 1959 dispensation. His change of stance may have been prompted by the compromise achieved between ULF and Congress representatives in the commission which led to accusations of the commission exceeding its brief. On 23 August, Bishwanath Upadhyaya announced that the draft of the new constitution would be submitted to the king on 31 August, and that the king would hand it over to the council of ministers for their perusal on the same day. He admitted that

---

[24] An Amnesty International mission visited Nepal in April 1990, and a Memorandum was sent to the Interim Government in June, recommending the incorporation of human rights safeguards in the new constitution.

[25] *Nepal Press Digest,* 34, 29; 16 July, 1990.

the members of the commission had not yet reached a decision on the issues of whether Nepal should be a Hindu or a secular state, and of how the army should be controlled.

From the end of August until the actual promulgation of the constitution on 9 November, the story is one of delay and controversy, and of several apparent attempts by the palace to water down the document and retain the maximum possible powers. On 31 August Justice Upadhyaya announced the completion of the draft, an outline of which appeared in the *Gorkhapatra* the following day. The constitution contained provisions for amending its three basic features: constitutional monarchy, multi-party democracy and the vesting of sovereignty in the people. Some newspapers interpreted this as evidence of republican forces having undue influence in the commission—not a very convincing argument since under the draft constitution any change to the status of the monarchy could only be made with the monarch's prior consent. Other papers suggested that this was the work of 'reactionaries', and commentators from all angles returned to the old theme of the palace stirring up controversy to delay promulgation and undermine democracy.

The most likely explanation advanced for the surprising inclusion of these provisions appeared in the *Gorkhapatra* on 1 September. The Nepali Congress had held the view for many years that the new constitution should enshrine the three basic features mentioned above. According to the *Gorkhapatra,* the ULF representatives on the commission announced at the eleventh hour that they had no faith in the first two of these. After a furious debate, the chairman achieved a compromise by including provisions for amendment of these three features, on the basis of a three-quarters majority vote in the legislature *and* a national referendum. He said, 'The constitution cannot be said to be binding on future generations. It *can* be amended, but a complex process has been adopted for amendments, in the belief that certain provisions should not be amended as easily as others'.[26] From this time onward the leftist parties, who believed that they had scored a victory with the inclusion of these provisions, demanded immediate promulgation without changes, while the Congress continued to look for an opportunity to make these concepts inviolable. The palace, meanwhile, found a chance to exploit these differences to its own advantage. Justice Upadhyaya presented the draft of the new constitution to the king on 10 September. The king then handed it to Bhattarai as agreed, but sparked further controversy by instructing him to consider suggestions put forward by constitutional organs and political parties which had not been represented in the Recommendations Commission. On the advice of the council of ministers, he then extended the term of the commission up

[26] *Nepal Press Digest,* 34, 38; 17 September, 1990.

to the day of promulgation. There were widespread objections to the king's directive, most of which emanated from the Left, which demanded immediate promulgation. It was protested that 'anti-people' elements would now have a say, and that promulgation would be endlessly delayed. The Congress, however, did not complain too loudly: its opposition to the provisions for amendment were widely known, and there were probably also objections to the king's right to appoint ambassadors and to an article that required a two-thirds majority in both houses for the ratification of treaties with foreign countries. On 26 September Girija Prasad Koirala said that it had been a 'suicidal' decision to put the basic features of the constitution into a 'state of uncertainty', since it would compel the king to engage actively in politics in order to safeguard his position.[27]

The council of ministers is said [28] to have made over twenty changes to the draft. The most important of these made it impossible to repeal or amend provisions if such an amendment contravened the spirit of the preamble, and another made it possible for parliament to ratify treaties by a simple majority, except those treaties which related to strategic or military alliances, or to the boundaries of Nepal. Apparently, ULF representatives had acquiesced to these changes after veiled threats had been made by the Congress to withdraw all co-operation if they did not. The constitution was submitted to the king by the prime minister on 11 October, and the king announced that he would study it, 'to determine to what extent it was positive in the exercise of democracy'.[29]

The Palace Draft: a Final Crisis
On 16 October, it was announced by the palace that the constitution would not be promulgated until after the national holiday of Tihar (i.e. after 20 October), and that consultations were still going on between the king and the prime minister. Some press reports suggested that the king had asked for improvements in the 'language and organisation' of the document, others that he had raised strong objections to a reference to the democracy movement in its Preamble. On 21 October, it became plainly apparent that the palace had had objections to many other features of the constitution, when a new draft was released to the press. It was claimed that this had been prepared jointly by the king and the prime minister. But it contained many fundamental differences from the revised draft submitted by the council of ministers: some of the changes made in its preamble are summarised below:

---

[27] *Nepal Press Digest* 34, 40; 1 October, 1990.
[28] *Nepal Press Digest,* 34, 42; 15 October, 1990.
[29] Ibid.

Original Draft	*Palace Draft*
'in accordance with the desire expressed by the people of Nepal through historic people's movement for constitutional change	clause removed
'Framed through the broad of the Nepali people in accordance with their desires	'Whereas the happiness and prosperity of Nepal and the Nepali people have always been our sole objective, and we are determined to achieve that objective, and whereas it is desirable to frame and promulgate a constitution…'

'We hereby proclaim and promulgate this constitution…

on the advice and with the approval of council of ministers.'	…in accordance with the constitutional laws, customs, usages and traditions of Nepal.'
'Whereas we have expressed the determination from time to time to run the polity in accordance with the popular will	'Whereas our revered forefathers and ourselves have been running a polity based on the public will
(Sovereignty vested in the Nepali people)	'The sovereignty of Nepal shall be vested in the Nepali people, including His Majesty'

According to the palace draft, there was to be a Raja Parishad (Council of State), to be appointed by the king, with duties prescribed by the constitution. A standing committee would offer advice to the king when requested, and submit an annual report to him. Emergency powers were assigned solely to the king, who would have to present his proclamation of a state emergency *post facto* before the legislature within three months. The executive, legislative and judicial powers of the kingdom were all vested in the king, and would be exercised 'in accordance with the constitution and current law'.[30]

The interim government was stunned. Ganesh Man Singh said, 'It is quite undemocratic to seek to promulgate a constitution similar to that of 1962. No sane person can do it'. Bhattarai told the king's Principal Secretary to convey his resignation to the king, since he would be unable to gain endorsement of the draft from the Congress party, the government or the people. Leftist parties, student unions and

[30] *Nepal Press Digest*, 34, 44; 29 October, 1990

professional associations took to the streets to denounce the 'palace conspiracy'. The palace feigned surprise at the ferocity of this response. Disingenuously, a press note expressed surprise at Bhattarai's offer of resignation, claiming that he had been fully consulted—something the prime minister denied. After hasty discussions between the king and Bhattarai, the palace backed down: a press note issued on 23 October said the royal draft was a 'proposed draft' only. Two days later, promulgation was promised for 9 November.

One of the most striking features of this story is the extent to which its final stage turned into a fundamental struggle over the constitution between the palace and the interim government. It was a simple matter, devoid of democratic or constitutional niceties, of putting pressure on the king to re-make the concessions that had officially been made several months before. Outside the palace gates, there was a general strike in Patan and a mass ULF rally in Kathmandu on 27 October, while leftists burned copies of the palace draft and threatened to launch a new republican movement if the original constitution was not promulgated on 9 November. Inside the palace, on 24 October, the king spent four and a half hours in talks with Congress leaders and Justice Upadhyaya. By the end of the day, agreement had been reached on the issues of multi-party democracy, constitutional monarchy, the vesting of sovereignty in the people, and human rights. The national anthem and the privileges of the royal family were still under discussion. G.P. Koirala warned, 'We must remain alert, since we cannot be sure of anything until the constitution is promulgated'.[31]

On 9 November it became clear that a compromise had been achieved that generally favoured the demands of the democratic movement, but still reserved important powers and privileges for the monarchy. Bhattarai described the 1990 constitution as 'an historic document' which guaranteed there would never again be 'one-man rule' in Nepal. The moderate leftist groups accorded it a qualified welcome, but the Nepal Communist Party (4th convention) and the ethnic and communal parties rejected it out of hand, since their demands had not been fulfilled. Proclaiming the constitution, King Birendra referred to the fact that democracy had been established in Nepal in 1951 'through the cooperation of the king and the people' and ended with the long-fought-over sentence 'We hereby promulgate and enforce with immediate effect *on the recommendation of the council of ministers the draft prepared by the commission* as the constitution of the kingdom of Nepal, 1990' (emphasis added).

The Main Features of the 1990 Constitution
An 'unofficial' English translation of the 1990 constitution is available, though unpublished, but only the original Nepali text has

[31] *Nepal Press Digest,* 34, 45; 5 November, 1990.

full legal force.[32] The quotations given below are my own translations.

The Kingdom of Nepal: Sovereignty, Religion and Language. Article 3 stated 'the sovereignty of Nepal is vested in the Nepali people', and was thus uncontroversial. However, Article 4(1) stated: 'Nepal is a multi-ethnic, multi-lingual, democratic, independent, indivisible, sovereign, Hindu, constitutional monarchical kingdom'. The terms 'multi-ethnic' and 'multi-lingual' were probably intended to mollify the minorities who had been pressing claims on behalf of their languages and regions for months. But many commentators have objected to the insertion of the word 'Hindu' here. They argue that, since the position of the Hindu king is safeguarded by Article 27(1), which states that the king must be a descendant of Prithvinarayan Shah, an upholder of the Aryan culture and a practising Hindu, there was no need for article 4(1) to make any statement whatsoever on either religion or secularism.

The 1990 constitution also adopted a somewhat ambiguous position on the question of language. Whereas Article 4 of the 1962 constitution simply stated 'The National Language of Nepal is the Nepali language in the Devanagari script', the 1990 document hedged its bets, by dividing its Article 6 into two clauses: 6(1) 'The Nepali language in the Devanagari script is the state language *(rashtrabhasha)* of Nepal. The Nepali language shall be the language of the workings of government.' (2) 'All languages spoken as mother-tongues in the various parts of Nepal are national languages *(rashtriya bhasha)* of Nepal'. Article 18(2) went rather further, stating, 'Every community shall be able to run schools so that education may be provided to children at the primary level in their mother-tongues.'

The above articles were probably drafted to appease linguistic and religious minorities, but it soon became apparent that groups such as the Nepal Goodwill *(Sadbhavana)* Party, who had demanded the status of a second national language for Hindi, and Christian, Buddhist and Muslim groups who had demanded a secular state, were far from satisfied. The dissatisfaction of the Christian minority had been compounded by the fact that Article 14 of the 1962 constitution which banned conversion had been retained as Article 19. This was likely to

---

[32] The Nepali text of the 1990 constitution was reproduced in the *Gorkhapatra* of 24 Kartik, 2047 (10 November, 1990) and later in booklet form by the publishers of the magazine *Antarrashtriya Manch (International Forum)*. 48 of the latter journal carries summaries on pp. 309-11 and pp. 350-4. See also 'Samvidhan: Kranti ki Agni Pariksha se Mila Praman Patra' in the newly-launched Hindi journal *Nava Nepal* 1, (pp. 6-12), and the 'Constitution Special edition' *(Samvidhan Vishesh)* of the monthly *Sindhu*, 21, 5, (December, 1990-January, 1991). (A published English translation of the 1990 constitution was made available just as this volume was going to press.)

lead to continued protests by Christian and human rights organisations since, if interpreted narrowly, it seemed to require one to follow the religion of one's ancestors, not that of one's own choosing, and thus, it has been claimed, contravened Article 18 of the Universal Declaration on Human Rights. [33]

The Council of State (Raj Parishad) was to be formed by the king as an advisory body, and to designate a regent in the case of his mental or physical infirmity. This Raj Parishad, which consists of members of the royal family, the cabinet and leading national figures, was modelled on the *Raj Sabha* of the old constitution, but holds fewer powers.

The Executive. The executive authority of Nepal was vested in the king *and* the council of ministers, and the constitution made it clear that all functions discharged by the king (other than those explicitly stated by the constitution to be discretionary) should be discharged on the advice and with the consent of the council of ministers. The king must appoint as prime minister the leader of the party or coalition of parties which wins a clear majority in the House of Representatives. These provisions contrast strongly with those of 1962: Article 20(2) of the old constitution began 'The sovereignty of Nepal is vested in His Majesty and all powers—executive, legislative and judicial—emanate from Him', while Article 24(2) stated, 'The question of whether His Majesty has consulted any person or authority under the provisions of this constitution...shall not be inquired into by any court'.

The Legislature. The legislature was to consist of three elements: the king; a House of Representatives *(Pratinidhi Sabha)* consisting of 205 members each elected from a district constituency; and a National Assembly *(Rashtriya Sabha)* consisting of 60 members. Of these 60, 10 would be royal nominees—reputed persons who have made distinguished contributions to national life—35 (including at least 3 women) would be elected by the House of Representatives, and 15 would be elected from the 5 development regions through an electoral college system. The term of the House of Representatives would be 5 years, while the National Assembly was to be a permanent body, with one-third of its members retiring every two years.

The form of the legislature represents a return to the constitution of 1959, which provided for a 36-member senate and an elected House of Representatives. In 1959, however, the king nominated 18 of the 36 senators, who served six-year terms, while the House of Representatives had only 109 seats. The king therefore has far less say in the membership of his government now than he did under the democratic constitution of 1959.

[33] Shaha, 1990.

The Judiciary. The constitution provides for a three-tier judiciary—a Supreme Court, appellate courts and district courts. The Chief Justice is to be appointed on the recommendation of a constitutional council, other Justices of the Supreme Court on the recommendation of a judicial council. The Supreme Court will have the power to declare any law *ultra vires* of the constitution.

Political Parties. There appears to be almost total freedom to form political parties. However, a party must conform to certain rules if it is to be permitted to stand in national elections: it must not restrict membership on the basis of religion, community, caste or region; its constitution and regulations must be democratic; its executive office-bearers must be elected at least once every five years; and at least 5 per cent of its candidates in elections must be women.[34]

Emergency Powers. Article 81 of the 1962 constitution entitled the king to revoke the constitution in its entirety and to assume to himself all powers of government—which is exactly what King Mahendra had done in 1960, under a similar provision (Article 55) of the 1959 constitution. There was, as a consequence, great concern lest the 1990 constitution should again grant emergency powers to the king. This it most certainly has not done, but commentators such as Rishikesh Shaha point out a number of contradictions and ambiguities. According to Article 115, the king can declare a state of emergency in the event of a 'grave threat to the sovereignty, unity or security of any part of Nepal, due to war, outside attack, armed rebellion or serious economic disruption'. The king's proclamation must be ratified by the House of Representatives within three months. Shaha claims that the constitution is not clear enough on the important question of whether the king is at liberty to proclaim a state of emergency without consulting his government: how, he asks, could the king 'be expected to act by and with the advice and consent of the council of ministers [as laid down in Article 35(2)] while giving *it* advice and encouragement?' [as laid down in Article 43(2)]. Shaha also claims that a clause which explicitly required the king to seek the consent of the council of ministers before declaring an emergency was deleted from the constitution commission's draft. But this may have been necessary in the event of an emergency arising when there is no council of ministers to give its consent, as can happen in a parliamentary system.

Amendments. Bills seeking to repeal or amend provisions of the constitution may be tabled in either house, providing they do not 'contravene the spirit of the Preamble'. Such amendments require a two-thirds

---

[34] Under these rules, three of the 47 parties that applied to the Election Commission for registration early in 1991 had their requests turned down.

majority and the king's approval, although the king must approve such bills if they are presented to him a second time.

The Royal Nepal Army. A compromise was reached on the matter of control of the Army. The king is to remain the title of Supreme Commander-in-Chief. He will appoint the Commander-in-Chief on the prime minister's recommendation, and a National Security council headed by the prime minister will take charge of all other military operations.

Conclusion: Did the Mango Tree Bear Oranges?

The new constitution did meet the demands of the democracy movement: political parties are free to organise, the proportion of the legislature that is directly elected is larger than it has ever been, and the power of the palace, though still substantial, has been greatly reduced. But communal groups have been granted only minor, non-fundamental concessions. Though Radio Nepal now broadcasts news bulletins in Hindi and Newari, full news summaries may only be heard in Nepali or English. Similarly, Nepali remains the language of government and post-primary education throughout the kingdom. Some concessions have been made to women's groups, but these are mostly nominal, while the demand for a secular state forced only one change: the granting of a right to all sects and denominations to run and maintain their own institutions. The demands of Tarai organisations have been largely ignored. Human rights groups have been more successful: the death penalty has been abolished, there is protection against discrimination on the basis of religion, race or gender, and protection against preventative detention. Some of these rights are granted only to Nepali citizens, while the constitution itself discriminates against women in its section on nationality: according to Article 9, the children of male citizens are considered Nepali by descent, while those of female citizens must reside in Nepal for 15 years before they can become citizens.

The 1990 constitution of Nepal represented something of a compromise between the palace and the Congress, and the Left was slightly marginalised. Republicans cannot be happy with a dispensation that still assigns considerable powers and privileges to the monarch and his family, and it must be admitted that the record of April to November 1990 did give cause for doubt over whether the palace had truly acquiesced to its semi-constitutional role, or would actually act in every instance after sincere consultations with elected bodies. This may often have depended on the quality of the advice received by the king himself. On several occasions, King Birendra acted decisively in line with public opinion, after the people had made their feelings known directly to him. It often seemed in the past, however, that the decision-making process in Nepal was dominated by the highly conservative palace secretariat.

The weakening of the secretariat that one assumes has followed the election of a new government can only strengthen democracy in Nepal.

Compared with the earlier constitutions of Nepal—and particularly with the 1962 dispensation—the 1990 constitution represented a dramatic advance in the evolution of a democratic, constitutional order in Nepal. Whether it will actually work in practice depends on whether the political parties can co-operate with one another, and with the palace, in its implementation, and whether the growth of communalism witnessed during 1990 will be recognised, understood and contained. Further struggles to amend the constitution are not impossible, though the precedent of 1960 which filled every Nepali politician's mind during 1990 seems to be fading from view. So far, it seems, the mango tree bears oranges of a sort: the earnest hope in Nepal after promulgation was that the palace would not reach out to pick them again, and that the constitution would not be tested by the Supreme Court to establish whether such fruits were forbidden.

REFERENCES

Agrawal, Hem Narayan, *Nepal a Study in Constitutional Change*. New Delhi, 1980.

Gaige, Frederick, *Regionalism and National Unity in Nepal*. Los Angeles and Berkeley, 1975.

Government of Nepal, *The Constitution of Nepal*. Kathmandu, 1983.

Joshi, Bhuwan Lal and Rose, Leo, *Democratic Innovations in Nepal*. Berkeley, 1966.

Koirala, B.P., *Melmilapko Sharta: Rashtriyata ra Prajatantra*. ('Arguments for Harmony: Nationhood and Democracy'). Kathmandu, 1982.

Mishra, Shashi P., *B.P. Koirala, A Case Study in Third World Democratic Leadership*. Bhubaneshwar and Varanasi, 1985.

Chapter 4

THE GENERAL ELECTIONS OF MAY 1991

John Whelpton

On 12 May 1991, just over one year after the triumph of the Movement for the Restoration of Multi-Party Democracy, the people of Nepal went to the polls in the first fully free election for 32 years. They marked the final repudiation of the panchayat era by restoring to power the Nepali Congress, which had won Nepal's first multi-party election in 1959, only to be robbed of the fruits of victory the following year. But there is a crucial difference between the 1959 and 1991 results. Although the Congress share of the total popular vote was much the same on both occasions (35.4 per cent in 1959, as against 37.8 per cent in 1991) in 1959 the splintered nature of the opposition parties and the geographical distribution of their support presented Congress with 74 out of 109 parliamentary seats. But now Congress has only 110 seats out of 205, and the Communist Party of Nepal (United Marxist and Leninist) is established as a strong opposition, with 69 seats and the prospect of support on some occasions from 13 other leftist members of parliament.[1] This survey of the 1991 election will pay particular attention to the new alternative to Congress, and to the way the balance of forces is likely to evolve.

The Electoral Framework

Nepal's 1990 constitution and the negotiations which produced it are discussed elsewhere in this volume, but it will be useful here to consider briefly its provisions on the electoral system.[2] These set the number of seats for the House of Representatives *(pratinidhi sabha)* at 205, to be distributed among the 75 districts in proportion to their population, but with the proviso that each district must be allocated at least one seat. There is consequently some over-representation of the thinly-populated far-northern region: the least-populated constituency, Mustang district, contains only 6,249 voters, while the one with the largest electorate, Kathmandu -1, has 102, 632.

Each constituency elects one member, using the 'first-past-the-post'

[1] Figures for the 1959 election are given in INSEC, 1991:70-1. Results for 1991 are from Election Commission 1991.

[2] An English translation of clauses relating to the legislature and the electoral process is given in INSEC, 1991:65-6. Versions quoted here are modified on the basis of comparison with the original Nepali *(Gorkhapatra,* 10 November, 1990).

system employed in India, and in the UK and USA. The decision not to
adopt any system of proportional representation appears to have been
taken almost by default. Since the election, some on the Left have
complained at the injustice of Congress gaining complete control of the
government with less than 40 per cent of the popular vote, [3] but no
party raised the issue while the constitution was being drafted. One
Nepalese political scientist, Chitra K. Tiwari, in conjunction with a
visiting Danish scholar, Jorgen Elklit, did advocate the adoption of proportional representation in summer 1990 but, judging from the reaction
at the Tribhuvan University seminar to which they presented their
views, there was no support for it among other Nepalese academics or
officials. [4] This preference for the traditional system was rooted in a fear
of instability if no party gained a working majority in parliament and,
for supporters of the two principal parties, in the hope that they
themselves would be the beneficiaries under the traditional system.

While in general there is now complete freedom for the establishment and functioning of political parties, clauses 112-114 of the constitution impose certain conditions for a party to be registered by the election commission and thus gain guaranteed access to government media
and other facilities. These conditions include the observance of democratic norms in the party's own organisation, at least five per cent of its
candidates nominated for national elections being female and, for every
general election subsequent to 1991, the party having obtained a minimum of three per cent of the popular vote in the previous election.
Registration is also to be denied to any political organisation which
opposes the multi-party system or is of a separatist character. The latter
exclusion, potentially the most controversial, is worded differently in
different sub-clauses:

(112.3): 'any party...on the basis of religion, community, caste *(jat)*,
tribe *(jati)* or regionalism *(kshetriyata)*'

(113.3) 'any political party or organisation if membership is prejudi-
cially denied to any citizen of Nepal solely on the basis of religion,
caste, tribe, language or sex, and also if the name, objectives, insignia
(chinha) or flag are of a religious or communal nature or of one promoting the disintegration of the country *(dharmik, sampradayik va deslai
vikhandit garne prakritiko)*.'

It is arguable that the outlawing of geographical or cultural separatism infringes the right to political organisation as it is understood in

[3] See, for example, Padma Ratna Tuladhar's call for a review of the
system in *Jhilko,* 16 (April-September 1991): 8.

[4] Chitra K. Tiwari, 'Electoral Systems and the Forthcoming Elections in
Nepal' and Jorgen Elklit, 'The Choice of an Electoral System and the
Consequences for the Political Parties', papers presented at the Political
Science Association of Nepal's National Seminar in Kathmandu, 3 August,
1990.

western democracies, but the approach is common to many Third World countries trying to weld an extremely diverse population into a single nation-state. In India it has been illegal since the 1950s for any organisation to advocate independence for a part of the country, while in Malaysia it is similarly an offence to promote the secession of one of the constituent republics. In Nepal's case, the electoral commission chose to interpret these provisions leniently, denying registration to the small Mongol National Organisation, but granting it to the Sadbhavana Party, which is a Tarai regional party, and also to the Nepal Rastriya Jan Mukti Morcha, which advances the claims of the hill tribes. The apparent principle is that a *de facto* regional or ethnic party will be tolerated so long as its name and constitution do not make its regional or ethnic nature explicit.

The Main Political Parties

The success of the democracy movement prompted a rush to establish new political parties and, according to one study, the total number had reached 74 by early 1991. [5] Of these, 47 applied for recognition by the electoral commission and 44 were accepted for registration and allocated election symbols. Only 20 parties eventually fielded candidates, only eight actually won seats, and only six obtained the three per cent of the national vote needed to retain their status as national parties in the next election. The eight parties with parliamentary representation will now be examined separately, with discussion of some of the minor organisations included in an account of the election campaign.

The **Nepali Congress Party** is Nepal's oldest continually functioning party and has also always been the dominant one.[6] It was founded in 1947 by Nepalese dissident exiles in India as the Nepali National Congress. Many of these dissidents had also been active in the Indian Nationalist Movement and, as well as adopting its name from the Indian National Congress, the party also adopted that organisation's basic principles: a combination of socialism and parliamentary democracy as its goal and Gandhian non-violence as its tactics. The name was changed to Nepali Congress in 1950 when it amalgamated with the Nepal Democratic Congress, an organisation set up by estranged members of the Rana family. The party played a leading role in the overthrow of Rana rule in 1950-51 and when it obtained a two-thirds

[5] INSEC, 1991:82.

[6] If continuity is not taken into account, the title of 'oldest party' should probably go to Tanka Prasad Acharya's Praja Parishad. Formed in the 1930s as a clandestine anti-Rana organisation, this functioned openly as a political party from 1951 to 1960 and was re-established in 1990. Acharya and Dilli Raman Regmi, who had similarly revived his Nepal Rastriya Congress, formed an alliance and then decided jointly not to contest the elections.

majority in the 1959 election it seemed set to become the 'natural' party of government, just as its Indian counterpart then was across the border. This situation was unacceptable to King Mahendra, who had envisaged a balance of power between the parties which would enable the monarchy to retain a dominant role. In December 1960, alleging that Congress had failed to maintain law and order and was compromising national independence, he used his emergency powers under the 1959 constitution to arrest the government and dissolve parliament.

Despite Mahendra's subsequent ban on political parties, the Congress continued to function and to oppose the royal move. Prime minister B.P. Koirala and his cabinet colleagues were kept in prison until 1968, but many party workers went into exile in India, which they used as a base for armed cross-border raids. The Indian government was strongly opposed to Mahendra's action and it tolerated the raids at first, but put a stop to them in 1962 when the outbreak of the Indo-China border war made a rapprochement with the king essential. In 1968, when Koirala and his colleagues were released from prison, a faction of the party led by Subarna Shamsher Rana decided to accept the Panchayat system and work constitutionally for its liberalisation, but Koirala himself and the majority of the party continued the struggle. There were sporadic attempts at further armed action, particularly during the first two years of Birendra's reign (1972-74), while tussles between pro-Congress, pro-communist and a small number of royalist students were a major feature of campus life.

In 1976, when Indira Gandhi's state of emergency had made India a less congenial place of exile, B.P. Koirala returned to Nepal, announcing his intention to seek 'national reconciliation', and although court proceedings were started against him in connection with the party's previous violent campaign, he was eventually released. In 1979, when student demonstrations led King Birendra to hold a referendum on the future of the Panchayat system, B.P. campaigned energetically for the multi-party side.

After the Panchayat system's narrow victory in the 1980 referendum and the introduction of direct elections for the Rastriya Panchayat, Congress was split on whether to have nothing to do with panchayat institutions until the ban on political parties was lifted or, as some leftist groups were doing, adopt an entryist approach. After boycotting the general elections of 1981 and 1986, the party participated in the 1987 local elections. Its candidate, accepting the legal fiction that he was standing as an independent, was elected *pradhan panch* (mayor) of Kathmandu, only to be removed from office by the government later in the year when he refused to take part in the official commemoration of the promulgation of the panchayat constitution. As economic difficulties, a succession of political scandals and, finally, the ill-judged

confrontation with India over trade and transit arrangements continued to
erode the position of the panchayat administration, the party finally
opted for direct confrontation in 1990, in conjunction with an ad hoc
coalition of communist groups called the United Left Front.

Since B.P. Koirala's death in 1982, the party had been dominated by
three figures: veteran politician Ganesh Man Singh, who had the cour-
tesy title of 'supreme leader'; general secretary Girija Prasad Koirala,
B.P.'s younger brother; and Krishna Prasad Bhattarai who had been
appointed acting president in 1981 on Ganesh Man's recommendation.
When the interim government was being formed, Ganesh Man declined
the premiership in favour of Bhattarai, whose conciliatory manner made
him more acceptable to the Left than the stridently anti-communist
Koirala.

Commitment to parliamentary democracy has always been the key-
stone of the Congress political creed. On the campuses of Tribhuvan
University, one of the few arenas where party politics could be kept
alive when the Panchayat system was at its most rigorous, the pro-
Congress faction among staff and students used to be known simply as
'the democrats'. In the months before the May election, the party continued to present itself as the key actor in the struggle to bring democracy to Nepal and also as the sole reliable guarantor of a democratic
future. It naturally pointed to the worldwide trend toward political
pluralism as vindication of its own traditional stance, but the
international triumph of its ideology perhaps made it less able to
provide the party with a distinct identity: when virtually everyone inside
and outside the country is proclaiming the virtues of political
pluralism, describing oneself as a democrat may seem tantamount to
saying one is against sin.

On economic issues, the party's stance is less clearcut. For the
Nepali Congress in its early days, as for the Indian Congress,
'socialism' meant state-control of much of the economy, albeit within a
democratic framework. The attraction of the Nehru-Mahalanobis model
has waned since then and, in so far as anything has replaced it, the new
economic vision is of social democracy along Scandinavian lines.[7]
There is in fact a range of opinion on this issue within the party,
perhaps partly coinciding with a division some observers see between
India- and USA-orientated blocs.

In assessing any party's economic intentions, it is of course necessary to look not just at its propaganda but at its activists and its support base in the country. Congress's left-wing opponents have long
characterised it as 'the representative of liberal zamindars and capitalists'
or in the simple phrase heard in summer 1990 from two young

[7] Arjun Narsingh K.C., Congress M.P. for Nuwakot-3, *Saptahik
Bimarsha*, 26 July, 1991.

communists in Pokhara and Kathmandu, *dhani manisko parti:* 'the rich man's party'. While the party was not set up with any such intention, and many activists are intellectuals and middle-class professionals, it is certainly true that many better-off Nepalese have aligned themselves behind the Congress, in the belief that it provides the best bulwark against the communists. In addition, both during the pre-1960 period of parliamentary politics and since April 1990, elite groups in rural Nepal naturally gravitated toward Congress as the best way of maintaining their local influence. Such people had equally naturally chosen to work within the Panchayat system during the interim, and the resulting rush of ex-panchas into the Congress ranks may have weakened the chance of a direct attack on the multi-party system by traditionalist forces, but has also enabled many on the Left to argue that there is little difference between Congress and the old regime.

The influx of these opportunistic elements into the party accentuated its basic structural weakness: an abundance of members and aspirant members eager for a share of the spoils, but not enough dedicated cadres willing to shoulder the day-to-day burden of political work. In the run-up to the election, one Congress leader put it candidly: 'The leaders and workers of the Nepali Congress are in general slow, lazy and inactive. Perhaps this is why the communists label us as the bourgeoisie'.[8] Similar sentiments were voiced by Ganesh Man Singh himself after the election.[9] It was a situation which left the party too dependent on the prestige of a few figures at the top as well as on loyalties formed in a previous generation.

In contrast to Congress the main opposition party, the **Communist Party of Nepal (United Marxist and Leninist)**, was formed only four months before the election by the merger of the CPN (Marxist) and the CPN (Marxist-Leninist). Its historical roots, however, are intertwined with those of Congress in the final years of the Rana period. In common with most of the sixteen or so communist groups in Nepal, the Marxist and Marxist-Leninist groups both claimed to be the true heirs to the original Communist Party of Nepal, founded in Calcutta in 1949 by Pushpa Lal Shrestha, a former secretary of the Nepali National Congress. The party was a marginal force during the 1950s, gaining only seven per cent of the vote in the 1959 election. After Mahendra's dismissal of the Congress government and banning of political parties, the communists split into an accommodationist wing under general-secretary Keshar Jung Raimajhi, who had initially welcomed the king's move as a 'progressive step',[10] and a more radical group favouring direct opposition to the royal régime. The radicals

---

[8] Rajan Panta, quoted in Krishna Hacchethu (n.d.)
[9] Ganesh Man Singh, interview in *Saptahik Bimarsha*, 14 June, 1991.
[10] Rawal, 1990-1:52.

managed to organise a convention in 1962, at which Tulsi Lal Amatya was elected general secretary, but ceased functioning in 1965.

During the late sixties separate attempts to re-establish the party were made by Pushpa Lal, by his brother-in-law Man Mohan Adhikari, and by Mohan Bikram Singh.[11] Man Mohan's group, based on the old party's eastern regional committee, was influential at first but, as it began to decay, its Jhapa district committee broke away and launched a campaign of assassination of 'class enemies' modelled on the Naxalite movement across the border in West Bengal. The authorities cracked down and a number of activists, including Mohan Chandra Adhikari, were kept in custody until January 1990. The group abandoned terrorism as a political weapon but continued its adherence to Maoist theories of armed revolution and became the nucleus of the Communist Party of Nepal (Marxist-Leninist), established in 1978. During the 1980 referendum campaign, in which Man Mohan's group was active in the multiparty cause, the CPN(M-L) held aloof, recommending neither participation nor a boycott. By the time of the second general election under the amended panchayat constitution, the party had modified its line on participation in constitutional politics and put up a number of candidates. These won four seats (in Kaski, Chitwan, Tehrathum and Jhapa), while a sympathiser (who later deserted to the panchayat camp) was elected from Ilam. In 1989, the party held its '4th Convention' (so termed to proclaim the gathering the legitimate successor to the 3rd Convention of 1962), formally abandoning Maoism and proclaiming its readiness for a combined struggle with the Nepali Congress against the Panchayat system. In 1987, Man Mohan Adhikari had combined forces with the Pushpa Lal group, (dominated since Pushpa Lal's death in 1978 by his widow, Sahana Pradhan), to establish the Communist Party of Nepal (Marxist).

When the Marxist-Leninist and Marxist factions combined in January 1991, the former were the stronger group, with a more extensive network of activists. Most observers agreed that the reins of power in the CPN (Unified Marxist and Leninist) were held mainly by a 'hardline' group from the Marxist-Leninists—principally Madan Bhandari, general secretary of the new party, Jhalanath Khanal, who served as minister for forests, agriculture and land reform in the interim government, and Madhav Nepal. Despite the standing conferred by their association with Pushpa Lal in the founding of the communist movement in Nepal, Sahana Pradhan and party president Man Mohan Adhikari were less influential, as also were the Mainali brothers, Radha Krishna and Chandra Prakash, prominent 'moderates' in the CPN (M-L). Former

[11] Details in this paragraph are based mainly on the account in CPN (M-L) 1989a: 50-7, and on an interview with Jeevraj Ashrit, Central Committee member, Kathmandu, 23 August, 1990.

workers of the CPN (M) were particularly unhappy and there were constant rumours that the new party would split again. However, they managed to maintain unity until the elections were over.

Despite its abandonment of the 'Maoist' label in 1989, the CPN (M-L) shared with the CPN (M) and with ultra-leftist groups such as Mohan Bikram Singh's an analysis of and prescription for Nepalese society identical to that presented for China in Mao Tse-Tung's 1940 essay, 'On the Doctrine of New Democracy' *(Xin-min-zhu zhu-yi lun)*. According to this theory, which naturally formed the centre-piece of the manifesto issued on the formation of the CPN (UML),[12] Nepal is a 'semi-feudal and semi-colonial society' requiring further development of indigenous capitalism before the transition to socialism is feasible. To achieve this, the proletariat (represented, of course, by the communist party) must ally itself with the peasantry, the petit-bourgeoisie and the 'national capitalists', viz. entrepreneurs seeking to set up productive enterprises within Nepal rather than 'comparador capitalists' merely acting as agents of foreign capital. The political system to be established by this alliance is known as *naulo janbad,* best translated as 'new people's democracy,'[13] in which the proletariat takes the lead but still shares power with the other classes.

There has long been controversy, both among communists and between them and their opponents, on the compatibility of *naulo janbad* with multi-party democracy. Mao's original concept of 'new democracy' certainly accommodated non-communist parties, and in fact the main elements of the theory were evolved in the 1920s precisely in order to provide a rationale for the Chinese communists' co-operation with the Kuomintang (Nationalist) party.[14] In the same manner, the CPN

[12] CPN (UML), 1991a. Although the party's official title includes the formula 'Marxist and Leninist', in practice it came to be referred to as 'Marxist-Leninist', to the annoyance of the ex-CPN (Marxist) element!

[13] In describing his system, Mao used *min-zhu,*the standard Chinese for 'democracy', whether of the bourgeois or proletarian variety. Nepalese communists preferred not to employ the usual Nepali equivalent, *prajatantra,* presumably both to distinguish their system from capitalist parliamentarianism and because *praja* ('subjects') implies the existence of a monarchy. Outside the context of Marxist theory, *janbad* normally carries the sense of 'republic', but analysed etymologically it correponds precisely to *min-zhu* and *demokratia,* all three combining elements meaning 'people' and 'power'.

[14] Brandt *et al* 1973:262. Mao was still arguing for a degree of political pluralism in his report to the 7th National Conference of the CCP in April 1945: 'China, throughout the period of her New Democratic system, cannot and should not have a system of government of the character of a one-class dictatorship or a one-party autocracy. We have no reason not to co-operate with political parties, social groups or individuals outside the CP, who adopt a co-operative, but not a hostile attitude' (ibid.: 305).

(M-L)'s 1989 convention, seeking a basis for tactical unity with
Congress, declared that *naulo janbad* would guarantee 'full freedom for
the ordinary people *(am janta)* to establish parties....on the basis of
their political beliefs'.[15] However, both Mao's vision and the CPN (M-
L)'s 1989 line seem to have fallen short of a full endorsement of
political pluralism. First, they probably had in mind a continuing
alliance between parties rather than a competitive struggle: such an
alliance still exists in the People's Republic of China between the CPC
and a number of nominally independent parties. Second, they
undoubtedly wished to restrict the political rights of their bitterest
opponents, those 'feudal' or 'comparador capitalist' elements against
whom 'the people's democratic dictatorship' was to be exercised.

However, following the formation of the interim government, the
CPN (M-L) began to modify its stance. A report approved by the
party's central committee in November 1990 accepted that an element
of political competition was essential for democracy.[16] When the CPN
(M-L) and CPN (M) amalgamated, their agreed programme stated
explicitly that *naulo janbad* would permit peaceful political competition
between parties with the governing party chosen in periodic general
elections; and this commitment to multi-party democracy was reiterated
in the CPN (UML) election manifesto.[17] Party leaders argued that such
competition was in fact in accordance with the Marxist principle of the
dialectic, and that the one-party system as it had been practised in many
communist countries was thus a perversion of communism.[18] The party
was less clear on the exceptions to this general right to political
activity. In July 1990 Madan Bhandari stated that no party opposed to
the principle of *naulo janbad* would be permitted.[19] A central committee
member I interviewed the following month preferred to speak of a ban
on 'reactionaries' and 'anti-nationals' and the same formula was adopted
by three district leaders shortly before the election.[20] In August 1991,
when I asked another central committee member who would determine
whether a particular party was or was not 'reactionary', he told me that
the 'people' would decide. As I pressed for a more precise answer, two
younger party members intervened to say that, as at present, the
election commission would decide which parties to recognise and the
restrictions enforced would only be those against sectarianism and

---

[15] CPN(M-L),1989b: 16.

[16] CPN (M-L),1990: 4, 94.

[17] CPN (UML), 1991a: 9-10; CPN (UML) 1991b: 6

[18] Modnath Prashrit, *Saptahik Bimarsha*, 21/6/1991; Madan Bhandari,
interviewed in *Nepalipatra*, 19 July, 1991.

[19] *Nava Yug*, 1-15 July, 1990.

[20] Interview with Jeevraj Ashrit, Kathmandu, 23 August, 1990; Krishna
Hacchethu, n.d.

separatism in Nepal's present constitution![21] In October 1991, however, after a central committee meeting had officially adopted 'multi-party people's democracy' *(bahudaliya janbad)* as the party line, Madan Bhandari was again to imply that only supporters of *janbad* would be allowed to organise.[22] Amid all these mixed signals, non-communists could point to the party's official backing for the Chinese government's supression of the 1989 democracy movement and its leaders' initial support for the attempted hard-line coup in Moscow as proof that they still hankered after old-style authoritarianism.

The reality behind the apparent confusion is that the CPN (UML) is a party continuing on the path from the ultra-leftism of the 1970s towards a *de-facto* social democratic stance. Like the Nepali Congress, it contains many divergent strands of opinion: some cadres remain at heart committed to the Maoist line of a people's war leading to a *de-facto* one-party state, others on the liberal wing of the party would be happy to abandon the name 'communist' altogether, though they are constrained from so doing by many of their supporters' attachment to the old name. In the middle, the 'hard-line' leadership combines rigorous party discipline and a continuing attachment to the rhetoric of the international communist movement with ideological flexibility on domestic politics. In this, they seem to be following the example of Jyoti Basu's Communist Party of India (Marxist) in West Bengal, with whom they have long had cordial relations.[23]

As with the Congress, the composition and support base of the CPN (UML) needs to be examined as well as its overt ideology. Despite its claim to represent the proletariat, the party's own 1989 report revealed that 60 per cent of its activists were drawn from the 'middle peasantry' and the urban 'petit-bourgeois'. Only a very small proportion is drawn from the landless, poor peasants, urban industrial workers or members of backward castes and communities.[24] Schoolteachers, students and unemployed youths are a mainstay of the organisation at grass-roots level.[25] The party does enjoy passive support from many disadvantaged groups, but also from the middle and lower-middle classes, including lower-level government employees.[26]

The CPN (UML)'s main electoral rival on the Left was the **United**

[21] Interview with Keshar Mani Pokhrel (secretary to CPN (UML) Central Committee), Ganesh Shyam Bhusal and Romani Bhattarai, Kathmandu, 24 August, 1991. Pokhrel was among those party members who resigned in December 1991 in protest against the adoption of 'multi-party democracy' as the official line.

[22] *Chalphal,* 27 October, 1991 (Nepal Press Digest, 35, 44: 415).

[23] On the CPI (M)'s evolution into a reformist force, see Kohli, 1987.

[24] CPN(M-L), 1989a: 71.

[25] Hacchethu op. cit.

[26] 'D.B.M.', 1991: 33.

People's Front (Nepal) *(Samyukta Jana Morcha Nepal)*, an umbrella organisation for a number of avowedly Maoist parties who agreed to co-operate with one another just before the January deadline for registration with the election commission. Since it is not a unitary party, the UPF has no post of president or general secretary, but Baburam Bhattarai, an architect and planner who also edits the Kathmandu Marxist journal *Jhilko*, acted as co-ordinator during the campaign. Lilamani Pokhrel, one of the leaders of the student protest movement in 1979, became the leader of the Front's nine parliamentarians after the elections.

Precise information on the Front's composition is a little difficult to come by, but the dominant element is the CPN (Unity Centre), formed in 1990 by the amalgamation of members of the CPN (Mashal) and the CPN (4th Convention). Mashal split from Mohan Bikram Singh's group, the CPN (Masal), in the mid-80s and has been the most influential of the 'hard-line' groups, rejecting the Marxist-Leninists' 'revisionism'.[27] The 4th Convention group emerged from another split in Mohan Bikram Singh's party in 1983, and was one of the seven parties in the United Left Front, but quit the ULF in December 1990. When 4th Convention leader Nirmal Lama was appointed a member of the commission which drafted Nepal's 1990 constitution, party colleague Lilamani Pokhrel took over the running of the group by mutual agreement. Following the formation of the Unity Centre, both Lama and Pokhrel seemed to be prominent in the leadership, along with 'Prachand' (the *nom de guerre* of the Mashal leader) and 'Comrade Nirman'.

Also included in the United People's Front at the time of the election were the recently-established CPN (Marxist-Leninist-Maoist), and Shital Kumar's group. The latter broke away from Mohan Bikram Singh's organisation during the campaign because they rejected Singh's policy of boycotting the election. Kumar and his colleagues maintained that they themselves, not Singh, were now the legitimate Masal leadership, and so they continued to use the party's name.

The United People's Front differs from the UML on three main points. First, and most importantly, it argues that *naulo janbad* is only achievable through non-constitutional means.[28] It is willing to contest

---

[27] *Masal* and *mashal* are alternative spellings of the same Nepali word, meaning 'torch'. The 's' and 'sh' represent Nepali consonants which were originally pronounced differently but are now indistinguishable in most people's pronunciation. When a word is spelled out orally the words *patlo* (thin) and *moto* (fat) are employed to distinguish the two letters. Hence Mohan Bikram's group is often referred to in conversation as *patlo masal* and Prachand's as *moto mashal*. In July 1991 the small CPN (People-Orientated) also joined the Unity Centre.

[28] Lilamani Pokhrel, interviewed in *Nepalipatra*, 14 June, 1991.

elections in order to gain a platform to 'expose' the inadequacy of the parliamentary system, but rejects the goal of securing a parliamentary majority. Secondly, whereas the UML sometimes suggests that the monarchy might be retained if the king does not stand in the way of implementing a popular progamme, the UPF rejects this entirely and calls instead for a constituent assembly to draft a republican constitution.[29] Thirdly, although willing to countenance a system in which 'popular forces' (but not 'capitalists' and 'exploiters') would have freedom to set up different parties, the UPF still seems attached to the idea of a one-party state and is less reconciled to the long-term desirability of multi-party politics.[30]

Also describing itself as Maoist, but outside the United People's Front, the **Nepal Workers and Peasants Party** gained just two seats and 1.25 per cent of the popular vote in the election and so will not be recognised as a party by the election commission in the next general election. The grouping is nevertheless of some importance as it has a strong hold on voters' loyalty in Bhaktapur, the third town of the Kathmandu Valley, and in part of Karnali zone. Its leader, Narayan Man Bijukche, usually known as 'Comrade Rohit', left Pushpa Lal Shrestha's group in 1975-6, after rejecting the latter's relatively pro-Soviet line and his insistence on an immediate alliance with Congress rather than first building up the communists's own strength.[31] Although himself from a traditional landowning family in Bhaktapur, Rohit's patient political work among the Jyapu cultivator caste of the town gained him a firm following. Following the introduction of universal suffrage for elections to the Rastriya Panchayat, the party was one of the first leftist groups to adopt an 'entryist' approach to the Panchayat system, winning the Bhaktapur seat in the 1981 general election. When its victorious candidate, Karna Bahadur Hyuju, broke with the party, allegedly after succumbing to the blandishments of Prince Dhirendra, a new candidate was put up successfully in 1986. Following the mob-killing of Hyuju in 1987, Rohit and many associates were kept in prison without trial until the victory of the democracy movement. The party was a member of the United Left Front until withdrawing in December 1990.

Despite his party's Maoist orientation, Rohit himself seemed to

[29] In an interview with *Saptahik Bimarsha* (1 June 1990), Mohan Chandra Adhikari of the Marxist-Leninist group stated that, while a republic was desirable, the party would not resort to violence if a constitutional monarch allowed it to implement its programme. The demand for a republic is re-stated in the UPF manifesto (UPF 1991: 8.)

[30] Lilamani Pokhrel, interviewed in *Nepalipatra,* 14 June, 1991; Nirmal Lama has condemned the setting-up of multi-party systems in socialist countries as a retro-grade step *(Saptahik Bimarsha,* 15 June, 1990).

[31] Interview with Narayan Bijukche, Bhaktapur, 19 August, 1990.

become quite enthusiastic about multi-party politics in the immediate
aftermath of the movement, remarking favourably in a May 1990 interview on the adoption of 'good aspects' of capitalism in Dengist China
and suggesting that Nepal might be able to go through a capitalist stage
and then to a socialist revolution, without any need for the intermediate
stage of *naulo janbad*.[32] In August the same year he told me that
'experience had shown that a single-party system did not work'.[33]
Nevertheless, his group moved closer to the UPF in the run-up to the
elections, probably because of what it perceived as the CPN (UML)'s
heavy-handed treatment of the smaller leftist parties.

The **Communist Party of Nepal (Democratic)**,which also
obtained two seats but failed to break the three per cent barrier, was
known until 1991 as the Communist Party of Nepal (Manandhar), after
its leader, Vishnu Bahadur Manandhar. When the original Communist
Party of Nepal split in 1962, Manandhar had sided with Keshar Jang
Raimajhi but split with him in 1981.[34] A member of the United Left
Front, the party was represented in the interim government by Nilambar
Acharya (law and justice, labour and social welfare, tourism), who was
once a student in the Soviet Union. The party remained within the ULF
after the exodus of four other parties in December 1990, but in the run-
up to the election was critical of the CPN (UML) for seeking a
dominant role. Manandhar's group, which, as the elections were to
show, did not have a strong popular base, differed from the large
communist group in its strongly pro-Soviet and also pro-Indian
orientation: its manifesto called for priority to be given to India in the
use of Nepal's water resources, in contrast to other leftist groups, who
demanded protection for Nepal's rivers from Indian rapaciousness.[35]

Presenting a challenge both to Congress and the communist parties
was former Rastriya Panchayat member Gajendra Narayan Singh's
Tarai-based **Sadbhavana (Goodwill) Party**,which was to win six
seats. Singh left the Nepali Congress in 1980-81, and established his
organisation two years later as the 'Nepal Sadbhavana Council' to com-
bat alleged discrimination against the *madeshis*, the people of Indian or
plains origin. He was particularly prominent in the opposition to Harka
Gurung's 1983 report which called for an end to the open border with
India, and for restrictions on naturalisation and the economic rights of
non-citizens. In addition to his long-standing demand for the recognition
of Hindi as an official language, his party's manifesto also called for a
federal system of government, job 'reservations' for under-privileged
communities, a liberal policy on citizenship for recent immigrants, and

[32] Narayan Man Bijukche, interview in *Saptahik Bimarsha*, 1 May, 1990.
[33] Interview with Narayan Man Bijukche, Bhaktapur, 19 August, 1990.
[34] Rawal, 1990-91: 66.
[35] Notes on CPN (D) manifesto compiled by Deepak Tamang.

a separate *madeshi* battalion in the army.[36]

The Sadbhavana Party's stance undoubtedly strikes a responsive chord in many *madeshi* hearts, but linguistic and caste differences make it difficult for the Tarai to function as a cohesive political unit. Singh's own Rajput caste makes him suspect to many, particularly in the light of the virtual caste/class war going on across the border in Bihar.[37] On the linguistic issue, most Tarai inhabitants of Indian origin are more comfortable with Hindi than Nepali, but some communities, in particular the Maithili people, would probably prefer a greater role for their own mother-tongues.

Following the abolition of the Panchayat system, many former panchas hastened to find a new home in Congress, or in one of the other parties which had taken part in the democracy movement. Other former activists, however, joined two parties organised by prominent politicians of the panchayat era, and these were the remaining successful contenders in the election, gaining four seats between them and each managing to establish itself as a national party for the next election.

The **National Democratic Party** *(Rastriya Prajatantra Party)* **(Chand)**, which gained three seats, was led by Lokendra Bahadur Chand, who served the last of several terms as prime minister in April 1990, between the dismissal of Marichman Singh and the appointment of Krishna Prasad Bhattarai. He had valuable support in the person of Pashupati Shamsher J.B. Rana. One of the more capable panchayat leaders, Rana had made no secret of his own ambition to become premier under the old dispensation, but as the grandson of the last Rana maharaja his appointment would probably have been too sensitive for the palace to risk. He enjoyed royal confidence, nevertheless, and took a leading role in the negotiations in April 1990 which led to the establishment of the interim government. Perhaps because the two leading figures had been so close to the king in the past, it was rumoured that the party had backing from the palace, including substantial funding from the queen.

The **National Democratic Party (Thapa)**,which gained only one seat,was led by Surya Bahadur Thapa. Thapa had been a close collaborator of King Mahendra, under whom he served as premier from 1966 to 1969. After Birendra's accession, however, he began agitating for reform within the Panchayat system and was imprisoned for a year. Following the 1979 disturbances he was drafted in again as prime minister and was one of the major architects of the panchayat side's victory in the 1980 referendum. He was removed in 1983 after a vote of noconfidence, generally seen as engineered by the palace, and replaced as premier by Chand. Presenting himself as a champion of the liberalised

[36] Notes on Sadbhavana manifesto compiled by Deepak Tamang.
[37] Interview with Siddhi Bahadur Khadgi, Patan, 20 August, 1990.

Panchayat system who had been brought down through the extra-consti-
tutional machinations of an 'underground gang' *(bhumigat giroh),* he
again proceeded to act as an opposition within the Panchayat system.
Although Thapa made unscrupulous use of government funds in the
referendum campaign and is widely seen as personally corrupt, his deter-
mination to make full use of the liberal features of the amended
Panchayat system did help to create the conditions for the restoration of
full democracy.

Though termed 'revivalists' and 'reactionaries' by the Left, neither of
the two parties advocated a return to the Panchayat system,but instead
proclaimed their own liberal democratic credentials.[38] Chand's party
offered the electorate remission of agricultural and earthquake relief
loans under 10,000 rupees and, like the Left, attempted to play the
nationalist card by criticising prime minister Bhattarai's statement
during a visit to Delhi that rivers flowing from Nepal into India were
'common'. Thapa's group concerned itself with generalities, including
advocacy of a mixed economy and national unity and a promise of
'fundamental change' in agriculture and the land-reform programme.[39]

Organisationally, the National Democratic Parties had the advantage
of a network of activists which was already established in every village
in the country, and which included a wider spectrum of Nepalese society
than the largely high-caste-dominated Congress and communist parties,whose strength often lay more in district towns than in outlying
settlements.[40] Most observers assumed that they still had considerable
popular support in more conservative areas, and that Chand's group in
particular would do well as 'the king's party' in the Thakuri-dominated
west.

The Campaign and Conduct of the Election

At the beginning of 1991, the first question that posed itself was what
condition the communist parties would be in on polling-day. Although
seven parties had managed to work together and with Congress to bring
down the Panchayat system, the four which were not represented in the
cabinet—the Nepal Workers and Peasants Party, the 4th Convention
and the relatively weak Verma and Amatya groups—pulled out in
December, alleging that the Marxist-Leninists were concerned with their

[38]For a rare post-April 1990 attempt to defend the principles of the
Panchayat system (though not every aspect of its implementation), see the
interview with Yogi Naraharinath, *Saptahik Bimarsha,* 12 July, 1991.

[39] *Rastriya Prajatantra Parti (Chand) ko Chunav Ghoshana Patra*
(Election Manifesto of the National Democratic Party (Chand), Kathmandu,
n.d. and *Rastriya Prajatantra (Thapa) ko Chunavi Ghoshana Patra* (Election
Manifesto of the National Democratic Party (Thapa), Kathmandu, 2048
V.S.(1991-2) (notes compiled by Deepak Tamang).

[40] 'D. B. M.', 1991: 33; Hacchethu, op.cit.

THE GENERAL ELECTIONS OF MAY 1991

own interests rather than those of the coalition as a whole. Nevertheless, all realised that without some co-ordination between them a split leftist vote would let Congress candidates through in many constituencies. Negotiations were therefore held to try to ensure *ek tham ek bam*—a single, agreed leftist candidate for each constituency. Most if not all of the other parties acknowledged that the CPN(UML) had the largest network of activists and should get the largest share of the seats, but it proved impossible to agree just how large that should be. The UML itself held out for 180 of the 205 seats, and this was rejected by the rest. In the end some arrangements were reached between particular parties and in other cases unilateral decisions not to stand were made, but no comprehensive agreement was concluded. This failure was to cost the Left as a whole 14 seats.[41]

In their election manifestos, almost every political party except the United People's Front proclaimed its acceptance of multi-party democracy, albeit with varying degrees of enthusiasm. But this consensus did not extend to all the details of the 1990 constitution. The CPN(UML) and other leftist groups wanted to amend the constitution to reduce the residual powers of the monarchy, and to declare the country a secular, rather than a Hindu state. Secularism for its own sake was not attractive to any outside a small intellectual elite, but for non-Hindu elements in the population it served as a symbol of opposition to high-caste Hindus and their dominant position in the social structure. While advocacy of a secular state could thus help to rally disadvantaged groups, it may also have cost the Left votes among more conservative and orthodox sections of the population, especially as some Congress workers were putting it about that the communists would suppress religious practice if they came to power.[42]

For the electorate as a whole it was naturally 'bread and butter' issues which were of most concern. In the Political Science Association of Nepal (POLSAN) survey of 1,000 voters in ten districts just after the election, unemployment, education, drinking water and irrigation were the problems most frequently mentioned by respondents.[43] Both Congress and the CPN (UML), though differing widely in their opening rhetoric, adopted a broadly similar approach to such development issues in their respective manifestos.[44] Each advocated a combination of state

[41] Narayan Man Bijukche, interviewed in *Saptahik Bimarsha*, 10 May, 1991; Kharel, 1991: 50, Table 3.

[42] Hacchethu, op.cit.

[43] Borre, 1991: 37, Table 5.

[44] In an interview with *Saptahik Bimarsha*, 19 July, 1991, the veteran communist Tulsi Lal Amatya bemoaned the similarity, in particular condemning the UML for proposing to accept foreign capital which would produce 'only development on the South Korean or Thai pattern'. The previous year, Nepal Workers' and Peasants' Party leader Narayan Man

planning and encouragement of private and foreign capital, and each
promised a long list of specific benefits for the population, only a
small proportion of which would be realisable by any administration in
one term of office. The UML were, as might be expected, more categor-
ical in their pledges on land reform, promising to lower (by an unspeci-
fied amount) the current ceiling on holdings and to abolish feudal rem-
nants such as the *kamaiya* system of semi-serfdom in western Nepal.[45]
Congress, which has trouble reconciling the views and interests of
different sections of its membership on the land issue, proposed to
introduce progressive taxation on large holdings rather than actual
redistribution, to end dual ownership of land 'in a manner satisfactory
both to landlord and tenant' and 'to adopt suitable laws to end the
oppression of *kamaiyas*'.[46]

In Nepal, as in much longer-established democracies, few of the electorate will have been familiar with the detailed content of manifestos,
and voting decisions had to turn on the general image which workers of
the different political parties succeeded in projecting. Propaganda was
inevitably simplistic and not over-scrupulous. Congressites claimed
that a communist government would confiscate all private property and
communists made easy promises of immediate work and bread for all.[47]

Compared with domestic issues, foreign policy questions were not
of great interest to the electorate as a whole: 'national sovereignty'
ranked only ninth in the list of concerns emerging from the POLSAN
sample.[48] However, foreign policy is of great importance for many in
the educated elite and the official pronouncements of political parties
have always reflected this. For Nepal, the 'yam between two stones' in
Prithvi Narayan Shah's celebrated formulation, foreign policy means in
the first instance relations with India and China. While all parties sub-
scribed to the rhetoric of non-alignment and friendship toward every
nation, Congress and even more so the Sadbhavana party stood for
closer ties with India, while most of the Left parties, including the
UML, had long made opposition to 'Indian hegemonism' a key part of
their platform. In the UML election manifesto the rhetoric was toned
down but the anti-Indian card was played quite strongly during the
campaign. Krishna Prasad Bhattarai was attacked for supposedly
surrendering Nepalese resources in his reference to 'common rivers'.

Bijukche stated there was little difference between the short-term economic
policy of the Congress and the Left Front parties (interview, Bhaktapur,19
August, 1990).

[45] CPN (UML), 1991b: 11-2.
[46] Nepali Congress, 1991: 12,15.
[47] Hacchethu, op.cit. The author is excessively kind to western democracies by suggesting that simplistic propaganda is solely a Third World
phenomenon.
[48] Borre, 1991: 37, Table 5.

One leftist banner depicted the Congress troika Ganesh Man Singh, Krishna Prasad Bhattarai and Girija Prasad Koirala in the guise of monkeys, with a dhoti-clad Chandrashekhar cracking his whip over them and instructing them in Hindi, 'Dance and say 'The rivers are common!'[49] As a Congress minister later pointed out, such pandering to hill prejudice against the *madeshis* contained a large element of posturing: it has long been standard practice for Nepali politicians in opposition to denounce the government of the day for kow-towing to India, only to hasten to seek an accommodation with Delhi themselves when in office.[50]

In the broader international arena, Congress feels a close affinity to the western democracies while the communists have traditionally presented their own struggle as part of an international crusade against the 'imperialism' of the USA and its allies. The old rhetoric was fully represented in the manifesto issued on the formation of the CPN (UML), but its election manifesto, athough still denouncing 'imperialism' and paying homage to 'international proletarian leaders' Mao Tse-tung, Ho Chi Minh and Kim Il Sung, did not attack the USA by name. It was felt by many that the party was anxious to mend its fences with the Americans, though without making too conspicuous a U-turn. However, Congress workers made the most of the argument that a UML government would be unable to ensure either the American or Indian co-operation which is vital for development programmes.

There is little doubt that both New Delhi and Washington were hoping for a Congress victory and the Left were quick to point to anything that could be presented as attempted intervention. The American ambassador in Kathmandu, Julia Chang-Bloch, drew flak when a grant was made to SEARCH, a Nepalese NGO, to carry out a programme of voter education in the run-up to the election. The organisation did in fact confine itself to acquainting villagers with the basic features of the multi-party system, about which many were very sketchily informed but, not surprisingly, the enterprise attracted some suspicion.[51]

On the Indian side, prime minister Chandrashekhar, who had attended the Nepali Congress conference at the beginning of 1990 (while himself in opposition), was widely believed to be personally committed to the Congress leadership. He may have tried to persuade Sadbhavana leader Gajendra Narayan Singh to merge his party with the Congress. During

[49] The banner is reproduced on the cover of *Jhilko*, 16 (April-September, 1991).

[50] Sher Bahadur Deupa, interview in *Saptahik Bimarsha*, 31 May, 1991. Despite its 'pro-Indian' label, the Congress Party itself attacked the M.P. Koirala government for surrendering control of Nepali territory in the Kosi River Project Agreement of 1954 (Shaha, 1990, 2: 305-309).

[51] SEARCH, 1991a.

the actual polling, the Indian authorities co-operated with Krishna Prasad Bhattarai's interim government to impose tight controls on the India-Nepal border to prevent any disruptive elements from crossing over, and also to stop Indian residents coming into Nepal to vote fraudulently. One Nepali claimed that such electoral fraud had taken place at the time of the 1980 referendum and that, had Rajiv Gandhi been in power, he would have allowed the same thing to happen again, with a consequent boost to the Sadbhavana vote.[52]

Another issue which attracted great attention among the intelligentsia, though actually ranking low in the list of problems voters mentioned to the POLSAN survey [53] was that of the relations between the different ethnic groups and castes in Nepal's culturally diverse society. The panchayat years had been marked by the exclusive promotion of the Nepali language and the cultural values of the Brahman and Chhetri castes. Official propaganda had rarely stated this preference explicitly, but the underlying ethos was reflected in an interview given in the summer of 1991 by the politico-religious maverick Yogi Naraharinath, almost the only ideologue to openly mourn the downfall of the Panchayat system: 'there should be a single language and writing system...one dress (bhesh),one aim and one leader'.[54] In a reaction against such an attitude, the period of the interim government saw an upsurge of ethnic assertiveness, with demands for mother-tongue education and for an end to disadvantaged status particularly prominent. In addition to the Tarai peoples, whose case has already been discussed, the groups mainly concerned were the various ethnic minorities in the hills, and the Newars. In terms of representation in the bureaucracy and education system, the Newars can be classed with Brahmans and Chhetris as members of the elite, but there has long been a feeling among many of them that such success, which in any case is largely confined to the higher castes, has been achieved at the cost of sacrificing their own cultural identity.[55] It is arguable that the virtual mass uprising in Patan which was crucial for the success of the democracy movement owed much to a sense of ethnic solidarity in a largely Newar town, and this is certainly an important part of the explanation for the strength of the Nepal Workers' and Peasants' Organisation in Bhaktapur.

One way to channel such feelings into political action was to create

[52] Interview with S. B. Thakur, Kathmandu, 16 August, 1991.

[53] Borre, 1991: 37, Table 5.

[54] Yogi Naraharinath, interview in Saptahik Bimarsha, 12 July, 1991; Naraharinath, a yogi of the Kanphata sect, played a part in the disturbances in the Gorkha area which were part of King Mahendra's pretext for the 1960 royal takeover. Though a fervent supporter of panchayat ideology, he later became very critical of King Birendra.

[55] On Newar 'cultural revivalism'; see Gellner, 1986.

ethnically-based or regional parties. Sadbhavana was the only such party
to win parliamentary representation, but there were also various smaller
groups. The Limbuwan Liberation Front, pressing for the restoration of
the autonomy originally promiseḍ to the Limbus by Prithvi Narayan
Shah in the late 18th century, boycotted the elections and its leader Bir
Nembang was arrested and detained in Ilam for a few days in April.[56]
The Mongol National Organisation and Khagendra Jang Gurung's Nepal
Rastriya Janajati Party (National Ethnic Party) both attempted to
contest, but fell foul of the constitutional ban on separatist parties. The
only party appealing specifically to the hilltribes which got past the
election commission's scrutiny was the Nepal Rastriya Jan Mukti
Morcha, which fielded fifty candidates. In 1990 its secretary general,
Gore Bahadur Khapangi, had called for the constitution to allow all
tribes and castes a proportionate share of political power.[57]

More mainstream parties also tried to garner 'ethnic' votes.
Congress and the UML both promised mother-tongue primary education, but the Left parties made the strongest bid. This was natural
enough since, while socio-economic stratification and caste/ethnic divisions do not always coincide (eastern Nepal does have some poor
Brahmans and some rich Rais and Limbus!) the *matwali* (tribal hill)
population is by and large among the 'have-nots'. Although only the
tiny Marxist-Leninist-Maoist group, a component of the United
People's Front, actually accepted the principle of self-determination for
all ethnic groups within Nepal,[58] the UPF as a whole and the UML
both called for 'reservations' (i.e. quotas in government employment)
for ethnic minorities and backward castes. The UPF offered use of the
mother-tongue at all levels in the education system and also in the
courts and administration, and the CPN (Verma) proposed free education
for backward groups up to university level.[59] Finally, realising that its
traditional opposition to Gurkha recruitment into the British and Indian
armies might jeopardise its electoral chances in some *matwali* communities, the UML pragmatically omitted from its manifesto the commitment to end this arrangement which had been included in its 1989
programme.

The various national and international observer teams who

[56] In an interview given while under arrest *(Nepalipatra,* 26 April, 1991)
Nembang denied having either separatist or republican aims and argued that,
unlike the Mongol National Organisation, the Front was advancing the
interests of an area, not an ethnic group. He explained that he was
boycotting the election because of the constitutional ban on regional
parties.

[57] *Nepali Awaj,* 15 June, 1990.

[58] Tamang, 1991: 30.

[59] United People's Front, 1991:10; notes on CPN (Verma) manifesto
compiled by Deepak Tamang.

monitored the elections all concluded that they had by and large been a fair test of popular opinion. While there is no reason to quarrel with that general verdict, there were a number of features of the campaign and of the polling process itself which do give some grounds for concern for the future, particularly in the light of the distortions which have entered the working of Indian democracy and which inevitably tend to seep over the border.

Violent clashes between opposing political factions were a problem (around a dozen people were killed in the course of the campaign), although they nowhere approached the scale seen in neighbouring Bihar. The former panchayat politicians were particular targets, and the disruption of Pashupati Shamsher J.B. Rana's canvassing in his Sindhupalchok-3 constituency was highlighted on the BBC World Service. Intimidation was not only practised by parties contesting the election but also by Mohan Bikram Singh's Masal group to enforce its call for a boycott of the polls. Masal activists forced prime minister Girija Prasad Koirala to abandon campaigning in their Pyuthan district stronghold, and intimidated the workers of the American-financed Voter Education Programme into moving to another district.[60] The average turn-out rate for Pyuthan's two constituencies was between 36 and 37 per cent, comparing with a national average of 65 per cent. Part of the explanation was genuine support for Mohan Bikram Singh among some of the local people, but fear of reprisals was certainly what kept many voters at home, both here and in some neighbouring districts.

There were frequent accusations of election funds being improperly obtained or improperly used. One organisation monitoring polling in twenty northern and middle-hill districts obtained clear evidence of party workers handing out money to buy votes in three districts, and reported unsuccessful attempts by workers in three other districts and rumours of votebuying in six. Several parties seem to have been involved but the National Democratic Party (Chand) figured frequently in the accusations.[61] Sahana Pradhan and Jhalanath Khanal were said by their opponents to have used their positions in the interim government to gather money for their party's campaign and, according to some, also for their own accounts. Rival communist leader Tulsi Lal Amatya accused the UML of fomenting strikes in industrial concerns and then privately informing companies that a return to work could be arranged in return for a donation to party funds.[62] Amatya also claimed that he had himself turned down an American offer of financial support, and supporters of the UML charged that 'national and international

[60] SEARCH, 1991a: 87-88.
[61] SEARCH,1991b. The NDP (Chand) was the target of accusations in Rasuwa, Humla and Dandeldhura districts.
[62] Tulsi Lal Amatya, interview in *Saptahik Bimarsha,* 19 July, 1991.

reactionary forces' had tried to boost the smaller communist parties in an attempt to split the leftist vote and facilitate a Congress victory.[63]

There was also a degree of laxness in the electoral process itself, despite the deployment of around 62,000 civil servants and about 70,000 regular and temporary police personnel. SEARCH monitors reported several instances of under-age voting, fraudulent proxy-voting and multiple-voting. The most blatant case occurred at a booth in Baglung district, where one person cast his vote 60 times. The election officer in charge of the booth later informed observers that he was unable to prevent it because supporters of one particular party were dominant at that booth.[64] The electoral roll may itself have been inaccurate in many constituencies. The SEARCH team reported cases of apparently genuine voters being turned away because their names had not been included on it. There is also evidence that names may have been wrongly included on the register in the past: in 1981 the national census and voter registration exercises were carried out within two months of each other, but the register was larger by 9.5 per cent than the census figure for the total population of voting age![65] The SEARCH report recommended reducing the scope for abuse by requiring voters to produce a citizenship certificate or similar proof of identity, but in a society where widespread illiteracy still exists this may prove difficult to implement.

The Results and Their Implications

Whether accurate or not, the election commission's register showed a total of 11,191,777 Nepalese citizens eligible to vote, of whom 7,291,084 (65.15 per cent) went to the polls. The percentage turnout was the highest in the nation's history, comparing with 42.24 per cent in the 1959 multi-party election, 52.27 and 60.38 per cent in the 1981 and 1986 panchayat elections and 61.16 per cent in the 1980 referendum.[66] 6,969,061 valid votes were cast and the table below shows the percentage distribution of these between the different parties compared with the number of seats obtained. As explained above, only the first six parties, with over three per cent of the total popular vote, will be recognised by the election commission at the next elections.

As can be seen from the table and from the map, Congress owed its majority to the electoral system which translated a plurality of votes into an absolute majority of seats, and it drew its greatest support from the Tarai and the western hills. Despite the talk from some in the party of repeating the two-thirds majority they had enjoyed in 1959, in the run-up to the polls some more neutral observers had been predicting a

---

[63] Amatya, loc.cit.; Kharel, 1991: 47.

[64] SEARCH, 1991b: 97.

[65] Aditya, 1991: 9-11.

[66] Figures for previous elections from Aditya, 1991: 8.

hung parliament, and therefore the result at national level ought not to have been too disappointing, especially as Congress had actually attracted a larger share of the popular vote than in the earlier election. However, its failure to reach the two-thirds mark meant that Congress would need the support of other parties to ratify major international agreements, including a deal with India over water resources on which the Left was unlikely to co-operate. Spirits were also dampened by setbacks in the eastern hills and in urban areas. The most striking reverses were in the Kathmandu Valley, where the party lost in seven of the ten constituencies. Of the five seats allocated to Kathmandu itself, the party won only one: prime minister Krishna Prasad Bhattarai and Haribol Bhattarai, the successful Congress candidate for *pradhan panch* of Kathmandu in 1987, were both beaten by UML general secretary Madan Bhandari, who, unlike Bhattarai, had taken the precaution of standing in two separate constituencies; while Ganesh Man Singh's wife Mangala Devi and son Prakash Man went down respectively to Padma Ratna Tuladhar, the 'independent leftist' now running with UML backing, and to Sahana Pradhan. Less unexpectedly, since Patan had long been something of a communist stronghold, Congress lost in all three constituencies, with Marshal Julum Shakya, minister of supply, construction and transport and target of corruption allegations, losing to UML Jyapu candidate Siddhilal Singh.

The rejection of Congress in the capital can be seen partly as a protest vote against the failure to achieve any marked economic improvement since the triumph of the democracy movement. Although the interim government had been a Congress-leftist coalition, the former party had supplied the prime minister and the largest number of members of the cabinet. This meant that the administration tended to be seen as a Congress one, whereas the communists were able both to run with the hare and hunt with the hounds, enjoying some of the patronage that went with office but still not seeming to be part of the establish-ment.[67] Congress's relatively poor organisation and lack of political spadework were also factors. In Kathmandu-1, where Krishna Prasad Bhattarai was standing, his UML opponent established a commanding lead in the rural areas, visiting almost every village in the constituency, while Bhattarai failed to motivate his potential supporters in the town to come out and vote.[68] Over-confidence and too much reliance on 'big names' also seem to have alienated voters. Ganesh Man Singh, who

[67] One researcher surveying village opinion in summer 1990 found many people not aware that the communists were in the government (Interview with Mohan Prasad Khanal, 30 July, 1990).

[68] Upadhyay, 1991. A month before the election, UML candidate Padma Ratna Tuladhar claimed that the communists had established their organisation in most of the Kathmandu Valley's 66 villages but Congress only in about 6 *(Saptahik Bimarsha,* 12 April, 1991).

once boasted that he could put up a walking stick for election in Kathmandu and it would win,[69] invited charges of nepotism when he encouraged (or, as he himself publicly maintained, allowed) his wife and son to stand. The victor in Kathmandu-3, Padma Ratna Tuladhar, was a popular figure in his own right, and well-known as one of the 'entryist' leftist candidates who had successfully stood for election to the Rastriya Panchayat.

With a total of 82 seats and 36.6 per cent of the vote, the Left generally could be well pleased with its performance, particularly in comparison with the mere 7 per cent polled by the United Communist Party of Nepal in 1959. The Left's percentage of the total vote was only 1.25 per cent behind that of Congress and, if leftist candidates standing against each other in 14 constituencies had not let Congress win by default, both sides would have had 96 seats each, leaving Congress with a choice between renewed power-sharing with the communists or forming a coalition with Sadbhavana or the National Democratic Parties.[70] The damage done to the Left as a whole by the failure to reach a comprehensive seat-sharing arrangement was limited by piecemeal understandings in particular constituencies, and because the electoral support of some of the groups proved to be so miniscule that they rarely harmed the chances of the larger communist parties against which they were standing.

The contrast between the relative communist success in Nepal and communism's collapse in Europe may seem puzzling. The election result has to be seen against the background of continual work at the grass-roots by activists within Nepal and also in the context of the regional situation. China remains professedly Marxist, and although Mao himself abandoned the economic prescription of 'new democracy' in the years of the 'Great Leap Forward' and the Cultural Revolution, the revival of some features of capitalism since 1979 does have something in common with the original theory and has had some success. Also important is the influence of the Indian political system, where parties calling themselves communists have long been in power in West Bengal and in Kerala and, at the very least, do not come off so badly when compared with non-communist Indian states as did the regimes of the former Soviet bloc in comparison with those of western Europe.

The UML, which had over 75 per cent of the total leftist vote, had succeeded where the Gorkha Parishad had failed in 1959 and established itself as a credible alternative to Congress. Its electoral support was concentrated more in the east and in urban areas, and was thus drawn from sections of the population better-educated and more politically

---

[69] *Nepalipatra,* 17 May, 1991. The remark was supposedly made in a reference to the 1987 local elections.

[70] Kharel, 1991.

conscious than the mass of voters in the relatively less-developed west who supported Congress. The party was also significantly more popular with younger voters: the POLSAN survey found 50 per cent backing for the UML among the 18-29 age group, compared with 39 per cent among those aged 30 to 49 and 30 per cent among the over-50s. The same survey also indicated that it was the UML's reputation as a new, radical force which appealed to an electorate increasingly eager for change. 64 per cent of those questioned thought the party stood for 'new ideas', as against only 18 per cent for Congress, while 50 per cent of the sample claimed the same orientation for themselves, only 15 per cent choosing to be described as 'traditional' and 30 per cent as 'in between'.[71]

Among the smaller communist groups, the UPF's relatively small but geographically-concentrated support base gave it a respectable nine seats. While it is not likely to become strong enough to challenge for power in its own right, it might in the future become an embarrassment to a CPN(UML) government by pushing for swifter and more radical action than the UML itself thinks desirable. A left-wing government's inability or unwillingness to restrain extreme-Left factions has in the past provided the excuse for right-wing intervention, as happened when the Indian central government removed the Popular Front government in West Bengal during the Naxalite campaign of the late 1960s and early 1970s.

Vishnu Bahadur Manandhar's CPN (Democratic) gained less than 3 per cent of the vote but secured two seats, with former Rastriya Panchayat member Bhim Bahadur Shrestha winning in Chitwan-2 and Vaidyanath Mahato in Sarlahi-4. In August 1991 the party merged with two groups which had failed to win any seats in the election, the CPN (Verma) and the CPN (Amatya). The new party, known as the CPN (United) was headed by Tulsi Lal Amatya as president, Manandhar as general secretary and Krishna Raj Verma as deputy general secretary. Verma, like Manandhar, had worked with Raimajhi in his pro-Soviet wing of the original Communist Party of Nepal but had broken with his old leader in 1983 when the latter accepted membership of the Raj Sabha (State Council) under the Panchayat system.[72] Amatya had been a leader of the anti-Raimajhi faction in the split at the beginning of the

[71] Borre, 1991: 35-36. Chaitanya Mishra has suggested that the UML's poor performance in the west might have been due to support for Congress from well-organised Indian army veterans in the region, rather than to economic backwardness.

[72] Rawal, 1990-91: 67. Raimajhi himself continued to collaborate with the palace and in 1990 was actually one of the two 'king's men' in the interim government. He then finally formally renounced communism and established his own party, the Janta Dal (Social Democratic) only to announce its dissolution after failure in the elections.

1960s but had become increasingly marginalised in the communist movement since then, and polled only sixteen hundred votes in his home constituency of Lalitpur-2, against 27,474 for the UML victor and 14,855 for the Congress runner-up, while no other candidate from his group even managed to reach four figures. The Verma group, whose electoral performance had not been quite so embarrassing as Amatya's, pulled out of the new party in April 1992 and Amatya's faction left in September. Manandhar is thus on his own once again, but continues to use the CPN (United) label. All three groups have been losing members to the UML and they are unlikely to survive for long.

The Nepal Workers' and Peasants' Party which is now represented in parliament by Rohit himself (Bhaktapur-1) and Dilli Bahadur Mahat for Humla in Karnali zone, managed only 1.25 per cent of the popular vote. However, it may in fact have a slightly better chance of survival than the CPN (United) because the intense loyalty of its followers in its Bhaktapur base makes it a political force within the Kathmandu Valley. Its candidate would also have won in the second Bhaktapur seat and in Dailekh-1 (Bheri zone) and Kalikot (Karnali) had the UML agreed not to stand in all constituencies where the group had substantial support.[73] In order to secure its future, and perhaps also out of resentment at the UML's behaviour towards it, the party has once again been moving closer to the UPF.

The performance of the two National Democratic Parties surprised most observers, who had been expecting a much stronger showing, something on the lines of the old Gorkha Parishad (the 'revivalist party' of the previous generation) which took 21 per cent of the vote in 1959. It was also a disappointment to some in Congress, including the new premier Girija Prasad Koirala, who would have felt more comfortable as a centre force with a large grouping to their right as well as to their left rather than appearing as the right-wing in a bi-polar system. As the results table is designed to show, the ex-pancha parties' performance is rather more respectable if they are ranked in terms of total votes cast, this criterion putting Chand in 3rd and Thapa in 4th place, whereas they are only 5th and 8th on the basis of seats won. The discrepancy reflects the fact that they had a low level of support right across the country in contrast to the Left parties, whose support was more locally concentrated. The Chand and Thapa parties were also at a disadvantage because they were unable to agree seat-sharing arrangements and therefore ended up standing against each other in many constituencies. Their combined popular vote of just under 12 per cent was still, however, unexpectedly low. The explanation seems to have been the (quite rational) decision by so many former stalwarts of the Panchayat system to switch to Congress (or, less frequently, to the UML), and

[73] Kharel, 1991: 50.

also confusion in the minds of many voters over what the two parties stood for: in the POLSAN voter survey 35 per cent and 28 per cent of respondents did not know where to locate the NDP(Thapa) and NDP(Chand) respectively in the conservative-radical spectrum.[74]

Thapa and Chand themselves both failed to gain election, but whereas Thapa's group managed only a single victory (Akbar Bahadur Singh in Darchula-2 in far-western Mahakali zone), the NDP (Chand) did rather better, winning three neighbouring constituencies in the hills north of Kathmandu. Pashupati Shamsher J.B. Rana held Sindupalchok-3, part of the constituency he had represented and carefully 'nursed' during the panchayat years, and Prakash Chandra Lohani and Ram Krishna Acharya took Nuwakot-1 and Rasuwa-1.

In February 1992 the two National Democratic Parties merged to form the United National Democratic Party with Lok Bahadur Chand as 'leader' and Surya Bahadur Thapa as 'president'. Even as a single force they face an uncertain future, because the Chand group's hold on its constituencies may have resulted from the direction of development funds towards the area during the panchayat era and the party is not in a position to continue to provide such patronage. However, if popular dissatisfaction with the Congress and the communist alternative grows, they may yet see an upturn in their fortunes.

The Sadbhavana Party, which had also nursed hopes of holding the balance of power between Congress and the UML, obtained six seats and 4 per cent of the national vote, or slightly less than 10 per cent of the vote in the 76 constituencies it contested, thus bettering the record of its predecessor, Bhadrakali Mishra's Tarai Congress, which failed to win a single seat in 1959. Nevertheless, it is still well short of being able to speak for the Tarai as a whole. Its support, like that of the smaller leftist parties, is highly localised: apart from party leader Gajendra Narayan Singh's own seat in Saptari-2 (forming part of the area he used to represent in the Rastriya Panchayat) all its parliamentarians are from Lumbini zone in the west-central Tarai. Furthermore, except for the large absolute majority won by Triyogi Narayan Chaudhuri in Nawalparasi-4, all the rest, including Singh himself, owed victory over a Congress runner-up to votes being taken by the two National Democratic Parties or the UML. Thus only in one constituency did a majority of the electorate fail to vote for parties with a national rather than regional appeal. As suggested earlier, this will have been partly due to apprehension over Singh's own high-caste status, and to a preference for mother-dialect over Hindi. The major factor, however, as with the NDPs, must have been the feeling that local interests would best be served by supporting a group that actually

[74] Borre, 1991: 37, Table 6. The 'don't know' percentages for Congress and the UML are 14 per cent and 28 per cent respectively.

had a chance of forming a government in Kathmandu.

For the future the Sadbhavana Party, like the Left, has the advantage of being perceived as a radical challenge to the status quo. It has higher support among younger voters (18-29 years: 6 per cent; 30-49: 4 per cent; 50 and above: 2 per cent) and its adherents express greater disapproval of higher-level government officials than do those of any other party.[75] In the next election it could pick up some of the right-wing vote which went to the Thapa and Chand groups, and it might make more substantial advances if disillusionment with both Congress and UML sets in, especially if future Indian governments are less sympathetic to the Nepali Congress than was the case this time. There is thus a challenge for all the nationally-based parties to try to ensure that Tarai interests are taken more fully into account within the existing constitutional framework.

It can certainly be expected that in the new House of Representatives Tarai claims will be advanced more loudly than in the past. The Sadbhavana members have already caused a stir by insisting on speaking in Hindi rather than in Nepali, a linguistic assertiveness which is paralleled by Newar representatives of leftist parties such as Padma Ratna Tuladhar and Narayan Man Bijukche (Comrade Rohit) who chose to take their oaths at the beginning of the session in Newari. The total percentage of *madeshi* members of the House is 20 per cent (76), so that the Tarai peoples, who account for about one third of Nepal's population, are still under-represented.[76] The traditional elite groups (Brahmans, Chhetri-Thakuris and high-caste Newars) still dominate, with 63.5 per cent of the seats. In the long term, however, the *madeshis* are in a stronger position than the similarly under-represented hill minorities and untouchables since, despite the heavy migration of hillpeople into the Tarai since the 1950s, the indigenous Tarai peoples still have the advantage of a relatively distinct territory while the hill minorities are interspersed with and often outnumbered by the high-caste hill groups.[77]

The most striking change in the caste distribution of members of parliament has been an increase in the percentage of hill Brahmans from 14.2 per cent in 1986 to 39.2 per cent, while the Chhetris have fallen from 40.2 per cent to 17 per cent. Within the cabinet, the Brahmans' predominance is even more striking at 47.1 per cent, lending some plausibility to Ganesh Man Singh's recent complaint about

[75] Ibid.: 35-36.

[76] Tamang, 1991: 31 (table).

[77] The hill minorities and untouchables account for about 25 per cent of Nepal's total population and the Brahmans, Chhetri-Thakuris and Newars for about 36 per cent (Based on advance figures from the 1991 Population Census (10 per cent sample), presented in Gurung, 1992.)

'Brahmanism'.[78] The palace-led Panchayat system naturally boosted the position of the traditional dominant caste, to which the royal family itself belongs. Party politics now, as in the 1950s, is more the province of the intellectuals and education has always been a pre-eminently Brahman sphere.

Soon after the general election, the Congress government and the UML opposition both became the targets of widespread dissatisfaction. Congress was able to consolidate its political position through sweeping victories in the local elections of May-June 1992, but even loyal supporters of the government admitted that this did not reflect positive enthusiasm as much as disenchantment with the Left, and the calculation that Congress local authorities would be in the best position to obtain development funds from a Congress central administration.

Soon after it came into office, the Congress government showed heavy-handedness in dealing with an agitation for improved pay and conditions in the civil service, and although the government seemed to have come out on top in the confrontation, its political standing was damaged. Another blow was the Supreme Court's ruling in December 1992 that the government had to seek parliamentary approval for a controversial understanding with India on the construction of a dam on Nepalese territory at Tanakpur. The government was also weakened by an open quarrel between Ganesh Man Singh and Girija Prasad Koirala. This turned on the distribution of appointments rather than on any matter of party principle, and the 'Brahmanism' jibe was made in this context. Krishna Prasad Bhattarai continued to act as conciliator, but some of his close associates were openly critical of the prime minister. At the same time, continuing economic difficulties guaranteed continuing popular grumbling, as under the interim government.

The UML was not able to gain political advantage from this, because of even worse problems of its own. Unlike the hard-line Maoist groups which had long since written off the Soviet Union as 'revisionist', the UML and its predecessors the CPN (M-L) and CPN (M), while critical of certain Soviet actions, had continued to regard it as a socialist country and an important partner in the international revolutionary struggle. Forming the 'correct' attitude towards foreign communist parties has always been an important issue for Nepalese communist groups, and one which has often played a critical role in the many splits and re-alignments within the Nepalese movement. It was therefore highly embarrassing for the UML when developments in Moscow belied its own previous hopes and expectations. Matters were made worse, of course, because UML leaders, like spokesmen for other communist groups, seemed to welcome the initial news of the coup.

Another worry was the exodus of many former members of the CPN

[78] *Deshantar*, 15 September, 1991 *(Nepal Press Digest*, 35, 38: 370).

(M) to re-establish their old party. This began in September 1991, amid allegations that the conditions of the merger between the Marxist-Leninist and Marxist parties had not been kept and that Pushpa Lal's concept of *naulo janbad* was being abandoned in favour of *bahudaliya janbad*—people's democracy based on a multi-party system; the latter formulation was in fact formally adopted at a Central Committee meeting in October 1991, in the absence abroad of the three most prominent former CPN leaders (Man Mohan Adhikari, Sahana Pradhan and Bharat Mohan Adhikari) and reportedly against the opposition of C.P. Mainali's faction of the former CPN (M-L).[79]

Party policy statements had long been acknowledging that different political parties could function under *naulo janbad*, and, since Madan Bhandari and others continued to suggest that there would be a restriction on parties radically opposed to the new system, the mere dropping of the word *naulo* did not amount to a substantive change in policy. It seems therefore that the real grievance of the dissidents was against the domination of the party by Madan Bhandari and his associates. Even if it lost all former CPN (M) workers, the UML would remain the largest of the communist groups, but its standing, and that of the communists generally, would be weakened.

Even more than internal dissension, it was the quarrels with other communist groups and the extremism of some of the latter that probably did the most damage to the UML. In spring 1992, when the Maoist United Popular Front launched an aggressive street-campaign against the government, the UML first gave a limited degree of support. Following police firings on 6 April and the consequent deaths of civilians, the party called for the resignation of the home minister but refused to join the UPF in its call for a general strike on 3 May. Most businesses in the Kathmandu Valley did close down on that day, but the UPF candidates' abysmal performance in the local elections showed that this observance of the strike had been the result of intimidation, rather than genuine support. The general disarray on the Left disheartened some of those who had campaigned for the UML at the general election while, despite the party's attempts to disassociate itself from extremism, many voters seem to have placed the blame for political violence on communists of all stripes.

Despite calls for the prime minister's resignation, or for mid-term polls over the Tanakpur issue, the Nepali Congress is probably still today (January 1993) in a secure position. However, the country still waits to see whether it can make constructive use of the power with which it has been entrusted, and whether its communist opponents can establish themselves as a credible alternative government.

[79] *Deshantar*, 27 October, 1991 *(Nepal Press Digest,* 35, 44: 415).

ELECTION RESULTS

Party	seats contested	seats won	per cent of total seats	per cent of total vote
Nepali Congress	204	110	53.6	37.75
Communist Party of Nepal (Unified Marxist-Leninist)	177	69	33.66	27.98
National Democratic Party (Chand)	154	3	46	6.56
National Democratic Party (Thapa)	162	1	0.49	5.38
United People's Front	69	9	4.4	4.83
Nepal Sadbhavana Party	75	6	2.93	4.1
Communist Party of Nepal (Democratic) *	75	2	0.98	2.43
Nepal Workers' and Peasants' Party	30	2	0.98	1.25
Nepal Rastriya Jan Mukti Morcha	50	0	—	0.47
Communist Party of Nepal (Verma)	36	0	—	0.23
Janta Dal (Social Democratic)	15	0	—	0.08
Nepal Rastriya Jan Party	4	0	—	0.08
Communist Party of Nepal (Amatya)	14	0	—	0.07
Rastriya Janta Party (H) **	28	0	—	0.06
Rastriya Janta Party Nepal**	9	0	—	0.06
Nepal Conservative Party	6	0	—	0.04
Bahujan Janta Dal	1	0	—	0.03
Janbadi Morcha Nepal	14	0	—	0.02
Akhil Nepal Sarbapakshiya Rajnitik Ekta Party	1	0	—	0.00
Dalit Majdur Kisan Party	1	0	—	0.00
Independents ***	291	3	1.46	4.17
TOTAL	—	205	100%	100%

NOTES * The CPN (Democratic) merged with the Verma and Amatya groups two months after the election to form the CPN (United).
** The original Rastriya Janta Party split into these two groups a few days before the deadline for registration with the election commission.
*** The three independent members joined the Nepali Congress in June 1991. At least one of them appears to have already been aligned with Congress, as the party put up no candidate of its own in his constituency.

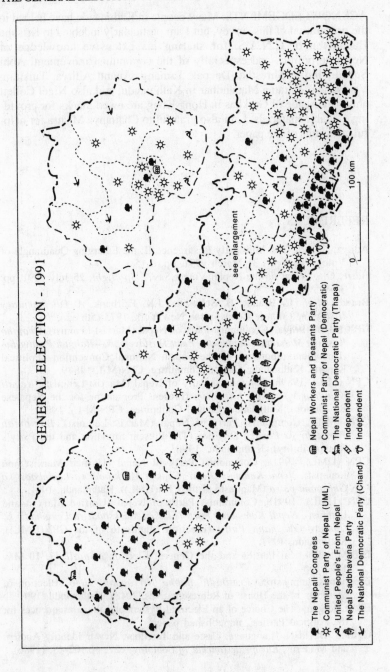

GENERAL ELECTION - 1991

The Nepali Congress

Communist Party of Nepal (UML)

United People's Front, Nepal

Nepal Sadbhavana Party

The National Democratic Party (Chand)

Nepal Workers and Peasants Party

Communist Party of Nepal (Democratic)

The National Democratic Party (Thapa)

Independent

Independent

100 km

see enlargement

ACKNOWLEDGEMENTS: Many people in Kathmandu have helped in the preparation of this survey, but I am particularly indebted to Krishna Hachhethu of C.N.A.S. for sharing his extensive knowledge of Nepalese politics and especially of the communist movement. Abhi Subedi, Indira Shrestha, Deepak Tamang, Anand Aditya, Tulsiram Vaidya and Triratna Manandhar in Kathmandu, and also Nigel Collett and the Brigade of Gurkhas in Hong Kong are owed thanks for providing valuable materials. I am also grateful to Chaitanya Mishra for helpful criticisms of the paper.

REFERENCES

Aditya, Anand, 'The Multiparty Resurgence II: the Emerging Quadrangle of Vote', *Spotlight,* 31 March 1991, pp. 6-15.

Borre, Ole, 'What do the Nepali Voters Say?', *Spotlight,* 25 July 1991, pp. 34-7.

Brandt, *et al.* C. Brandt, B. Schwartz, J.K. Fairbank, *A Documentary History of Chinese Communism,* New York, 1973 (5th ed.).

CPN (M-L), 1989a, Communist Party of Nepal (Marxist-Leninist), *Chautho Rastriya Mahadhiveshandwara Parit Dastavejharu—Rajnitik Prativedan* (Documents approved by the Fourth National Convention—Political Report), Kathmandu: Central Committee, CPN(M-L), 1989.

CPN (M-L), 1989b, Communist Party of Nepal (Marxist-Leninist), *Nepali Krantiko Vartaman Karykram* (Present Programme for the Nepalese Revolution), Kathmandu: Central Committee, CPN(M-L), 1989.

CPN (M-L), Communist Party of Nepal (Marxist-Leninist), *Bartaman Paristhiti ra Partiko Dayitwa* (The Present Situation and the Party's Responsibility), Kathmandu, 1990.

CPN (UML), 1991a, Communist Party of Nepal (Unified Marxist and Leninist), *Nepal Kamunist Parti (Ekakrit Marksbadi ra Leninbadi) ko Ghoshana-patra* (Manifesto of the CPN(UML)), Kathmandu, 1991.

CPN (UML), 1991b, Communist Party of Nepal (Unified Marxist and Leninist), *Nepal Kamyunist Parti (Ekakrit Marksbadi ra Leninbadi) ko Chunav Ghoshana Patra* (Election Manifesto of the CPN(UML)), Kathmandu, 1991.

D.B.M., 'Political Parties and the General Election', *Spotlight,* 10 May 1991, pp. 32-4.

Election Commission, *Pratinidhi Sabha Nirvachan, 2048* (Election of Members of the House of Representatives, 2048), Kathmandu, 1991.

Elklit, Jorgen, 'The Choice of an Electoral System and the consequences for the Political Parties', unpublished paper.

Gellner, David N, 'Language, Caste and Territory, Newar Identity Ancient and Modern', *European Journal of Sociology,* 27, pp.102-48, (1986).

Gurung, Harka, 'Jat-jatibare prarambhik tathyanka' (Preliminary statistics on castes and ethnic groups), *Saptahik Bimarsha,* 31 July 1992.

Hachhethu, Krishna, 'Challenge for Democracy in Nepal', unpublished paper.

INSEC, *Nepal and its Electoral System,* Kathmandu, 1991.

Kharel, Balmukhund, 'Nepalko Am Nirvachan 2048 ra Bam Ektako Prashna' (Nepal's 2048 General Election and the Question of Leftist Unity), *Jhilko,* 16 (April-September 1991), pp.45-51.

Kohli, Atul, *The State and Poverty in India: the Politics of Reform,* Cambridge, 1984.

Nepali Congress, *Nepali Kangresko Chunav Ghoshana-patra—Mahanirvachan* (Nepali Congress Election Manifesto—General Election), Kathmandu, 1991.

Rawal, Bhim, *Nepalma Samyabadi Andolan—Udbhav ra Bikas* (The Communist Movement in Nepal: Origin and Development), Kathmandu, 2047 V.S. (1990-91).

SEARCH, 1991a, *Strengthening Democratic Processes in Nepal—Voter Education Program,* Kathmandu, 1991.

SEARCH, 1991b, *Strengthening Democratic Processes in Nepal—General Election Monitoring Program,* Kathmandu, 1991.

Shaha, Rishikesh, *Modern Nepal—A Political History 1769-1955,* New Delhi, 1990.

Tamang, Deepak, Summaries of 1991 election manifestos (unpublished.)

Tamang, Pashuram, 'Sansadiya Am Nirvachan 2048 ra Janjati' (Parliamentary General Election 2048 and Ethnic Groups), *Jhilko,* 16 (April-September 1991), pp.27-33.

Tiwari, Chitra K., 'Electoral Systems and the Forthcoming Elections in Nepal', unpublished paper.

UPF, United People's Front, Nepal, *Chunav Ghoshana Patra* (Election Manifesto), Kathmandu, 1991.

Upadhyay, Akhilesh, 'Taking the People for granted', *Rising Nepal* (General Election Supplement), 22 May 1991, p.8.

Kathmandu media: *Gorkhapatra; Nepal Press Digest; Nepali Awaj; Nepalipatra; Saptahik Bimarsha.*

Chapter 5

THE NEPALI LITERATURE OF THE DEMOCRACY MOVEMENT AND ITS AFTERMATH

Michael Hutt

> However much you scream with pain,
> Standing in the street in opposition to God,
> However many songs you sing
> In praise of life, distracted with joy,
> It will all be in vain:
> You cannot touch anyone, you cannot
> Wake anyone, you cannot tell anyone anything.
> Those who are engrossed like snakes in self-love
> Do not hear your songs,
> Do not hear your poems.
>
> I know that you incessantly tell
> The stories of the age, tales of joy and sorrow,
> Forever telling of your pride,
> Shaping into verses the knots of your heart,
> Seeking the cadence of life in your poems,
> Humming the story of wrongs and barbarity,
> Playing the ragas of your existence
> From beginning to end.
>
> But what can you do, my dear singer ?
> Serpents don't listen to songs.
> None of the snakes in this whole wide world
> Will attend to your poems.[1]

Sakar's poem was published sometime during the 1980s, and sums up the political position in which Nepali writers found themselves after the national referendum of 1980. In 1970, Nepal's intellectuals were dismissed as 'a band of economically castrated and socially limping angels beating the drums of their respective fads' (Malla 1979: 204) but over the next twenty years their numbers grew, and the disjuncture between their private and public discourse also became more profound, until a point of fracture was reached in 1990. Until then, Nepali poets could write what they liked, so long as they wrote allegorically and recognised that their 'songs' would be ignored.

The long-held view of Nepal as a conservative, peasant society in

---

[1] Shailendra Sakar: 'Serpents Don't Listen to Songs' *(Sarpaharu Git Sundainan)*, Sakar, 1990a: 49-50.

which the educated elite plays an unrepresentative, even fraudulent role, is becoming outdated. Nevertheless, two indisputable facts must be acknowledged. The first is that Nepal is still indeed an agricultural society: of a total working population of ten million in 1981, almost seven million were self-employed farmers. The second is that Kathmandu, where most Nepali intellectuals live, and where all important national decisions are made, is quite unlike the rest of Nepal:

> Kathmandu can no longer mean
> The whole of Nepal.
> Now feet should cross the passes,
> Now eyes should gaze on all the mountains,
> Now the birds of this generation
> Should fly towards fixed goals,
> Now the voices of this generation
> Should erupt like volcanoes.
> Now we have to move ahead,
> Feeling our way through the thorns,
> Now Kathmandu should spread
> Throughout all the hills.[2]

On several occasions since 1960, political developments have exposed the unrepresentative nature of Kathmandu society. Strong demands for a multi-party system and a greater degree of democracy emanated from the capital and the larger towns of the Tarai, but until 1990 these concerns did not seem to be of any great interest to the 90 per cent of the population which lives in rural areas. In 1980, the results of the national referendum demonstrated that the urban centres and much of the Tarai had voted for a multi-party system, while rural hill regions preferred the status quo. The concepts of participative democracy and a civil society are barely forty years old in Nepal, but the national literacy rate has leapt from 2 per cent to an estimated 39 per cent since 1951, despite a doubling of the population, and graduates have poured forth in ever-increasing numbers since the establishment of Tribhuvan University in 1955 and the proliferation of its campuses all over the kingdom ever since. In a period of such rapid change, it follows that what was true in 1980 did not necessarily apply ten years later.

By 1990, the mood of the country as a whole was closer to that of the Kathmandu intelligentsia than it had ever been before. The democracy movement began in the Valley towns, but quickly led to demonstrations of discontent throughout Nepal. In a sense, the Panchayat system's opponents had declared that they would no longer be parties to a

---

[2] Krishnabhushan Bal: 'Now Kathmandu Alone Cannot Carry Kathmandu' *(Kathmadau Eklaile Aba Kathmadau Bokna Saktaina)* in Sharma (ed.), 1983: 44-5.

conspiracy which maintained the fiction of a partyless state in which banned parties operated freely on a private level, but could not be mentioned in public, and in which academics, writers and poets could publish their political sentiments in a kind of semi-transparent code, but were required to pay repeated public tribute to a system they despised. The emperor wore no clothes, and Nepal's intellectuals were weary of pretending that he was magnificently dressed. Within the space of ten years, the gulf between private and public, real and pretended, conscience and necessity yawned ever wider, and at last the structure cracked and crumbled. These disjunctures were perceived most acutely by the urban intelligentsia, for whom they were a feature of daily life, but the fact that the fundamental dishonesty of the situation became apparent to people other than student activists and radical poets accounts in some part for the movement's success.

Modern Western scholarship on Nepal has often represented the attempt of the Bahun-Chhetri-Newar hierarchy to evolve a national culture with the Nepali language at its heart as an effort intended to erode the ethnic and cultural identities of minority groups. This has undoubtedly been one of its effects—an effect recognised by many communities, who have recently begun to try to counter it with political action. But the character of this putative national culture, and the political significance of its growing pervasiveness throughout Nepal, have not been analysed objectively or in depth. Writers, and particularly writers of poetry, occupy an important position in this culture, and it is indeed strange that many foreign scholars continue to produce accounts and studies of Nepali society without having read anything written by members of that society in their own national language. One can barely imagine a similar situation in reverse. To attempt to begin to redress this imbalance, my discussion here is based on conversations with Nepali writers and academics which took place in Kathmandu during four visits between 1987 and 1991, and on readings of published Nepali sources over the same period. I cannot say how representative of the Nepali intelligentsia my informants have been: though I can locate them with a modicum of accuracy at various points across the broad spectrum of Kathmandu's literary and political life, it is important to remain alert to individual prejudices, and to the sound of axes being ground.

Literature and Political Protest
After 16 December 1960, when King Mahendra revoked the democratic constitution of 1959, abolished the elected government and exiled or imprisoned its leaders, Nepalis were not free to engage in party political activities or to criticise the actions of the king. To stand for election to the panchayat units set up under a new constitution in 1962, they had to enlist in one of five, or latterly six, class organisations, and the

system became less and less representative, accountable and responsive to public opinion. Alienated from the political establishment, and subjected to professional demotion, imprisonment or, latterly, police brutality, if they criticised it too publicly, a very large proportion of the new generation of educated Nepalis turned their minds to literature. In 1988 a lecturer at Kirtipur Campus remarked, 'In England you can join a political party, or write to the press. Here we can't—or at least it's difficult—and all our finest minds are in literature. It's just not balanced'. Though the literary community still centres on Kathmandu, it now extends to many other towns. Tribhuvan University produces graduates, many of whom have literary pretensions, from scores of campuses nationwide, and literary movements launched in the capital inevitably reverberate elsewhere. Such movements invariably possess a political dimension.

The 'Rejected Generation' and 'Boot Polish' Movements

During the 1960s and 1970s, Kathmandu writers launched several movements with literary and socio-political objectives. The founders of each were young male graduates, and the same names recur in the journals and anthologies their movements generated from the late 1960s right up to 1990. My understanding of the first two of these movements, the *Aswikrit Jamat* (Rejected Generation) and Boot Polish, is hampered by a lack of published documentation. A brief reference to the former in Taranath Sharma's standard history of Nepali literature is absent from a second, revised edition.[3] Nevertheless, I have gleaned some information from conversations with those who were involved.

The Rejected Generation movement began with the publication of a collection of short stories in the Bhojpur journal *Sanjivani* in 1968-9, and involved writers such as Shailendra Sakar, Kavitaram, Parashu Pradhan and Ramesh Shreshtha, all of them in their twenties. They espoused a kind of socialist realism and sought to produce literature which was secular in its content and informal in its tone. Thus they rejected the romanticism of the generation of older poets who still dominated the literature, erased all references to gods and demons, and opposed the fashion then current in Nepali poetry of referring extensively to world mythology. Sakar described this small but concerted effort to encourage simple, unpretentious, secular writing as 'a search for the basic human being'.

The Boot Polish demonstrations of 1974 were a response to the government's Back to the Village National Campaign *(Gaon Pharka Rashtriya Abhiyan)* and to a censorship clampdown which banned most non-registered newspapers and magazines, and de-registered many others. In Kathmandu, writers and editors gathered under the old pipal tree on New Road—the hub of the city's literary life, where papers and

[3] Sharma, 1970: 251; Sharma, 1982.

pamphlets are sold, gossip is exchanged, and shoes are polished by professional shoecleaners—and these intellectuals cleaned the shoes of the passers-by for a week. Their aim was to demonstrate their feeling that educated Nepalis had no avenues of gainful employment, and no views that were worthy of notice. Activists in other towns quickly followed suit.

> A black sun has risen in front of my eyes,
> Eyes accustomed to watching
> Beautiful dawn from the window each morning...
> ...I need say nothing more.
> People will remember this day,
> This new generation which began true poetry,
> Which raised small questions about hunger,
> Poverty, inequity, joblessness,
> In the face of our country's
> Pervasive selfishness.[4]

The Street Poetry Revolution

The most significant campaign of the decade was the Street Poetry Revolution *(Sarak Kavita Kranti)* of 1979. It preceded, but became linked with, the student demonstrations that led to violent disorder, and eventually to King Birendra's declaration of the national referendum. Led by the same young writers, the movement also drew in more established poets, such as Mohan Koirala. At its climax in Kathmandu, some two hundred writers were reciting poems on street-corners, demanding the abolition of the Panchayat system. The poets at the forefront of the Street Poetry Revolution were all involved in the democracy movement ten years later: Vol. 2 No. 12 of the magazine *Swatantrata* (Freedom), a Street Poetry Special issue from 1979, included poems by Ashesh Malla, Govind Giri, Vinay Raval, Bimal Nibha, Shailendra Sakar and many others who are now among the most innovative Nepali writers. The tone of these poems is striking when they are read with the benefit of hindsight. They display none of the caution and employ little of the coded, allegorical language which typified the poetry of the 1980s when the Panchayat regime, considering itself vindicated by the results of the referendum, suppressed dissent more vigorously. These young poets were obviously confident that their point of view would prevail:

> This street on which we stand was not ours,
> This land where we were born
> Did not belong to us either.
> We were not citizens,

[4] 'Boot Polish' from Sakar, 1979: 156.

> We were not human beings.[5]
> We just watched the elders' blood flowing,
> We just watched the demon-dance
> Of our exploiters and oppressors.
> Helpless and forced to survive,
> We became weak and effeminate.
> Friends, is this life ?
> Why did we not rip apart
> The long black night of these nineteen years,
> Why did we not throw it away?[6]

This movement spread to some fifty towns in Nepal, and poets from Kathmandu travelled out of the Valley to encourage their peers elsewhere. Sakar relates that he recited his poems on the streets of Bhojpur, and was ordered to leave the town by the local district officer.[7] Many poets were assaulted, and several lost their jobs once the results of the referendum had been declared. Sakar, who worked for the Agricultural Development Bank, found himself transferred from Kathmandu to a junior post in the remote Sunsari district. Mohan Koirala's membership of the Royal Nepal Academy was not renewed when it expired in 1979.

Between 1979 and 1990, Nepali poetry became more politicised than it had ever been since the anti-Rana campaigns of the late 1940s. At the same time, its language became bare and simple—a consequence of the 1979 movement and the great popularity of the satirical poet Bhupi Sherchan. As the 1980s wore on, writers and editors were reprimanded, fined or imprisoned with increasing frequency. Keshav Raj Pindali, erstwhile editor of leading periodicals such as the government daily *Gorkhapatra,* the independent weekly *Saptahik Bimarsha* and the literary monthly *Madhuparka,* described such incidents in an interview:

Newspapers bear a greater responsibility [than literary magazines]. During the panchayat era, I went to jail twice. This was because I stressed democracy and discussed it a great deal. I had to go to the zonal commissioner's office to account for my actions about fifty times. Then the Ministry of Communications filed a case against me. The journal was shut down and its registration was withdrawn. I was jailed because of a poem by Rup Chand Bista. It had already been read out in public and published scores of times, but when I published it I went to jail. It probably wasn't the real cause at all. Someone had ordered that I should be locked up, and the poem became the pretext.[8]

The poem in question appeared to criticise the king, warning against

[5] Om Mani Sharma, 'From the Pilal Tree' (*Sandarbha Pipal ko Botbata*) *Swatantrata* 2, 12: 8.

[6] Vinay Raval: 'Still Something Else Remains to Occur' (*Ajhai Kehi Huna Banki Nai Cha*), ibid.: 10-11.

[7] Sakar, 1990b: 96.

[8] Pindali, 1990: 101.

the activities of the 'clique' of twenty-eight royally-nominated members of the National Assembly. The cases of Pindali and Rup Chand Bista, who was himself a member of the National Assembly, were highlighted in the report published by Amnesty International in 1987.

Double Lives and Compromise

The Panchayat system could hardly expect to be maintained by the lip-service of a sophisticated elite with highly-developed democratic leanings. Nevertheless, as one university lecturer remarked, 'The language of a considerable number of academics became one of sycophancy, and a small repertoire of phrases and cliches was employed to carry out the communication among themselves'.[9] This double-life could be observed in its most chronic form inside the Royal Nepal Academy.

The academy was founded by King Mahendra in 1959 and is the kingdom's foremost institution for the promotion of literature and the arts. The fact that the king himself was the academy's Chancellor meant that palace favour played a significant role in the selection of members, despite King Birendra's expressed willingness to allow the vice-chancellor complete discretion. Members who acquiesced to the culture within the academy usually had their memberships renewed after the initial five-year term, but others did not. The academy's critics called it a graveyard of artists or a common dance hall *(nach ghar)*. But there were some surprising members: the late, great Bhupi Sherchan, whose grand and ironic satires made him a formative influence on younger poets, was a member until his death in 1989. Here, perhaps, the role of the academy had been to absorb a dangerous talent. Its success in achieving this is evident if one compares his poem 'Long Live Birendra' *(Birendra Jindabad)*, written for the academy's own poetry journal in 1986, with the political fury of his poem 'In Search of Serpents', the last poem Sherchan published before he became an academy member:

I am in search of serpents, yes,
I am in search of serpents.
For a long time now I have been out looking
For those venomous snakes...

An age has passed while I have walked
From alley to alley, from market to market,
From street to street, through forests and jungles,
In search of those serpents,
Carrying a stick in my hand.
But instead of snakes I have found those places,
Those forests, markets, alleys and streets,
All bitten and poisoned instead.

[9] Subedi, 1991a.

So now I search with greater care,
Tracking down those disguised serpents
That adopted civilised forms
And struck at civilisation,
That turned into priests and struck at the gods..........
I have even seen them in the darkness,
But before I could strike they fled down their holes;
Their lairs I destroyed, but then they fled
Down even bigger holes.
These too I have destroyed,
But even as I pursued them, they escaped
And went to hide behind walls.
I knocked down the walls,
But shame ! The walls that sheltered them were so tall
I could not climb them, breach them, or enter within.

I know my campaign is in vain: leave aside killing a snake,
I might even be bitten myself.
Even so, I sit snoring asleep, lying in wait by the walls.
Because I am seeking those serpents
Which time after time are striking
And striking and striking and striking
At this beautiful land.[10]

The compromises that Nepali academics had to make under the Panchayat regime were clearly evident in the affair of Chandani Shah. This was the pen-name adopted by Queen Aishwarya, whose romantic and patriotic lyrics were published in 1987 and entered a second edition the following year. The second edition consisted of 27 pages of poetry followed by 323 pages of laudatory essays commissioned by the editor from thirty leading literary scholars. Chandani Shah's songs no doubt possessed considerable charm, but all critical faculties were suspended and all pretence to objectivity abandoned as writers and academics vied with one another to heap the most extravagant praise upon them. One poet offered what she considered the ultimate paeon of praise when she described Chandani Shah as a latter-day Mirabai, only to find herself attacked ferociously by a leading academic on Nepal TV, for belittling the queen's contribution.

The 1990 Revolution
Shortly before the democracy movement was launched, the Congress leader Ganesh Man Singh met pro-democracy writers to ask for their support. As a result, a slim volume of poems appeared on 18 February, the day the movement began, entitled *The Search for Spring (Vasantko Khoji)*, followed by a second collection of political poems, *Melting Even from your Heart (Paglera Pani Timro Mutubata)*, published in

[10] Sherchan, 1984.

April when the movement was well-advanced. The editor and publisher of *The Search for Spring* were anonymous, but its title-page carried a quotation from B. P. Koirala ('My principle is to create an atmosphere in which writers and artists may think freely'), followed by a publisher's statement:

Literature can never remain within the narrow sphere of politics. Nor should it do so. Whenever the political life of any country has been conducted narrowly and behind walls, literature has not tolerated the situation even for a moment. Nor shall it in the future. So literary life is bound up with the question of liberty. This collection of poems is a manifestation of the desire for liberty which has existed ever since the human race first evolved. It may be considered proof of the active involvement of freedom-loving Nepalis in a journey down a road the whole world is walking now. But the collection represents nothing more than a desire that humanity should continue its ancient journey, and that we should wait for the brilliant world of tomorrow and the complete human being it will bring.

The tone of this statement was cautious: in the political context of the time, the message was clear enough, but it was couched in broad generalisations. The same caution was reflected in the oblique nature of most of the eighteen poems' messages. Apart from Mohan Koirala, all the contributors were from the post-1968 generation of poets, and their allegories were transparent enough. Govind Singh Ravat represented the exclusiveness of Nepali political life as a locked room:

> Who knows how long it's been locked,
> That room: it's been shut
> For as long as I remember.
> Though I tried, I could not discover
> The secret inside that room:
> Some say there's a soul locked inside,
> Some say there's a voice.
> People's desires are locked away
> In the room where the Buddha
> Lit a lamp of peace.

(Govind Singh Ravat: 'Closed Room'*(Band Kotha)*

The only poem that resembled a call to revolution was Vinay Raval's 'Once Fists are Clenched' *(Hat Mutthi Kasepachi)*, which also referred to developments abroad that inspired many of the younger elements within the democracy movement:

> Once fists are clenched,
> Even the Berlin Wall falls down;
> Once fists are clenched,
> The events of Tienanmen Sqaure take place,

> Once fists are clenched,
> Even Mandela is freed...
> Why are we the only ones
> Who do not clench our fists,
> And seek to be prisoners of history ?
> Has the man inside us died ?

The Nepali press came under severe pressure during the early days of the movement. For many years journalists had been prohibited from reporting the activities of the banned political parties, while the doings of the royal family dominated the headlines, particularly in the government-subsidised papers *Gorkhapatra* and *The Rising Nepal*. Between 15 February and 26 March, 1990, police confiscated the print-runs of privately-owned newspapers on at least eighteen occasions, and about forty-five journalists and editors were detained. *Gorkhapatra* and *The Rising Nepal* published long articles and editorial statements in defence of panchayat democracy, and attacked 'foreign elements' (meaning India) for meddling in Nepal's internal affairs. It is clear from several confessional articles published in the twenty-fifth anniversary issue of *The Rising Nepal* (18 December, 1990) that most of the journalists employed by the newspaper felt profoundly uncomfortable in their role as apologists for the Panchayat system. It has been suggested that the extreme, even excessive deference shown to members of the royal family in reports published while the movement was in progress may have been the journalists' own sarcastic, muted protest.

The Aftermath

Kathmandu's writers were not at the forefront of the democracy movement. After April 1990 there were recriminations and arguments over who had, and who had not, played an active role. Those who were felt to have compromised too enthusiastically with the old order were strongly criticised. But some writers had added their voices to the tide of protest against the suppression of the movement. On 3 April, the revered poet Kedar Man Vyathit resigned from the Council of State *(Raj Sabha)*, expressing his support for the movement and his opposition to the government's 'medieval and barbaric' policy of repression.[11] A group of forty writers issued a press statement which called for an impartial inquiry into human rights abuses[12] and many others paraded through Kathmandu wearing black gags, to stage a sit-down protest in a city-centre street near the palace.

Most of the predictable flood of revolutionary and pro-democracy poetry that is available now in published form appeared during the months after the movement had been called off. There was an obvious

[11] Ghimire, 1990: 17.
[12] Ibid.: 16.

urge to identify with the movement and to express solidarity with the
young men and women who had lost their lives. These were
characterised as 'martyrs' *(shahid)* and were thus identified with the
members of the Praja Parishad executed by Juddha Shamsher Rana in
1941, who are now commemorated in the Martyrs' Gate at Bhadrakali
in Kathmandu. There was no longer a need to express a dislike of the
old order obliquely—indeed, the writers felt obliged to disassociate
themselves from it as categorically as possible—and the Panchayat
system was universally condemned as 'despotic', 'feudal', and 'bestial.'
Three anthologies of poetry represent this literature well. They are *Long
Live, Down With (Jindabad, Murdabad), Movement Poems (Andolan
Kavita)* and *Martyrs/Poetry (Shahid/Kavita),* all published during the
summer of 1990. The tone of their editorial statements differs markedly
from the cautious generalities of *The Search for Spring:*

Our national people's movement proves that the raising of voices against
atrocities, repression, suffering and unjust despotism, and in favour of justice and freedom, is not a phenomenon limited to any one region of the
world (Jangab Chauhan in *Martyrs/Poetry.)*

For writers and artists to attack despotism is an old tradition in Nepali literature. Through long years of suffering and penance, they motivate the
people, and this becomes evident on the streets. The conscious writer does
not merely prepare the ground but becomes a part of the movement and tries
to give it a definite direction... The 1979 movement made Nepali poets more
aware of the importance of insight and communicability. Now we realise
that obscurity and sloganeering are both forms of extremism (Rurdra Kharel
in *Movement Poems).*

These statements exaggerate the importance of the role played by poets
in the 1990 movement, but they do show that many Nepali writers
believe their work to have relevance in the process of political change.
Many of the poems in these three anthologies, which were still available from Kathmandu street-stalls early in 1991, read like celebrations
written after the event. But there are some notable exceptions. For
instance, Shyamal provides a neat description of the political role of
poetry in early 1990:

> Now poetry's not found in solitude,
> You meet it in demonstrations,
> Now poetry isn't written on paper,
> You find it running down the street.[13]

Bimal Nibha's 'Patan' contains the kind of emotion that one would
expect in a poem composed while the population of Patan was erecting

---

[13] 'Poetry in Processions' *(Julusma Kavita)* in *Martyrs/Poetry* (Shahid/
Kavita):1).

barricades at the entrances to the town, and declaring it a 'zone of democracy':

> Excitement, anger and revolt
> And protests against injustice
> Are prohibited by written order,
> Murder has become legal.
> The red blood that flows from your breast
> Is anarchy...
> 'Consciousness' is an unconstitutional word.
> No kind of restlessness will be tolerated now.
> People of Patan,
> Your lives are declared illegal.[14]

Bikram Subba, in *Martyrs/Poetry*, equates revolution with patriotism:

> I spat and I pissed many times
> In this country's face,
> Not once did it object with its laws.
> But when I began to love my country
> Prisons and jails were made ready for me.[15]

After the establishment of an interim government, many individuals in academic and cultural institutions found themselves in a precarious position. On 22 May, 1990, every member of the Royal Nepal Academy but one resigned, explaining that all memberships were invalid since they had been granted by the discredited regime. The historian Naya Raj Pant claimed he owed the Panchayat system nothing, and withheld his resignation.[16] Pant was later vindicated, but all the other members probably resigned because they expected their memberships to be rescinded anyway.

On 22 July the academy was reconstituted, with members selected by the Prime Minister, Krishna Prasad Bhattarai, on the recommendation of his Minister for Education and Culture. The new Vice-Chancellor was Dr. Ishwar Baral, who had held a lectureship in politics at Jawaharlal Nehru University at Delhi for many years, but was better-known as a literary scholar in Nepal. The other members were three poets (Mohan Koirala, Bairagi Kainla and Ishwar Ballabh), a critic and essayist (Krishnachandra Singh Pradhan) and the historian Naya Raj Pant. The composition of the new membership, and the mode of its selection, were strongly criticised. The main complaint was that it was dominated by male pro-Congress Nepali literateurs, and that no other languages or political views were represented.[17] Demands were made for the immediate dissolution of the academy and its reconstitution through

---

[14] From *Movement Poems* (*Andolan Kavita*):1.
[15] 'The Martyr's Message' (*Shahidko Sandesh*).
[16] *Madhuparka* 23, 5: 63.
[17] *Janmat* 7, 6: 24-25.

a democratic process, and for the establishment of a separate academy for non-literary arts. A group of leftist writers and artists organised a protest march and presented these demands to the interim prime minister in September 1990.[18]

The individuals to whom memberships were granted were each worthy of some such honour, in view of their contributions to Nepali literature in the main. Nevertheless, there is a real danger of the cultural traits defined by Bista as 'bahunism' and 'afno manche' continuing to influence such nominations. (See Macfarlane in this volume.) It is likely that the academy's membership will change in years to come, and possibly it will be enlarged, but a government dominated by the Nepali Congress or any other party is not likely to honour artists and writers who are not in its fold. In this and many other fields of national life, considerations of who is and who is not favoured by the palace may be replaced by the equally pernicious factor of party political loyalty. Neither will ever augur well for the democratisation of Nepali culture.

A more positive aspect of the aftermath of Nepal's revolution has been an atmosphere of greater freedom of expression. Many articles have appeared in newspapers and elsewhere which would have exposed their authors, and the papers' editors, to a range of punitive measures prior to mid-1990. In one such article in the *Saptahik Bimarsha* of 14 December 1990, Raghu Pant mocked the excessive deference to royal sensibilities required of flightcrew on RNAC flights when the king and queen were on board. According to Pant, staff were not allowed to be seen walking to the aircraft lavatory, and had to urinate into bottles in the cockpit. In an essay entitled 'Chandani Shah and Pieces of Silver', Khagendra Sangraula suggested that those who had praised the queen's poems so immoderately only a few months earlier were hurriedly donning the clothes of democracy: 'Now the brave Nepali people are praised to the sky, while all talk of Chandani Shah has fled down a hole. It's amazing! Who was where yesterday, and where are they today?'[19]

Nepali journals and pamphlets contained numerous examples of such post-revolutionary rhetoric at the end of 1990. Many writers were understandably anxious to prove their democratic credentials, and to pour scorn on the contemporaries they accused of having collaborated with the Panchayat regime. The censorious and oppressive tendencies of that regime have perhaps been somewhat overstated since its downfall: there were periods of clampdown, of course, particularly during the early 1960s and late 1980s, but there were also periods of comparative laxity. The development of Nepali literature was not wholly retarded during the three decades of the Panchayat system. In fact, the existence of censorship (which was, more often than not, self-censorship) produced many

[18] *Madhuparka* 23, 5: 63.
[19] Sangraula, 1990: 23.

great and memorable works of allegory. As long as their poems employed the well-known codes, Nepali poets could express dissent. But now that there is no longer a need for elaborate symbolism, many are at a loss. 'What to write?' said Mohan Koirala in December 1990, 'It's hard. There's no need to hide anything from anyone. Democracy arrived so suddenly that we're in a state of confusion'.

The Crisis of Acceptance

In a survey of the Nepali literature of 1990-91 (B.S.2047), Abhi Subedi concluded:

Our journey is from the street to the canvas. Until yesterday we spoke in symbols. Now the challenge is to speak clearly. Now the images and veiled references will all collapse. Writers must announce how closely they intend to relate literature to life. The streets can return to mentalities and experiences, or the reverse can occur. Whatever happens, we are in a period of transition. Soon we should see the inevitable.[20]

Krishnachandra Singh Pradhan analysed the situation in more detail in an article entitled 'The crisis of acceptance within the rejectionist revolt',[21] basing his discussion on one of the more interesting works to have appeared in Nepali since the movement's success. This is a collection of highly unorthodox short stories by Ram Bahadur Shreshtha (b.1948), who writes as 'Kavitaram' and was involved in the 'Rejected Generation' movement of 1968. The stories date from a twenty-year period, 1970-90, and the following summary of one of them, 'King Haribhunge and Minister Bhatabhunge', first published in 1973, brings this discussion to a close.

The story describes an absurd, topsy-turvy world where many ludicrous laws are enforced. For instance, the market price of every commodity depends solely upon its colour. Thus, silver, flour and milk all cost the same, because each is white. One day, a man approaches the rulers of the kingdom and complains that he has sustained a near-fatal blow to the head at the house where he is staying as a guest, because its entrance is too low. The king and his minister ordain that the door should be brought to them and punished. But the owner of the house pleads for his door, and blames the carpenter who made it. So the carpenter is summoned, but he in turn defends himself by blaming a young woman who distracted him with the jingling of her anklets while he was making the door. The woman is brought before the rulers to answer for her crime, but she blames the blacksmith who made the anklets. Blacksmiths belong to a lowly caste, and the thin, cowering specimen who is presented for punishment inspires pity in the king and the minister. They decide that the person punished should be fat, not

[20] Subedi, 1991b.
[21] Pradhan, 1991.

thin—and a corpulent yogi is summoned. The author points out that yogis grow fat on traditions such as entering through doors, wearing anklets and the like. A death sentence is passed upon him, but the yogi smiles. When asked why he smiles, he explains that he happens to know, through yogic insight, that the next person to be executed will become king in the next life. So the king and his minister volunteer for execution, and are put to death instead. 'No-one knows', concludes Kavitaram, in what is surely a reference to what he considers the absurdity of his country's politics, 'how many Haribhunges and Bhatabhunges have met with the same sorrowful end. Let us see what the fate of the Haribhunges and Bhatabhunges of this age will be'.[22]

REFERENCES

Amnesty International, *Nepal. A Pattern of Human Rights Violations.* London, 1987.

Bista, Dor Bahadur, *Fatalism and Development. Nepal's Struggle for Modernisation.* Madras, 1991.

Ghimire, Kapil, 'Jan Andolanka Dinharu' (The days of the people's movement) *Madhuparka*, 23, 5: 9-17 (1990).

Kavitaram, *Mukti Prasangka Aswikrit Kathaharu* (Rejected Stories of the Context of Freedom). Kathmandu, 1990-91.

Malla, Kamal Prakash, *The Road to Nowhere.* Kathmandu, 1979.

Pindali, Keshav Raj, Interview in *Samashti*, 23, April-June 1990, Kathmandu.

Pradhan, Krishnachandra Singh, 'Aswikrit Vidrohabhitra Swikritiko Sankat' (The Crisis of Acceptance within the Rejectionist Revolt) *Samakalin Sahitya* 1, 2: 87-93, Kathmandu).

Sakar, Shailendra, *Shailendra Sakarka Kavita* (The Poetry of Shailendra Sakar). Kathmandu, 1979.

—. 1990a, *Sarpaharu Git Sundainan* (Serpents Don't Listen to Songs: poems). New Delhi and Jaipur, 1990.

—. 1990b, 'Jivan Jasto Cha....' (reminiscences) *Samashti*, 23, 1990.

Sangraula, Khagendra,*Jan-Andolanka Charraharu* (Shots from the people's movement: essays). Kathmandu, 1990.

Shah, Chandani, (ed. Narendraraj Prasai) *Aphnai Akash, Aphnai Parivesh* (My own sky, my own environment: poems). Kathmandu, 1988.

Sharma, Taranath, *Nepali Sahityako Itihas* (History of Nepali Literature). Kathmandu, 1970, 1982.

—. (ed.) *Samasamayik Sajha Kavita* (Contemporary Nepali Poetry: an anthology). Kathmandu, 1983.

[22] Kavitaram, 1990-1: 24.

Sherchan, Bhupi, 'Birendra Jindabad' ('Long Live Birendra') *Kavita,* 20, Kathmandu, 1986-7.

—. 'Sarpako Khojima' ('In Search of Serpents') reprinted in *Unnayana,* 2, 4 Kathmandu, 1984.

Subedi, Abhi, 1991a, 'Presidential Address to the Eleventh Annual Conference of the Linguistic Society of Nepal on November 20, 1990' in *Nepalese Linguistics,* 5-8 (November 1991).

—. 1991b, '2047 salma nepali sahitya-kalako moda' (Trends in Nepali literature during 2047) *Gorkhapatra* Chait 30 2047.

Chapter 6

THE BRITISH GURKHA CONNECTION IN THE 1990s

Nigel Collett

This paper discusses aspects of change currently affecting the British Brigade of Gurkhas, and the ways in which these have effect in their turn in Nepal. Development and political change in Nepal have accelerated the pace of change in the society from which Gurkhas are recruited. In Britain, large-scale changes now underway in the size and shape of the British armed forces will have a severe effect on Gurkha numbers and will accelerate changes to their lives within the Service. Consideration of the effects of these changes is therefore timely.

Some background information will be useful at this stage. In early 1991 there were slightly over 7,400 Gurkha soldiers serving in the British Army, and these were accompanied in Hong Kong and Brunei by about 4,800 dependants and nearly 150 Nepali civilian employees (teachers, religious instructors, goldsmiths and midwives). The soldiers were organised as follows:

a) Five infantry battalions, which are:
   1st Battalion and 2nd Battalion 2nd King Edward VII's Own
   Gurkha Rifles
   6th Queen Elizabeth's Own Gurkha Rifles
   7th Duke of Edinburgh's Own Gurkha Rifles
   10th Princess Mary's Own Gurkha Rifles.

b) Three supporting regiments, as follows:
   Queen's Gurkha Engineers
   Queen's Gurkha Signals
   Gurkha Transport Regiment.

c) A training depot in Hong Kong which trains recruits and acts as a school of instruction.

d) Two demonstration companies attached to the Army schools of instruction at Sandhurst and Brecon.

e) Lines of communication troops in Nepal, including a Headquarters in Kathmandu and a recruiting centre in Pokhara.

f) A Headquarters of the Brigade, a central Manning and Record Office and a pay office, all in Hong Kong.

For historical rather than military reasons, the majority of these troops are stationed in Hong Kong and Brunei, though about 20 per cent are stationed in the United Kingdom. About 300 soldiers are recruited annually in two groups, once every six months. They are recruited in traditional areas, in the west mainly from Rapti, Gandaki and western Central Zones, and in the east from Sagarmatha, Koshi and Mechi Zones. For reasons of homogeneity the British Army continues the traditional policy of recruiting from 'martial' jats. In the west these are Gurungs, Magars, Thakuris, and some Tamangs and Thakalis. In the east they are Limbus, Rais, Sunwars, Gurungs and Tamangs. Small numbers of other jats are recruited, in particular for clerical and technical posts requiring more educated men; Chhetris and Newars are often recruited for these fields. The impact of this recruiting is not fully quantifiable in terms of the proportion of the population who have come into contact in some way with the British Army, due to the non-availability of the records of pre-1947 Indian Army servicemen and their surviving families. As a rough estimate, a figure is used of something over 100,000 ex-servicemen surviving in Nepal, 88,000 of whom were recruited prior to 1947. The British Army pays pensions to those who served for 15 or more years and currently has a total of 21,000 pensioners on its books.

On behalf of the Gurkha Welfare Scheme, a charitable organisation that administers funds for the independent Gurkha Welfare Appeal and is supported in part of its administration by the Ministry of Defence, the Brigade carries out a considerable amount of welfare activity in its recruiting areas. The Scheme aims to benefit ex-servicemen, their families and the communities in which they live, and disburses £1.5m annually for projects such as village water supply, bridge construction, and the building and furnishing of schools. Additionally, the Brigade administers British ODA grants to a total of £1.3m for water projects. The Scheme provides educational grants for 321 students and 67 schools, and pays 2,956 welfare hardship pensions, in the main to those whose service was too short to entitle them to a pension. The Scheme has 23 welfare centres distributed throughout Nepal, mostly in the hills, which are staffed by teams of between three and six ex-servicemen.

The exact financial contribution the Brigade makes to the Nepalese economy has not been fully calculated. However, it is estimated that pay, pensions, contracts for air movement and the recurring costs of British establishments in Nepal currently amount to some £30m per annum. The benefit of this sum to the country is enhanced by the way almost all of it is applied to the areas from which our servicemen come in ways which benefit the population directly.

The Brigade's ties with Nepal are therefore strong, and it is self-evident that changes in the country have effects upon that connection and within the Brigade. To analyse the effect of social developments on the Brigade, and particularly to come to an assessment of whether these developments impinge upon or even threaten the connection, it is necessary to understand what, apart from the pressure of history itself, makes Gurkha recruiting attractive to the British Army.

Firstly, the Service values the type of men found in the hills of Nepal, particularly for infantry work. Strong, enduring, used to discomfort and hence uncomplaining, the Gurkha is physically an ideal soldier. The traditional hierarchical society of Nepal fits the Gurkha well to take a place in a disciplined organisation based upon a rigid hierarchy and the need for obedience. These traditional ideal attributes for servicemen in all armies are with some difficulty coupled with the slightly more recent requirement for intelligence and sufficient education to cope with more complex weapons systems and equipment, and for individuals to act on their own initiative in smaller groups and more complicated situations. The fact that the British Army is able (through terms of service which are highly attractive in Nepal) to recruit the best part of a generation in the areas of recruiting means that these conflicting requirements can be met readily in Gurkha recruits. Secondly, the British Army continues to set much store by the cohesion within a regiment which stems from ties of common areas of origin, family and historical tradition. Within the Brigade these ties are particularly strong. British Gurkhas are often related to other soldiers at least by marriage, and come from similar home areas in Nepal. Thirdly, ease of recruitment of good quality men is of value to the Army. Nepal, due, sadly, to its poverty, is an almost inexhaustible source of recruits. It continues to supply high quality soldiers in whatever numbers the British government needs.

As society changes in Nepal, modernisation and reform affect the characteristics which make Gurkhas attractive to recruit. The major change affecting the Brigade is the steady spread of education throughout the hills. Our recruits have long been 100 per cent literate, but now are almost all educated to Class 9 or 10, and in many cases have studied to Intermediate level or even beyond. On arrival, all already have had some modicum of language training, and all have acquired a much more open view of the world than many of their predecessors. They are used to absorbing knowledge and learning skills, have often been more widely travelled in Nepal than earlier recruits were (and sons of old soldiers may have been brought up in Malaysia, Singapore or Hong Kong), and throughout their youth have had at least some access to world news through the radio. These factors work both for and against them from a military point of view. The Army now benefits from the increased speed at which it can train soldiers in more technical skills based upon their earlier education. The standard of English now achievable is much improved, and within a further five or so years will be such as to enable Gurkhas to take their place in British Army schools of instruction alongside their British counterparts. Gurkha soldiers are becoming sharper of wit and more capable of acting on their own initiative and responsibility. The reverse of this is a gradual loss of the simplicity and ruggedness of character that has always been valued. Open minds may be more prone to question or even to criticise, and Gurkha soldiers as a result will require more effort to command than has been the case in the past. Clearly, though, this is a small price to pay for the improvements in responsiveness which are the result of this process. Commanding Gurkhas will for the foreseeable future remain a joy for those lucky enough to be given the task.

The drift of population from country to town and from the hills to the plains of the Tarai does cause the Brigade some problems. The Brigade aims to recruit from the hills, but finds itself taking a gradually increasing number of recruits brought up in the somewhat (though in a British context this is a comparative term only) easier life of the town or the plain. The physical robustness and stamina of potential recruits suffers somewhat, and the very process of sitting in a classroom for nine or ten years will inevitably produce a physically less sturdy man than a youth spent on the farm or roaming the hills. As a result, slightly more physical training may be required to bring recruits up to the right standard. Nevertheless, the recruitment tests are formidable, and no weakling passes through them. Part of this problem of the drift of population is the settlement of many of our soldiers on retirement in the towns or plains. Life is easier, there is often electricity, shops, buses, clinics and telephones. Schools are better, and in particular almost all the English medium boarding schools are located down from the hills. The children of soldiers settling in these places therefore grow up in an environment that lessens their suitability for recruiting. Additionally, the welfare system is currently organised throughout the hill recruiting areas, and is thus misplaced to deal with the welfare problems that arise after the end of a man's service. The system will now need to be stretched to cope with this problem, which will involve great expense. Whilst the growth of population in the hills makes recruiting there still feasible and attractive, the trend of retirement settlement is pushing the welfare organisation down the hill. The Brigade is in the forefront of the drift of population in that the cream of a generation from the hills is taken and deposited, enriched, upon the plain some 15-20 years later.

The political changes of the last two years have perhaps the greatest potential for affecting the Brigade's connection with Nepal. The Nepali Crown and its governments of whatever complexion had, since 1947, treated Gurkha service very favourably, encouraged recruiting and raised no political objections to the use of Gurkhas in any theatre (it is noteworthy here that any restrictions placed upon the use of Gurkha troops in theatres such as Northern Ireland have been imposed by the British government, not the Nepali). Whilst the corruption and inefficiency of

the old system affected British Gurkhas as part of the population as a
whole, the stability of the old order, and the ability that monetary
wealth had to manipulate it, benefited the acquisition by British soldiers
of a place in society. At village and sometimes at district level, ex-
servicemen were able to play active roles in local affairs and put their
experience to the benefit of the community. British service gave status
and some local influence. Some of this is inevitably put at risk by
political change. However, the increase in political freedom and the
institution of democracy in Nepal have been widely welcomed in the
Brigade. Service abroad has given Gurkha soldiers a view of many
wealthy, stable, honest and open societies, and the absence of many of
these things in Nepal had become bitterly resented. The functionaries of
the old system had increasingly battened upon the servicemen of the
Brigade who were wealthy, but politically unconnected. Bribery, extor-
tion and corruption of soldiers by high-placed officials aiming to mis-
use the facilities of overseas travel provided by the Brigade, all occurred.
There has been general satisfaction throughout the Brigade with the
changes that have taken place in Nepal.

With political freedom goes the possibility of change, and this in
itself raises the issue of the durability of the Brigade's connection with
Nepal. The current government has proved as firm a supporter of the
connection as its predecessors. Opposition parties are less favourably
inclined, and in some of the more extreme communist factions, openly
hostile. Whilst it would seem that views opposing the connection will
not be held by those in power for some time, if ever, support for them
in the political arena will ensure that they are periodically aired. This
will be particularly the case whenever British interests and those of the
Non-Aligned Movement can be portrayed as different. The British government will need to continue to be robust on the issue of its unfettered
deployment of Gurkha troops. Any loss of freedom to use Gurkhas
anywhere alongside British soldiers would lessen their utility and thus
endanger the connection itself. There is no sign, luckily, of any change
in this situation at the moment.

The Brigade itself has an effect upon Nepal and the changes that
have, and are taking place there. In the capital our usefulness to the
country and wide connections within it make the British embassy an
informed, committed, and useful source of assistance to the Nepali
government. The British presence is also of use to Nepal as a balance to
the heavy political influence of its neighbours, particularly India.
British influence, however while not dependent on the size of the
Gurkha connection, will no doubt diminish somewhat as the size of the
Brigade reduces.

There is no evidence so far that ex-servicemen have entered the political arena at the national level. However, at district level and below,
many ex-servicemen took part in the Movement for the Restoration of

Democracy and remain prominent in local political parties. The Brigade discourages serving soldiers from participation in politics (other than exercising the right to vote or express a view) as is the case in the rest of the British Army. Clearly, the Brigade cannot be identified through its members with any political party or opinion; to be so identified would drag the Brigade into controversy which would inevitably harm the connection.

The economic contribution that the British connection makes to Nepal is significant, but will inevitably decrease as the size of the Brigade reduces. Our contribution to the infrastructure of the country reduced in 1989 with the closure of the cantonment, and with it the hospital at Dharan, and with the imposition of commercial contract procedures for air movements arrangements. These, whilst resulting in savings to the MOD budget, have decreased the contribution it makes to the Nepali economy. Conversely, with the increase in Gurkha wages which will soon bring Gurkha terms of service to the level of their British counterparts, and with the continuance of the Welfare Scheme, the usefulness of the connection to Nepal's economy will continue beyond the reductions in the Brigade's size. Locally it is even possible that the significance of this contribution, by being more concentrated and therefore more noticeable, will increase. The way that Welfare Scheme aid is channelled through ex-servicemen alone will continue to ensure the local importance of the British connection.

Whilst the British continue to recruit and train Gurkhas, there will be a continual flow of men leaving the service at the ages of 33-45 who have served for much of their lives in Western societies and have become accustomed to the benefits they have found within them. Their dependants will also have spent some time in these environments and some of their children will have been brought up and educated in no other environment at all. The return to Nepal can be a great shock to these men and their families. Many men seek continued service abroad, in Brunei, the Gulf or other countries. Some continue to educate their children abroad and even settle overseas themselves. The vast majority return home to Nepal, but decreasing numbers return to the hills; it is not surprising, therefore, that the soldier's relative affluence and knowledge of better standards of hygiene and style of life are diluted and of little effect in most of the villages of the hills. The conservative, hierarchical nature of rural society, coupled with a lack of resources and facilities, makes the task of any serviceman settling back in his village and seeking to overturn the old ways almost impossible. However, where groups of servicemen gather in relatively accessible places, physical improvements to village buildings, paths, sanitation and water supply are made and are gradually accumulating. Down the hill, in the major towns or local centres such as Damauli, Butwal or Dharan, ex-servicemen are noticeably to the forefront of community life and in improvements in local society. Service children provide a large source of pupils for private boarding schools in such places. It is likely that the growing number of ex-servicemen investing their savings in such local communities in the plains or town is a significant contributory factor to the large increase in land and house prices in these regions. Gurkha servicemen view investment in property in much the same way as their British counterparts, and prefer to invest in the relatively safe areas of land and housing rather than in the more risky and certainly less familiar field of commercial enterprise. Nevertheless, partially encouraged by resettlement courses in commerce, and partially by the general, if slow, increase in commercial activity throughout Nepal, the number of ex-servicemen entering some form of business activity is gradually increasing. Activities in the hotel and catering trade have proved particularly suited to ex-soldiers used to contact with Europeans. Other activities involving ex-servicemen include joint trading ventures (usually in small luxury or electrical goods) and in some cases more extensive businesses like bus and haulage companies, small automated food processing plants, and the construction industry. A small number have found employment with international aid agencies.

In a more general sense, British service is in the forefront of the spread of Western culture as opposed to the Sanskrit/Hindu culture spreading before. Ex-servicemen tend to set trends in Western dress, music and fashion. Western ways of thought and behaviour become to some extent ingrained during military service and spread imperceptibly at home as a result. In the long run, this may prove one of the most far-reaching of all influences the British connection brings to bear.

Changes in current British defence policy following the substantial diminution of the Soviet threat to the NATO countries have been rapid, and will continue to have repercussions within the services up to the middle of the decade. Reductions in the size of the Army will be considerable. The Brigade of Gurkhas is affected simultaneously by the withdrawal of the garrison from Hong Kong, which is due to be completed by mid 1997. As a result of this general retrenchment it has been announced that the Brigade will reduce to about 2,500 men by about 1997. The five infantry battalions will reduce to two and form a single regiment. The supporting regiments of engineers, signallers and drivers will reduce to a squadron each. What remains will be based in the main in the United Kingdom,with a battalion in Brunei and lines-of-communication troops in Nepal. The reductions in manpower necessary to achieve this will be made continually from now until 1997, and the number of soldiers recruited to sustain the new Brigade will reduce proportionately. The British connection will therefore diminish by two-thirds in terms of the number of serving soldiers. The British financial contribution, however, will not diminish by anything like that amount as the pay of those continuing to serve is expected to more than double over the next few years. The contribution made by the Welfare System will, if anything, increase during this rundown, and the infrastructure in the camps in Kathmandu and Pokhara will continue. At the end of the rundown the military movement organisation may have considerably fewer passengers to transport, but any diminution will be offset by plans to grant annual as opposed to tri-annual leave in Nepal. It is likely, therefore, that the real financial contribution made by Britain to Nepal will not diminish greatly in the near future. Indeed, British service is likely to increase its attractiveness, and entry to it is likely to become even more competitive than before as emoluments increase and numbers drop. In terms, though, of the effects that British service has on the community, the influences brought to bear by the British connection will inevitably decrease as numbers of serving soldiers fall.

Despite the current rundown in the British Army's Gurkha contingent, the connections with Nepal that are embodied in the Brigade of Gurkhas are likely to remain of value to the Nepali government, and to remain attractive to the British Army well into the next century. Continuing changes to society in Nepal and to the employment of Gurkhas in the British Army will continue to affect the soldiers we recruit and the society to which we return them. As long as the effects of both types of change continue to be manageable, the connection of the British Brigade of Gurkhas with Nepal is likely to be maintained to the mutual benefit of both.

Chapter 7

FATALISM AND DEVELOPMENT IN NEPAL

Alan Macfarlane

It is possible to take very different views about the way in which Nepal is currently heading.[1] An optimistic assessment culled from official statistics and superficial impressions could be made. In contrast to India there appears to be little absolute poverty, with no begging and no real shanty towns. Famines are infrequent. There is a notable absence of violence; the police are few, crime rates are low, and political violence has been limited.

These impressions could be backed by impressive statistics. From a standing start in 1950, when the Ranas were overthrown and Nepal began to be transformed from a medieval oriental despotism into a modern nation-state, a great deal has been done. An all but roadless country in 1950, Nepal had built more than six thousand miles of properly paved highways by the late 1980s. Between 1950 and 1980 the cumulative growth in various sectors has been estimated as follows: '70 times in power generation, 13 times in irrigation facility, 134 times in school enrolment, 12 times in number of hospital beds'.[2] Epidemic diseases have been practically eliminated. Infant mortality rates have been halved. Piped water has been brought to most villages. An international airline has been started. Nepal now exports goods worth more than 25 million US dollars a year. A large tourist industry has been created, with over 300,000 tourists (other than Indians) a year. A literacy rate of two per cent in 1951 had been increased to over 40 per cent by the late 1980s. There are more than 150 university campuses. Kathmandu and other towns have grown remarkably and now have many facilities, including television, computers and many modern goods and services. All this has been achieved with no significant revolution or bloodshed. It looks like an economic and social miracle.

Yet an equally convincing case could be made to support a

[1] This article was originally published in Cambridge Anthropology, 14: 1 (1990). I am grateful to the Editors of that journal for permission to reprint it in this collection. Some of the fieldwork upon which it is based was funded by the Economic and Social Research Council. Sarah Harrison gave valuable advice on earlier drafts of the article and helped with the fieldwork. Some interesting comments on an abbreviated form of the article are contained in a letter by David Seddon to the London Review of Books, 16 August 1990.

[2] Gurung, 1926: 246.

pessimistic assessment. Despite a long-established family planning
policy, there has been little success in controlling population. In 1800
there were less than two and a half million people in Nepal. By 1941
there were about six million. By 1971 the population had nearly
doubled to eleven and a half million. It is currently over eighteen
million and is projected to be at least twenty-five million by the year
2001. It will thus have increased four-fold in sixty years. At present the
population is growing faster than almost anywhere in Asia, at 2.7 per
cent per annum, and the use and knowledge of contraception is lower
than in any other Asian country.[3]

This population pressure is particularly worrying because of the ecological situation. The population density in relation to cultivable land
is as high as in many of the far more fertile Asiatic deltas. People press
on land that is usually a thin covering of soil on extremely steep rocky
slopes, swept by torrential monsoon rains. The growing numbers
exploit the remaining forest ever more intensively for firewood, fodder
and grazing. The results are very serious. Moddie concludes that 'Nepal
provides the most dramatic example of the spread of desertification....
In a flash, within the decade ending 1971, Nepal had lost 50 per cent of
its forest cover....'[4] Eckholm claimed that Nepal faces 'the world's
most acute national soil erosion problem'.[5] One expert estimated that
Nepal was losing 164,000 cubic inches of top soil each year.[6] A figure
quoted by the Annapurna Conservation Area Project suggests that 'one
hectare of cleared forest loses 30-75 tons of soil annually. In Nepal,
approximately 400,000 hectares are cleared each year....' As Seddon
puts it, 'the country now faces a crisis whose major components
include serious over-population, ecological collapse in the densely
populated and highly vulnerable hill areas...and overall declining yields
in agriculture....'[7] In one hundred years, with present trends, the
mountains will be stripped of forest and soil, and a population of over
one hundred million will be forced to live in absolute poverty or
migrate elsewhere.

These facts are well known and easily visible. Less obvious is the
serious deterioration in the material standard of life of a majority of the
population, despite the massive inflow of 'aid'. One of the most omi-
nous developments in the last thirty years in Nepal has been the way in
which the formerly rice-surplus middle hills have become grain deficit
areas. The western hills, for instance, became short of grain before
1976, with an average of up to three per cent decline in food production
per annum over the last few years. (It is predicted that the food deficit in

[3] Seddon, 1984: 1, 87.
[4] Quoted in Gurung, op.cit.: 191.
[5] Quoted in Seddon, op.cit.: 72.
[6] Gurung, op.cit.: 192
[7] Seddon, 1979: 46.

Nepal will increase at least ten times between 1985 and 2000.[8] Hill
farmers, who once produced a surplus, now only survive with the help
of a steady flow of outside grains. Harka Gurung quotes a recent
estimate that 'in comparison to the 2.12 per cent annual increase in
population during 1964-78, annual agricultural growth was only 0.78
per cent and this indicated a reduction of annually 21 kg. per head in
food consumption'.[9]

What these general trends mean for individuals is best seen in one
central hill village where data has been collected over the last twenty
years. Between 1970 and 1990 there has been an almost 50 per cent
drop in grain production as the land loses its fertility and goes out of
production. In 1970 most families had enough rice for themselves and
practically no rice was bought outside the village. By 1990 only a quarter of the villagers had enough rice for their needs; rice had become a
luxury rather than a necessity and a large amount was being bought
from the south.

The number of animals has also dropped by half. This means that
less manure is available for the fields, hence there are reduced crops. It
also means a worsening of the diet. Twenty years ago people in mid-
dling families had a protein-rich diet, eating meat every two or three
days, drinking milk at almost every meal. Now they eat meat only once
or twice a month and drink milk occasionally. Their personal wealth
has visibly declined; the women have sold their gold ornaments, the
clothing is less adequate, the houses and paths are deteriorating.

This growing impoverishment reflects a dramatic decline in the
return on labour. It is estimated that the maize equivalent (the poor eat
maize) of wage rates fell by roughly 30-60 per cent in the period 1968-9
to 1976-7 alone.[10] In the sample hill village, there has been an
approximate halving on the returns on labour during the last twenty
years, thus a halving in the standard of living. For instance, in 1970 it
took just over a day's work to earn enough to buy a chicken. In 1990 it
takes two to three days work to do so. A day's hard work in the fields
produces grain worth 15-20 rupees (30-40p sterling in 1990); this is
certainly not enough to feed a family, let alone clothe, house, marry,
bury, nurse and educate it. Many villages are propped up by money
from migratory labour in the army or civilian work in India.

Thus, on the one hand, we have the national statistics of growing
literacy, improved health, water, roads, trade, while on the other the majority of the population are year by year growing poorer and worse fed
and the environment is rapidly deteriorating. A strange contradiction.
Furthermore, the contrast between a small affluent minority in
Kathmandu and other towns, who enjoy almost First World standards,

[8] Gurung, op.cit.: 182.
[9] Ibid.
[10] Seddon, 1984: 115-6.

and the 95 per cent who live in growing poverty, is growing ever sharper.

In fact, the contradiction between progress and impoverishment is not as dramatic as it seems, for behind the impressive statistics, the actual progress is far less notable. The figures giving total numbers of schools, hospitals, health workers, miles of road constructed, are meaningless without taking into account the quality of what is being developed. Those who have worked in Nepal all have their own stories. The following tiny set of examples, all taken from one small valley over a short period of time, could be multiplied a million-fold.

The school statistics are impressive and some of the private schools are good. But the average village school is very badly equipped, often not even having benches or blackboards; it teaches a curriculum which is of practically no use to the children unless they obtain one of the scarce office jobs in a town. Many of the teachers do not understand the language of the ethnic group they are working with and are disillusioned and homesick. Much learning is by rote, there is high absenteeism, and a high failure rate in exams. Attempts to reform the educational system have been unsuccessful and the general standard is very low. Likewise the universities are very poorly equipped, the staff badly paid and in constant turmoil. Education is avidly sought by the wealthier, who send their children to expensive schools, thereby using up all their own capital and producing an alienated middle strata who find it impossible to reintegrate into the basically agrarian economy.

There has been a massive foreign investment in medical improvements and a superficial counting of the number of medical personnel or health posts would suggest a country going through a medical revolution. Yet if one visits the hospitals and health posts, or talks to villagers who have tried to use them, there is an overwhelming impression of a waste of resources and considerable inefficiency. The government hospital in the second largest hill town, Pokhara, is notorious for its absentee doctors, poor hygiene, careless operations, shortage of medicine. The wrong limbs lopped off, all the nurses absent when women are in labour, totally inaccurate diagnosis and prescription, the siphoning off of time and medicines to private stores, all are endlessly alleged. Even allowing for exaggeration and gossip, there seems to be much to be concerned about.

Likewise, the health posts are over-staffed, but under-equipped. One near the sample village has ten workers, but anyone seeking the simplest medicine for sores or cuts will be told to walk a day and buy their own in the bazaar. There are two nurses, but neither has even the simplest of gynaecological instruments. Other large villages have no health post or health worker and women die needlessly in childbirth, unable to make the eight hour journey to the nearest nurse. The government contribution in one such village of a thousand people is one rupee per year (less than 2p sterling in 1990). This is the reality of medicine in Nepal.

The situation with agricultural development projects is broadly similar. Most of the budget goes on constructing buildings, often in the towns, and on paying staff. Very little reaches the villages and fields for which it is destined. The staff themselves are often disinterested in agriculture. As Bista writes, 'Agricultural training institutions are built yet farmers are not the ones who go there for training. People who have no interest in the soil are the ones who get degrees in agricultural science'.

A typical example in the related field of veterinary medicine concerns the location of the nearest veterinary station to the sample village. When I asked why it was located in the plain, two thousand feet below any of the villages where the animals which it was to treat were located, I was told that the expert who worked there lived in a nearby town. He did not want to walk up the steep hill to his office. It is not surprising, with no animals, that it is seldom used. Furthermore, villagers allege that they are unable to find anyone present most of the time. When there was a chicken epidemic and they enquired about vaccinations, the official demanded a large amount for merely walking to the village, let alone payment for the injections. They did not bother and almost all the chickens in the village died.

Another example could be taken from the massive effort to install piped water. A large system, starting in the sample village, is currently being built. It is in its early stages, but is already a catalogue of inefficiency. The pipe joints are inappropriate and will soon break, the junction pipes are set at the wrong angle, the pipe is left exposed at crucial points to be punctured by passing livestock, the inflow and outflow pipes in the tank are at the wrong level. After a few months, a landslide fell and blocked the top reservoir entirely, and a rock fell a little lower down and severed the pipe. This was quickly reported and a team came to investigate. Eight months later, nothing has been done and no engineers have been seen. The water dribbles down to only one or two of the taps in the village.

Again, there are constant complaints about the working of minor bureaucrats, who need bribes, are insolent, and are usually absent from their offices. Villagers commonly allege that even for the most minor business they are told to come back another day, unless they produce extra cash, when the business will be quickly done. There are fears of the police, who can be brutal, undiscriminating and not accountable for their behaviour.

As for the transport revolution, many of the bridges are unfinished or badly maintained, the roads soon deteriorate into a bad condition, the public transport is ramshackle, public facilities scarce.

The question then is, why is Nepal heading towards economic, ecological and demographic crisis, and why has foreign aid had so little impact? Two possibilities can be immediately ruled out. The first is that the people themselves are incapable of developing. In fact, the country is rich in human talent. For a century and a half the middle hills have supplied the Gurkha troops in the British and Indian armies. With training, leadership and organisation, these hill soldiers have earned a reputation as one of the most efficient, brave, hard-working and efficient fighting forces in the world. They are full of initiative, practical, flexible, quick to pick up new ideas. These qualities, if effectively harnessed, could have turned Nepal into a small example of the southeast Asian economic miracle. The religion, social structure and egalitarian values are very similar to what are called the 'confucian cultures', which have been so successful. Yet this is not happening.

Another possibility is that aid has not been at a sufficiently generous level. Again this does not seem to be the case. It is probable that in terms of its Gross Domestic Product, Nepal has received more foreign aid per head than any other country in the world. Its strategic position as a zone between two power blocks, with India and China competing for friendship, and Russia and America for cold war influence, is combined with the sentiments of the Gurkha association and Swiss-like environment which bring in British and European aid. This means that Nepal has been flooded with aid and advice. Nepal was only able to spend less than 65 per cent of the total allocated aid budget during the first five year plan period of 1956-61. During the two decades 1951-2 to 1969-70 foreign aid totalled more than 178 dollars.[11] If we remember that at that time the total exports of goods were worth less than an average of 10 million dollars a year, we can see that money from aid far outstripped all foreign earnings. There can be few countries in that position. Since 1970 the amount of aid has grown substantially. Of course, much of the money went back to the donor countries in the form of large salaries to their 'experts' and to pay for machinery and goods from the donor country. But even after this, there has been a great deal left to spend. Combining this money, the offered expertise and the natural talent might have led to real advance. As it is, while the towns grow and a small segment of the rich get richer, the population rockets and the number in considerable poverty grows daily. How and why has this happened?

The conventional wisdom comes in two main forms, demographic-ecological-geographical, and politico-social. The first argument is as follows. Nepal is a barren, mountainous country with little good agricultural land. Furthermore, there are few useful mineral resources, coal, oil, gas, metals. Communications are very difficult because the country is long and thin, from east to west, while the ridges cut across this from north to south. There is no sea access and trade has to pass through India. All these geographical considerations make it unlikely that Nepal would become wealthy.

[11] Gurung, op.cit.: 61.

On top of this is the rapid and uncontrolled growth of population which has already been documented. It is truly a Malthusian situation, and it is not surprising that Malthus himself quoted Turner's 'Embassy to Tibet' to the effect that 'It certainly appears that a superabundant population in an unfertile country must be the greatest of all calamities, and produce eternal warfare or eternal want'.[12] It is argued that the combination of growing population and poor resources is enough to account for most of the problem.[13]

While it would be foolish to ignore such arguments, and they do indeed provide some of the essential explanatory frameworks, they do not account for all the present trends. The Malthusian argument only suggests possible tendencies, what will happen if all else is equal. But, of course, all else is not equal. As Malthus himself argued in the second edition of his 'Essay on Population', people can control their population if they wish. Furthermore, since Malthus wrote, the equations have been altered by the industrial and scientific revolutions, which allow production to expand exponentially with the application of non-organic energy. Consequently, population and resources are not determining, they condition the situation. We only have to look at Holland, Japan, Singapore, or Hong Kong, to see how an inauspicious environment can be transformed into a centre of wealth through human ingenuity. In principle, there is no reason why this should not happen in Nepal. We therefore have to seek other causes.

A second set of arguments concerns the political economy of Nepal. In a series of studies, Blaikie, Cameron and Seddon have extensively documented what they call 'Nepal in Crisis'. They give detailed evidence to support many of the impressions noted above. They quote the Fourth Five Year Plan (1970-75) to the effect that 'although a number of development works have been undertaken in different sectors of the economy, there has not been virtually any noteworthy change in the basic condition of agriculture'.[14] Most of the money from foreign aid and the surpluses generated in the villages is siphoned off to the Kathmandu valley. They quote Rana and Malla who wrote that 'in terms of development expenditures, a disproportionately large part of the total investment in the last two decades has gone to Kathmandu and its surrounding areas....'[15]

They show that much of the wealth has been used to produce a massive expansion in the bureaucracy, a 'combination of rural neglect with massive redistribution of State revenues in the form of salaries and rents to government officials and offices in urban areas'. They quote Caplan's study which showed a 32-fold expansion in the number of

[12] Malthus, n.d.: i, 122.
[13] Macfarlane, 1976.
[14] Blaikie *et al*, 1980: 63.
[15] Ibid.: 78.

civil servants in one district in 35 years, whereas administrative income had only increased three-fold. They contrast this bureaucratic growth with what has been achieved: 'given the massive increase, both proportionately and absolutely, in officially 'development oriented' government departments situated in the (West Central) Region, the extremely feeble impact they have had to date on rural economy and society in West-Central Nepal is all the more serious in its implications'.[16] They show how Indian manufacturing has crushed indigenous manufacturing in Nepal, and how little real development is occurring. They conclude very pessimistically. They 'see no reason to believe' that the peasantry (or anyone else) will act collectively in time 'to save millions of people from impoverishment, malnutrition, fruitless migration, and early death'.[17]

While the detailed statistics and analyses are very useful in providing an objective picture of Nepal's serious position, the explanatory framework they offer is only partially satisfying. They acknowledge the geographic and demographic difficulties of Nepal, but then proceed with two other kinds of explanation. The first is an application of 'dependency theory' as developed by various economists and historians in the 1970s. They summarise their argument as follows. 'We follow more closely the general direction of dependency theory, which argues that underdevelopment is a consequence of the incorporation of a pre-capitalist system into the global capitalist system dominated by 'western' economies and 'western' powers'. What this means in Nepal's case, which they equate with that of Afghanistan, Lesotho and Ethiopia, is described as follows. 'Neither fully incorporated as a colony, nor genuinely isolated, Nepal suffered...the stagnation that is a product of its specific form of partial incorporation as a semi-colony of the British Raj and more recently within the political economy of India....'[18] Elsewhere they write that this 'experience as a 'semi-colony' ensured a degree of 'forced stagnation' in production and productivity which led to increased population pressure on marginal land, emigration, and ecological decline'.[19]

In this last quotation the line of causation is made explicit. The semi-colonial status is the cause of the demographic and agricultural problems.

The idea of core and periphery, or metropolis and satellite, is applied in two ways. Firstly, in relation to India, their studies do indeed show that Nepal's development is constrained by India, though we may wonder whether it might well be that Nepal would be a net loser if Indian aid, markets, grain and employment were not available. Be that as it

[16] Ibid.: 122.
[17] Ibid.: 284.
[18] Ibid.: 187.
[19] Ibid.: 5.

may, it is not a new or particularly major advance to portray Nepal as
dependent on India. It is clear that such dependency is again not determining, but just one of the constraints within which the Nepalese are
forced to operate.

A second application of dependency theory is within Nepal. While
India is a periphery of the first world, and Nepal a periphery of India,
most of Nepal is a periphery of the Kathmandu valley. Again this is
certainly true, and has often been affirmed, though not usually as well
documented. But again this is largely a descriptive statement; it
explains little, in itself needing explanation. Here dependency theory
gives out, unless we take it to be axiomatic that predatory international
capitalism will inevitably have such effects.

The authors themselves are aware of some of the limitations of this
approach and admit that 'concepts of centre and periphery...are not by
themselves able to provide the complete framework....'[20] In order to do
that, they argue, a class analysis is also needed. Thus they try to
provide such an analysis. Here they are immediately in trouble. Firstly,
as they admit, it is practically impossible to isolate or delineate classes
in Nepal. One can very roughly talk of a 'ruling class', but its edges are
very blurred and it is not at all clear that it has any sense of class-
consciousness or monopolises the ownership of the means of
production. It would be much more appropriate to call it a powerful
elite. As for the bourgeoisie, 'in so far as it can be identified', it is said
to consist almost exclusively of the larger merchants 'and those
involved in such recent growth areas as tourism and construction'.[21]
This constitutes a rather feeble bourgeoisie and furthermore 'it is
difficult to distinguish individual members of this merchant class'.[22]
As for the petty bourgeoisie, they are 'notoriously difficult to define',
and in Nepal especially so. Only with the 'peasantry', who constitute
the majority of the population, do we seem to be on safe ground.
Unfortunately for the future of Nepal, they argue, the peasantry have no
class consciousness or unity.

The difficulties of a class analysis are not limited to the impossibil-
ity of finding classes, or finding any real class consciousness. There is
also the fact, noted several times, that caste and ethnic allegiances cross-
cut any class identity and are often more powerful. All this means that a
significant analysis in terms of the dynamics of class conflict is really
impossible. While the authors assert that 'the interests of the different
classes outlined above are distinct and in some cases in overt conflict
with each other', not a single instance of overt conflict is given.[23] It
would appear that beyond the general statement that different people and

[20] Ibid.: 84.
[21] Ibid.: 86.
[22] Ibid.: 87.
[23] Ibid.: 89.

groups have differing access and control over the means of production, class analysis is really inappropriate in this setting. It explains very little.

Thus we are left with an enriched description of Nepal's plight, and a deeper awareness of the influence of India and of the inequalities between Kathmandu and the rest of Nepal. But we still do not know why Nepal is in its present predicament.

Most of the theories about Nepal's problems have been put forward by outsiders. Here we may consider a novel and interesting hypothesis put forward by Dor Bahadur Bista (Bista 1991). Bista is both an outsider and an insider. He has an unrivalled width of experience in relation to Nepal. As a young man he travelled over most of Nepal in the company of the distinguished anthropologist Christoph von Furer-Haimendorf. On the basis of this experience he wrote the standard survey, *The Peoples of Nepal* (1967). He is trained in anthropology and became the first Professor of Anthropology in Nepal. Combined with foreign travels, this gives him the comparative framework which allows him to see his country in perspective. It has distanced him from his own culture.

Yet he also knows the culture from the inside. As a member of the Kathmandu elite, with powerful family and friendship connections, he knows the centre, as well as the periphery of the village. He knows the political and diplomatic world intimately, having one son who has been the Minister of Education and having himself been the Nepalese Consul General in Tibet. He knows the educational world, having begun his career as a High School Headmaster in 1952 and later through his Professorship at Tribhuvan University. He has experience of the international aid world through his own and his son's involvement in the International Centre for Integrated Mountain Development. He knows the world of business and trade, having been involved in setting up several businesses, a brick factory, carpet factory, metal crafts manufactory, and experimental dairy farm. He knows the world of hierarchy and caste, himself being near the top of that hierarchy as a member of an old family within the Chhetri caste.

This multifarious life experience of over thirty years has been distilled into this book, which is an attempt to give a portrait of a society. It attempts to diagnose Nepal's ills through the eyes of a sympathetic yet critical insider. It has something of the flavour of other such attempts; De Tocqueville's *Ancien Regime,* Weber's *Protestant Ethic,* Taine's *Notes upon England.* It is worth considering at some length because of its insights and because Bista, as an insider, can say things which no outsider could say. The Nepalese are a proud and sensitive people and the kind of analysis Bista makes, striking at the heart of many cherished institutions, could not be borne from an outsider. But these things need to be raised, and only Bista can do so.

Bista starts with the same problem, namely the patent failure of

Nepal to make substantial progress. He approvingly cites Pandey, writing that 'enormous financial resources are devoted to bureaucratic planning with very little demonstrated results. A former high level bureaucrat has even commented that, in spite of almost four decades of foreign assistance, agriculture has not benefited; the poor have been bypassed; the needs of women have not even been understood; the relations of production and distribution have become worse; and technical assistance has not contributed to the improvement of administrative capability'. He points to the 'snowstorm of statistical wizardry' embodied in numerous reports 'without any inkling of how these abstract figures relate to the conditions of the bulk of the people'.

Bista provides plenty of instances of waste and corruption. For instance, in relation to education, he gives a very useful survey of educational development up to the present. The expansion in the 1950s led to a 'certificate orientation' and in the 1950s and 1960s 'education was becoming quickly a symbol of status, as high school and college degrees were used simply for the purpose of acquiring higher status positions'. An attempt to reform the system in the National Education System Plan had collapsed by 1979; 'students sabotaged the examination system through widespread and large scale cheating, which was largely ignored by supervisors and teachers'. He notes that figures of educational expansion are 'impressive', 'but they belie the abuse and misapplication of educational qualifications....' Education is not directed to any practical ends, but merely to enable people to get a job where they will be able to do as little work as possible.

In the field of agricultural development, he cites the Pokhara Crop Development Project as an example of a total waste of time and resources. Those who are trained as agricultural specialists 'loathe agriculture and hate soiling their hands with the earth. What they learn is never applied'. The picture is a familiar one. What is novel is Bista's explanation of why it is thus.

Although Bista concentrates on the internal, cultural and social context, he does also refer to the external pressure of foreign aid which 'reinforces a sense that Nepal is basically a weak and helpless country'. He notes that massive foreign aid has helped to mask widespread economic abuse and corruption and points to the ethnocentricism of foreign advisers, who are 'often insensitive to the peculiarities of the cultural system in Nepal'. But it is this cultural system that he wishes to expose. For, while others such as Lohani point to 'powerful external others' as the root cause of Nepal's problems, Bista considers this as yet another example of that evasion of responsibility and fatalistic attitude which itself is 'the root cause of the problem'.

Let us first look at some of the features of that cultural system. It is a complex of factors which Bista labels 'fatalism' and locates in the Bahun (Brahman)—Chhetri minority which dominates Kathmandu and other towns. He does not give statistics, but this disproportionate dominance is shown by a figure given by Blaikie et al, namely that while 22 per cent of the population in 1972 were Chhetri/Brahman/Newar, these groups held almost 93 per cent of all the higher civil service and political posts. It is this culture, which Bista contrasts strongly with that of the Mongoloid peoples of the hills and Tarai, which dominates Nepal's development. As a member of this culture, Bista attempts to analyse its working.

The complex has a number of castes and a number of manifestations. At its heart there lie two inter-acting principles, namely fatalism and caste. The most important feature is fatalism, the belief 'that one has no personal control over one's life circumstances, which are determined through a divine or powerful external agency'. This partly arises from the Hindu notion of *karma*, that one's fate is written on one's forehead at birth and there is nothing that can be done to alter it.

This fatalistic belief undermines personal responsibility: 'under fatalism, responsibility is continually displaced to the outside, typically to the supernatural. There is a constant external focus for the individual. The individual simply does not have control'. Bista contrasts this to the situation in western societies and Japan where people have an internalised sense of responsibility. The current dominant value system does not teach people to accept responsibility for their failures or to accept defeat with dignity and grace. They characteristically blame others. 'Altruism is suspect. Similarly, one is never obliged to anyone for anything because everything occurs as it should. No sense of obligation is instilled'.

The second main thread is hierarchy, or caste. Bista argues that the caste principle is not intrinsic to Nepal; 'Nepal's native Hinduism has not included a belief in caste principles...only in the last 135 years has the caste system gained any kind of endorsement....' But now it pervades all parts of the elite, who feel themselves superior to the majority of the population. In particular, it makes the elite identify with the anti-practical, non-work, ideals of the Brahman priests, who abstain from all physical work and depend on the charity of others. This ideal has been secularised and re-directed through education, so that 'as a career objective in modern Nepal, every Nepali tries to have a *jagir*, a salaried job where one does not have to work but will receive a pay cheque at the end of each month'. In Brahman belief, the material world is *maya,* an illusion, hence 'there is no dignity in labour. High caste people have always despised physical labour and are accustomed to believing, as well as teaching others to believe, that erudition and ritual are the only important things'.

While despising those below them, the hierarchic mentality produces sycophancy and dependence on those above; 'whenever Nepalis receive good treatment from anyone and become comfortable, they begin to identify that individual as a father figure'. The institution of *chakari,* or institutionalised sycophancy, is one important manifestation of this hierarchical tendency.

Chakari, originally 'to wait upon, to serve, or to seek favour from a god', was institutionalised in the nineteenth-century court of the Ranas. As in all despotisms, whether in Rome or Versailles, a court system was instituted whereby potential over-mighty subjects were forced to be constantly visible, and constantly spying on each other by attending daily on the most powerful rulers. Later, 'government employees had to perform Chakari to ensure job security and in order to be eligible for promotion'. The system has flourished behind the facade of modern bureaucracy; the vast expansion of the salariat, which feeds off foreign aid, merely exacerbates the tendency. 'Though it will be commonly denied, today Chakari remains a solid fact of social life, and is evident at all levels of government'. It is a way for information to pass informally through the organisation, endless gossip and back-biting is encouraged as each morning junior officials wait around their seniors, 'paying court' and offering small presents. This leads to widespread paranoia, as each person maligns others whom he thinks may be gossiping behind his back; an alternative to the anonymous poison pen letter which is so prevalent in India.

The Chakari system also interferes with the development of a Weberian 'rational' bureaucracy, by warping appointments and decisions. The superior is forced to recognise some of the chakariwalas and receive their gifts and servile courtship. This 'leads to a point where the patron is forced into actions that he would not normally perform, and that are not in the best interests of his higher obligations to the organisation of which he is a part' in other words, corruption. Decisions are often made on the basis of the needs of chakari. Bista concludes that chakari is a 'built-in guarantor of incompetence, inefficiency, and misplaced effort'.

Chakari is a vertical relationship, a particular manifestation of those widespread, personalised, dyadic ties, called patron-client relations, which anthropologists have widely documented in Mediterranean, South American, Indian and other societies. The description by Bista fits well with these accounts, adding the special courtly feature of bureaucratic organisations, namely that the main service of the client is to provide information, and his main duty is to spend long periods of time attending on his patron.

Complementing chakari and flowing from it, but lying on a horizontal rather than vertical social axis, is the other main institution, *afno manchhe.* There is a strong distinction made between 'us', who are trustworthy, loyal, to be helped, and 'them' to whom one has no responsibilities, and who deceive and are to be deceived. In Bista's words, 'Afno Manchhe is the term used to designate one's inner circle of associates—it means 'one's own people' and refers to those who can be approached when need arises'. Almost every activity is influenced by it: the length of time it takes to cash a cheque, whether one receives a permit, the treatment one receives in hospital, one's child's success at school, all are influenced by afno manchhe connections. 'Afno manchhe is a critical institution. It is integrally connected with the smooth running of society'. Sometimes it is institutionalised into Rotary Clubs, Leo Clubs, Lions Clubs and the numerous equivalents of western masonic-type associations. But usually it is just a circle of mutually-supporting associates, whose personal ties cut across and through the supposed impersonalities of bureaucracy.

The workings of a combination of fatalism, hierarchy, chakari and afno manchhe are examined in studies of education, politics and government and foreign aid. We have seen that education becomes a path to non-manual jobs which are secure and work-free. In the burgeoning bureaucratic and governmental system, 'the practice of chakari is so ingrained in the modern situation that an attempt to by-pass it or eliminate it is treated as an act of social deviance....' In the growing Ministries, based on an Indian model, 'chakari was rapidly institutionalised as an integral part of all the ministries'. There is a ritualised use of 'meetings' and 'conferences' and 'seminars' to cover over the fact that nothing much is being done, just a lot of talking.

One central feature is the fear of decision-making and the taking of responsibility. 'As the level of responsibility increases within the administration, the fewer the decisions actually made. Making decisions can be a risky business. In a fatalistic society people are not thrown out for not making decisions but for making bad decisions.... People do not really expect things to happen.... But doing something means taking responsibility for it'. Anyone who has tried to get anything done in Nepal will know how true this is. Requests are passed from place to place and years may pass before a simple decision, to release some corrugated iron or bridge-building cable or cement, which has been agreed in principle, can be taken. 'A variety of not doing work which might entail risk, is to pass it on to a higher level'. Often this means that the simplest of decisions on small matters goes right up to the top, to be decided by the King or a senior Minister. Passing the buck is an endless, and often infinitely circular, game.

Fatalism and hierarchy also influence the impact of foreign aid. Firstly they heighten the sense of powerlessness and dependency which aid on such a huge scale is in any case likely to instil. Foreign aid donors 'are seen as father surrogates; the only active agent of development becomes the foreign party'. The infatuation with speculative, abstract, non-practical and ritualistic thought deadens action. Those who go abroad and see alternative systems are soon defeated by the fatalistic attitude when they return. Often they leave the country, those who remain 'become cynics and adapt to Chakari and Afno Manchhe culture'.

Within this corrupt and corrupting system there is a massive squandering of resources. Putting it charitably, 'the Nepali foreign aid civil servant operates from Kathmandu, and is oriented to the Kathmandu valley as the real hub of national life. The welfare of ethnic villagers in remote places is hard to identify with.'. Thus the many dangers of foreign aid, the political motives of donors, the over-paid and ethnocentric advisers, the high degree to which aid is 'tied', the absence of any involvement or consultation with those for whom the aid is supposedly designed, are compounded by the administrative system through which the development effort is filtered. It is not surprising that, as Bista writes, the National Planning Commission's five-yearly planning document 'is worth very little', since it has little power; 'roads and schools get built, but most often in areas not designated by the NPC.' Development is uncoordinated and ill-planned, reflecting the random interests of donors and local patronage networks. 'The size of such administrative machinery requires a vast amount of resources for its maintenance', but, Bista writes, 'the contribution of such an apparatus to real development has been negligible'.

It is a brave man who reveals these characteristics; it is an even braver one who honestly tries to explain the source which he believes is poisoning a potentially viable development. Bista locates two main causes, which are again interconnected.

According to Bista, the root cause of fatalism and hierarchy is 'bahunism' or Brahmanism. 'Bahunism' is a cultural configuration combining caste and fatalism. To demonstrate this, Bista provides an overview of Nepalese history from ancient times, showing the gradual spread of Brahmanic values. Caste principles began to be seriously introduced into Nepal in the fourteenth century, and were strengthened by Jang Bahadur Rana in the nineteenth. An overview of caste principles in each region of Nepal is provided. Various features of priestly Brahmanism are stressed; its dislike of manual labour, its hierarchical view of the world, its dependence on ritual and magic as opposed to practical behaviour. For instance, in relation to education, 'Being educated, then, has a superstitious connection with high caste, and the act of being educated becomes the magical act that draws forth a sympathetic and supernaturally supported result of being treated as a Bahun...education is another form of ritualistic behaviour....' The belief in fatalism arising from the idea of *dharma,* the chakari system arising from the seeking of favour from a god, the strong distinctions between 'us' and 'them' in afno manchhe, all stem from priestly Brahmanism.

One needs to add the adjective 'priestly', because Bista is not talking about the majority of Brahmans, hard-working farmers who do not practise as Brahmans and who work alongside the other ethnic groups in apparent harmony. It is a small stratum, which also includes higher-class Chhetris and some Shreshta Newars and Thakuris, of whom he is writing.

Bista examines how the upbringing within such 'Bahun' houses contributes to the fatalistic and hierarchical attitudes. Young children are brought up without much discipline; long breast-feeding on demand, an absence of any parental control or strong standards lead, he believes, to an absence of an internalised morality. 'There is no moral pressure or guilt feeling regarding immoral acts, because there is little sense of morality instilled in children: a sense of social responsibility is simply not internalised and social sanctions are only effective in an external form'. Only fear leads to good behaviour, and fear can be mitigated by building up a network of friends, afno manchhe, and a dependency on outside forces. Bahuns grow to adulthood 'being self-righteous but without an ability to be self-critical'.

Much of this picture of relaxed child-rearing applies to most ethnic groups in Nepal. What differentiates Bahuns is their attitude to women. 'Women in Nepal generally have equal status except among Bahun-Thakuri and some middle and upper level Chhetri'. Whereas Gurung women, for instance, control their husband's purse, are consulted on all major decisions, are not considered inferior or impure, work at similar jobs to men; none of this is true of the Bahun culture. Bahun women are part of the hierarchical system, impure and inferior, given no control of money, often badly beaten, often carrying huge loads while their load-free husbands walk ahead of them. This applies to hill Brahmans as well.

This attitude to women affects the family at a particular point. High-caste sons, who have formed a deep bond with their mothers, are suddenly taken from them and taught to treat them as second-class, polluting, inferior: 'relations are autocratic, with females subservient to males'. A Bahun father, on the other hand, is an autocrat whose power remains very strong throughout a son's life. A son thus learns both dependency and autocracy in his family and applies this to the world outside. The system of partible inheritance, which shields all sons from the world, leads to 'a protective and patronising attitude towards junior children, especially the youngest' which 'helped develop the dependence syndrome to the extreme....'

Thus Bista's explanation combines sociological and psychological features arising from the Brahman priest's role and his family system. During the last hundred and fifty years, this small group has taken control of Nepal politically and bureaucratically, submerging the majority whose ethics and attitudes are much closer to the protestant values of hard work, honesty, equality and internalised conscience, which Bista clearly admires.

Two other insights are worth considering. One concerns the attitude to time in Nepalese culture. Time is seen as a river, with no sense of past, present and future. It is circular rather than progressive. There is thus no idea of time as a 'commodity', no idea of 'wasting' time, little idea of being able to plan or control future time, little interest in past time or history. Bista's account reminds one of many discussions of the contrasts between protestant and catholic, 'modern' and 'medieval', 'agricultural' and 'industrial' attitudes to time and work discipline. Certainly the relaxed lack of punctuality, the 'timelessness', which tourists often find so attractive, is less appealing when it is found within an attempt to introduce modern bureaucratic methods. The absence of a strong sense of the future, and the fatalism and lack of any sense of control, combine to make forward planning, saving, invest-ment, weak. 'They squander whatever food, grain, or money they get at once without any consideration for the future. Being highly consumma-tory, no savings take place and there can be no investment. The society must remain dependent on foreign investment in the future....'

Another important side-effect of Bahunism is on the relations between individual and group. Bista argues that under the pressure of western models, 'traditional group orientation' is being replaced by 'individualism'. But it is not that individualism which De Tocqueville perceived in America, namely 'a mature and calm feeling, which dis-posed each member of the community to sever himself from his family and his friends...', but rather the earlier form, which De Tocqueville calls 'egotism', namely, 'passionate and exaggerated love of self, which leads a man to connect everything with his own person, and to prefer himself to everything in the world'. 'Nepali individualism operates largely at the more primitive egotistic stage'.

This egotism is the worst solution to the problem of individual-group relations. It leads to a mild version of the Hobbesian war of all against all, where there is no sense of public duty or service. 'Very few people take high positions responsibly, as a duty to society at large'. Although there is a residual sense of the local community and the fam-ily, 'by contrast, the public, the state, the nation, are all abstract con-cepts' which mean little to most people. One effect of this is visible in the corruption and laziness of those in positions of responsibility, whose main goal is to promote their private and sectional interests. Another is in the field of development.

Bista points out that despite the rhetoric of 'grass-roots develop-ment', 'back to the village', 'community participation', the vast major-ity of 'development' projects are undertaken with little involvement or consultation with local communities. Bridges, roads, dams, health posts are built often with serious disadvantages to particular communities. They are perceived by local inhabitants as 'the whimsies of the foreign project directors'. When the bridge, road, dam, has been built and the facility has been left as 'public' property, supposedly to be maintained by 'the public', 'people lack any sense of either pride or of possession, as they would towards things they build through their own efforts'.

Bista argues that 'locally initiated projects, when funded by the central authorities, have the greatest chance of success'. This is certainly true. But the absence of a sense of the 'public good', which is a very unusual and abstract idea which took many centuries to develop in the west, is even deeper than this. The idea of 'citizenship', of doing a job for the good of an association larger than the family, is little developed throughout Nepal. Thus in the villages, each development initiative fails as the individuals employed to carry it out take their salary to be an entitlement to do the minimum amount of work. The tree nursery is allowed to fade away; the young trees are not watched by the paid watchers and are eaten by animals; the water bailiffs fail to inspect the water pipe and it leaks badly; the health workers at the local health post sell off the best medicine privately and refuse to visit sick villagers without large payments; the schoolmasters appropriate school funds and absent themselves frequently. These are widespread activities. Of course, there are honourable exceptions, but the pressures of insecurity and family need are usually much stronger than some abstract idea of generalised good. The acts of religious merit, the making of resting places, of temples, of paths, are quite frequent. But the idea of merit, the nearest equivalent to the protestant idea of 'calling', does not seem to be applied to the new tasks generated by development. It is almost as if the payment of a salary automatically deadens any sense of public responsibility. It is a social equivalent to the well-known finding that, contrary to classical economic laws, the more people are paid for their labour in pre-capitalist economies, the less they work.

Much of Nepal thus seems to be in a position where primordial loyalties, to family, neighbours, oneself, are very much stronger than impersonal ones; people see no benefit in putting their efforts into doing things well for the general good. Anthropologists have investigated 'amoral familism' quite extensively, a morality where people only apply ethical rules within their own family. One might well apply the concept here. But in the Nepalese context, and especially in the ethnic communities of the mountains, the community of moral and responsible behaviour is wider than the nuclear family of the Mediterranean and South American examples where the concept of 'amoral familism' was developed. All villagers are bound together through marriage, kinship, friendship, work associations and patron-client ties and hence will work together in what is perceived as their mutual self-interest. But this only applies to traditional activities where mutual support is essential. It is an entirely different matter with something which an individual, paid by the State, is expected to do for some larger abstract entity such as 'the community', 'the country,', 'the nation'. In calculating the best course of action, the individual state servant finds that the advantages of leisure or private reward far outweigh any feeling that he has a duty to help such abstract entities, or that he should do so because he is paid for his services.

The idea of 'paying back' something to a society, which lies behind a vast amount of vaguely altruistic voluntary behaviour in western societies, of the *noblesse oblige* variety, such as justices of the peace, jury service, voluntary associations and institutes to do good works, is absent. For instance, only a tiny proportion of the large amount of money brought back to Nepal by returning British Gurkhas, million-aires by local standards, is ever spent on public works in the villages where they were brought up and their families live. If one hundredth of this money had been productively invested in the villages, they would have been transformed. But such ideas are not at all familiar. They would probably be considered luxuries, only suitable to societies which had escaped from the knife-edged insecurities of subsistence living.

Examples from non-Bahun ethnic villages suggest one type of criti-cism that could be made of Bista's explanation. He tends to idealise non-Brahman groups. He does this for two main reasons. Firstly, he uses them as a stick to beat the Bahuns with, a way of pointing up the insidious and powerful, but ultimately 'un-Nepali' character of their cul-ture. The majority of the population are not hierarchical, but hard-working, with a conscientious discipline, a sense of guilt and respon-sibility and a practical attitude to life. The village is 'an efficiently productive and harmonious social group'. Secondly, Bista sees these ethnic groups as providing an alternative to the present disastrous tendency; the only real hope for Nepal lies in giving their culture priority over the recently-imported Hindu culture of priestly Brahmanism. 'Among the ethnic peoples, then, are located some very significant human and cultural resources. These people are hard-working, persevering and long suffering, co-operate well and work with a dedication towards collective well-being, and have the qualities necessary to be successful merchants'. But instead of cherishing their cultures, Bista argues, they are belittled, ignored and destroyed by the spreading Bahun culture.

Bista would probably argue that the instances of lack of public spirit instanced above are the result of the spread of Brahman values into the villages. Everyone has become aware of the corruption, laziness and inefficiency that pervades most of the salariat. There is widespread cyni-cism and a lack of any models for hard-working and public-spirited activities. Each individual feels disinclined to make marginal sacrifices of his short-term good for the long-term general good when he thinks noone else is doing so. Everyone believes that all others are 'on the make'. Even if an individual shows some deviant altruism, his family and friends would soon put great pressures on him to desist.

This idea of the spread of egotistic values is partly true. But it is a little over-simple. The features described are very widespread in agricultural peasantries which almost everywhere have little idea of the public good. But Bista is right that if the elite had by some extraordinary accident shown a very different and more 'rational-bureaucratic-protestant' character, then the response at the village level as the new institutions were developed would have been very different. One can see this from the enormous difference between the behaviour of Gurungs when in the British army, self-disciplined, hard-working, altruistic, co-operative, and when they are working in government employment in Nepal where they are often listless, unmotivated and as prone to pursue their self-interest as the most acquisitive Brahman or Chhetri. There is nothing intrinsic about the differences, but Bista is right that the tendencies of Brahman-Chhetri culture and the Mongoloid cultures of Nepal are very different, and the balance is swinging towards the former.

In assessing the degree of success of Bista's analysis it is important to distinguish three levels of problem. In order to understand Nepal's predicament one cannot ignore the gross geographical and demographic facts. Scarce, land-locked, resources pressed on by a very rapidly growing population are bound to make the task of development difficult. This is one type of explanation, a necessary but not sufficient one. Ecology and demography, for instance, do not explain why many aid schemes fail, or bureaucracy is so clogged. But cultural explanations do not account, in themselves, for the shrinking of the forests and the soil erosion.

At a second level, Bista is right to say that it is not sufficient to blame outside forces, international capitalism, neo-colonialism, Indian imperialism or whatever, for all of Nepal's ills. They do not explain the waste and inefficiency in local health posts or aid projects. But they do help to explain why Nepalese manufactures have been so unsuccessful, why hill agriculture is withering, why Nepal is a minor dumping ground for medical drugs, drinks and tourists. It is an incomplete explanation which does not take the international politico-economic context of Nepal into account.

At a third level there are the social and cultural factors which have largely been left out of account until Bista was prepared to state them. Many of his observations are tacitly accepted, but as with the Emperor's invisible new clothes, no-one has dared to say them out loud. They help to explain a good deal. But there are qualifications to be made even at this level. To start with, they do not explain many of the pressures on the Nepalese, which are undoubtedly demographic, economic and external. Secondly, it is not clear how much of the phenomenon of fatalism/hierarchy is due to Brahmanism.

It is indeed true that the only Hindu kingdom in the world, Nepal, is to an exceptional degree dominated nowadays by a Brahman-Chhetri elite and their values are as Bista describes them. The problem is that anyone familiar with other developing societies, whether in Africa or Asia or Latin America, will recognise many identical features. Much of the lack of western 'rationality' appears to be an integral feature of such societies. In particular, anyone familiar with India will recognise a good deal of Bista's world in the pages of Kipling, Paul Scott, V.S.Naipaul or Varindra Vittachi.

We might expand Bista's argument to say that certain structural features of a society with little experience of competitive, individualistic capitalism, suddenly thrown into such a world, have been combined with pressures which are more generally Indian, rather than specifically priestly Brahman. The thesis would then probably be nearer the truth. Much of the educational, political and bureaucratic system of Nepal is modelled on India, and it has inherited the defects, as well as a few of the merits, of that land. Nepal is thus a periphery of a periphery in another sense also.

What Bista does show, and this is his major argument against fatalism, is that it need not be so. If present trends continue, Nepal will grow more and more impoverished and dependent on foreign aid, as Blaikie and his collaborators argue. But there is nothing inevitable about this. Miracles have happened before, and in particular in cultures not dissimilar to Nepal. In the 1950s, most professional commentaries were still predicting that Japan was doomed to poverty and insignificance, would never recover and so on. In a relatively short time it has become the most powerful economy in the world. No-one could have predicted the success of Singapore, Hong Kong, Taiwan, Thailand and other 'miracles'.

Current prophecies of Nepal's imminent collapse could prove equally wrong in this rapidly changing world. The sudden demise of international communism and the Cold War; the new scientific discoveries which may make it possible to properly harness Nepal's one immense natural resource, hydro-electric power; new international communications which suddenly open up Europe and the Far East to Nepalese products, avoiding the Indian stranglehold, all these may have unforseeable consequences.

Yet they are unlikely to do so unless those who decide Nepal's future, both insiders and outsiders, are prepared to take seriously the grave defects of present developments and try to change course. It is too early to say whether the result of the recent elections will make this easier or more difficult.

What is clear is that it will be tempting to dismiss Bista's work, even though he cannot be swept aside as an ignorant outsider, or as a jealous member of an inferior caste. But it is important that his arguments , as well as those of others who love Nepal and care for its future be heard. Their anger at the wasted potential, the unnecessary deaths, the

grim future, arises not from malice but from a genuine care for one of
the most beautiful countries and peoples in the world. Furthermore,
Nepal's fate is part of all our fate. Ask not for whom the bell tolls.

REFERENCES

Bista, Dor Bahadur, *Fatalism and Development: Nepal's Struggle for
Modernisation.* Madras, 1991

P. Blaikie, J. Cameron and D.Seddon, *Nepal in Crisis: growth and
stagnation at the periphery.* Oxford, 1980.

Gurung, Harka, *Dimensions of Development.* Kathmandu, 1986.

Macfarlane, Alan, *Resources and Population: A Study of the Gurungs of
Nepaa.* Cambridge, 1976

T.R.Malthus, *An Essay on the Principles of Population.* (Everyman edition,
no date), 2 vols.

D. Seddon, P. Blaikie and J. Cameron, *Peasants and Workers in Nepal.*
Warminster, 1979.

Seddon, David, *Nepal: A State of Poverty.* (University of East Anglia
Monographs in Development Studies, 11, April 1979).

Chapter 8

DEMOCRACY AND DEVELOPMENT IN NEPAL

David Seddon

There is nothing more uncertain of success nor more dangerous to manage than the creation of a new order of things (Machiavelli).

Men make history but not under conditions of their own choosing (Marx).

There is a tide in the affairs of men, which, taken at the flood, leads on to fortune; omitted, all the voyage of their life is bound in shallows and in miseries. On such a full sea are we now afloat; and we must take the current when it serves, or lose our venture (Shakespeare).

Introduction

After a decade of increasing dissatisfaction with the partyless Panchayat system, sharpened in urban areas by the social impact of the government's economic policies, a structural adjustment programme initiated in 1986, and the effects of the Indian trade embargo during 1989, Nepal entered the 1990s in economic and political crisis.

The roots of this crisis run deep, as has been argued elsewhere,[1] but by the end of the 1980s the underlying contradictions of a stagnant economy and a restrictive political system were becoming ever clearer. As I suggested in the mid-1980s—in contrast with the 'radical pessimism' of some earlier work—'despite this grim picture, however, there are grounds for some hope; the crisis itself, which so threatens the lives of the mass of the Nepalese people in an immediate and tangible sense, also threatens the old structures of power and inequality. In the face of a deepening crisis, fundamental contradictions emerge more clearly and the possibility—indeed, the necessity—of significant change increases accordingly. Today, there are indications, at least in the political sphere, that such change is imminent.'[2]

It was my own view in the late 1980s that 'a broad popular front in which different and even conflicting interests might be able to organise and express themselves openly, would constitute the initial and most effective basis for fundamental transformation at this time'[3]. Such a popular front would be able to provide some credible response to the deep-seated worries and frustrations of the mass of Nepalese peasants and, more particularly, those of the workers who would constitute the

[1] Blaikie et al, 1980; Seddon, 1987.
[2] Seddon, 1987: back end paper, also cf. ibid.: 273-4.
[3] Seddon, 1988: 1

crucial basis for any effective and sustained democratic movement, as
well as to the urban middle classes' dissatisfaction with the government's economic policies and restrictions on civil rights. I argued that
'a great deal will depend on the ability of organised opposition
movements to translate this frustration into political action; but a
crucial factor in organising effective political opposition will be the
relationship between these political movements and industrial workers
in Kathmandu and in the Tarai: workers' support will be of critical
importance and it will be gained by providing a real hope of improving
conditions at work and more generally in the economy, as well as by
encouraging greater participation in democratic politics at all levels'.[4]

I had in mind a broad alliance drawn from different social classes, but
relying heavily on support from among the working class and progressive sections of the middle classes, including Nepali Congress and
communist supporters. These would rally round issues of democracy
and civil rights as a first stage in a process of political change leading,
possibly, to a genuine popular democracy. It seemed unrealistic, given
the class structure of Nepal at that point,[5] to expect or to advocate any
mass 'revolutionary' movement of whatever kind. In the event,
precisely such a broad-based movement did emerge during the latter part
of the 1980s, culminating in the creation of the democracy movement
in 1990 and the overthrow of the Panchayat regime.

The political forces which gave rise to the democracy movement
were generated largely from within Nepalese society (although one cannot discount entirely the effect of changes taking place elsewhere in the
world, notably in central and eastern Europe) and can be shown to have
grown out of the economic and social contradictions of the previous
decades. The fact that the political leadership was provided by self-
declared socialists and communists of different persuasions, as well as
by democrats, is to be understood very much in terms of the historic
role of these political groupings in opposition to authoritarian rule in
Nepal (although, here again, the influence of Indian oppositional
politics was also significant). But it is also essential to recognise that
the political movement was rooted in growing alarm among a wide
range of different social groups regarding the future of the Nepalese
economy and the prospects for their own survival. It was, in short, the
very development and dynamic of Nepalese society that produced 'the
democracy movement', with all its strengths and weaknesses. If we are
to appreciate the historical context of the dramatic events of 1990, and
to begin to delineate the broad outlines of what may be to come, it is
essential that we recognise the extent to which the opposition to the
government that developed and grew in the 1980s was rooted in the

[4] Seddon, 1986: 23.
[5] See Seddon *et al*, 1979: 35-43; Blaikie *et al*, 1980: 84-98.

deepening economic crisis of the 1970s, and in the ways that different
sections of Nepalese society responded to that crisis.

The Crisis of the 1970s

At the beginning of the 1970s, given the relative stagnation in agricultural production, the growing pressure of population, and a rapidly
increasing trade deficit, Nepal faced an economic and environmental
crisis. In 1973, the World Bank reported that 'over the past decade,
growth in aggregate output has been more or less neutralised by the
population increases; moreover, the rate of population growth appears
to be accelerating. This poses a particularly difficult problem in the
hills, which have a limited resource base and which have long suffered
from over-population. The slow pace of economic growth has taken
place despite increasing public investment in agriculture and
infrastructure. Slow growth of food-grain production and rapid
demographic growth have resulted in a rapid decline of the rice surpluses
produced in the Tarai and exported to India, which finances a large part
of Nepal's substantial import requirements'.[6] It was reported that
Nepal's food grain production had increased at a rate of only 0.7 per cent
a year during the previous decade, while the hill regions had experienced
an actual decline in food production of some 2.1 per cent.[7] The
implication was that 'Nepal is poor and is daily becoming poorer'.[8]

By the middle of the decade, however, some commentators were
more pessimistic: 'Nepal in the mid 1970s is not just a very poor
country.... The country is now in a period of crisis, a crisis whose
major components, over the next decade, will include serious over-
population relative to employment opportunities, ecological collapse in
the densely populated and highly vulnerable hill areas (where 30 per
cent of the cultivable land supports 60 per cent of the country's rural
population), and the elimination of certain important 'natural' resources
(eg timber), both in the hills and in the plains. These will be associated
with an increasing inability to pay for imported commodities, with
growing food shortages, and consequently with the development of
widespread unrest in both rural and urban areas'.[9]

The political significance of this deepening economic and environmental crisis was considerable. In the latter part of the 1960s and early
1970s there had already been sporadic outbursts of popular protest, particularly in the Tarai, and in the mid-1970s, Frederick Gaige warned
that 'the potential for increased opposition is very real in such towns as
Bhadrapur, Dharan, Biratnagar, Rajbiraj, Bhairawa, and Nepalganj, as
lower-echelon bureaucrats, small-scale businessmen, industrial labour-

[6] World Bank, 1973: 3.
[7] FAO, 1974.
[8] ARTEP, 1974: 1.
[9] Blaikie *et al*, 1980: 13-4.

ers, teachers, students, and unemployed graduates become increasingly frustrated by their political impotence'.[10] Over the next five years, there were clear signs of increasing dissatisfaction with the existing political system and of growing unrest, particularly—but not only—in the urban areas. This was undoubtedly linked to the failure of the Nepalese economy to show any real signs of growth (with the implications of increasing pressure on fragile physical resources), and the effects of this economic stagnation on the livelihoods and living standards of a wide range of less privileged social groups and classes. It was argued, on the basis of research carried out in the mid-1970s, that 'it seems likely that before long, if economic and social conditions do not improve rapidly, such unrest will become more pervasive and better organised'.[11]

The economic situation failed to improve and indeed continued to deteriorate in the last years of the decade. Even in the mid-1970s it was possible to predict that, without any significant increase in productivity, Nepal would become a net food deficit country by the end of the decade (cf Blaikie, et al 1976), while towards the end of the decade it was evident that, even on relatively optimistic projections, 'for the next development decade, 1980-90, the situation with respect to the gap between demand and supply for 'total food grains' would be most distressing'.[12]

In fact, agriculture stagnated in the years between 1973 and 1980 (World Bank figures suggest a growth rate of zero) and foodgrain production declined at an annual rate of nearly one per cent while the population continued to increase at over two per cent a year. An overall drop in food grain production of 14 per cent was recorded for the period 1975-80. In 1978, World Bank estimates for future per capita food supply suggested that, without dramatic changes in output, per capita consumable production would decline from 133 kgs in 1978-79 to 126 kgs in 1982-83, and 119 kgs by 1986-87. A year later, IFAD argued that 'unless there is a substantial acceleration in the growth rate of food production over the 1968-78 production trend, there will be a deficit exceeding 250,000 metric tons by 1990 (measured in terms of wheat equivalent) even if incomes fail to grow and 1976 consumption levels remain constant'.[13]

One of the most depressing features of Nepal's economic crisis was the stagnation of production in Nepal's 'grain basket', the Tarai. Hope for the future has always tended to focus on the possibility of increasing productivity through greater use of 'modern' farm inputs, particularly in the Tarai. In the second half of the 1970s, roughly 60,000 hectares were

[10] Gaige, 1975: 189.
[11] Blaikie *et al*, 1980: 45.
[12] Pant and Jain, 1980: 166-7.
[13] IFAD, 1979: 2.

added to the area under irrigation, fertiliser consumption increased by
around 40 per cent and the area under high-yield varieties (HYVs) rose
from virtually zero to nearly 700,000 hectares. Nevertheless, it was
suggested in the sixth five year plan (for 1981-86) that the poor performance of Nepalese agriculture during that period could be attributed to a
combination of bad weather and the failure to achieve any real break-
through in the use of 'modern' farm inputs in the Tarai. In 1976, it had
been predicted that the Tarai's surplus would be maintained until the
mid 1980s and then decline;[14] but in 1979 it was clear that overall
production in the Tarai had declined and yields had slumped.[15] The
situation was worse by the end of the decade than even the 'radical
pessimists' had foreseen.

Growing Pressure for Change: 1979-1989

In 1979, the return of veteran Nepali Congress leader, B.P. Koirala,
stimulated renewed calls from the outlawed opposition—and more
widely among the increasingly vocal middle classes and the small but
important working class (cf. Seddon 1986)—for civil rights and political change as the precondition for economic and social development in
Nepal. In March, Koirala declared that 'without an understanding
between the monarchy and the democratic forces, we cannot survive as a
nation'.[16] Student strikes and demonstrations during April 1979
increased the political tension and in May the king announced that there
would be a referendum to choose between the partyless Panchayat
system or a return to the multi-party regime of the 1950s. Meanwhile,
press freedom and the right to hold political meetings were officially
granted for the first time in nearly twenty years, as was an amnesty to
all political prisoners, except those (including most of the communist
leaders) charged with criminal offences.

In December 1979, the king publicly stated his own proposals for a
future constitution. These included: universal adult suffrage as the basis
for elections to the national legislature; the appointment of the prime
minister on the recommendation of the legislature; and the responsibility of the council of ministers to the elected legislature. He added that
the day-to-day administration of the country could best be undertaken by
the people's representatives. These proposals were taken by some as
recognition by the king of the need for a more genuinely democratic
system, even under the partyless Panchayat regime, and as opening up
the way for political reform, without the need for a referendum.[17]

In the event, a national referendum on the future of democracy in
Nepal was held in May 1980, in which voters were asked whether they

[14] Blaikie *et al*, 1976.
[15] World Bank, 1979: 14-5.
[16] Quoted in *The Economist*, 10 March, 1979.
[17] cf. Shaha, 1991: 75-97.

wished to retain the 'guided democracy' of the existing system or to introduce a multi-party system. Over two thirds of the eligible voters (4.8 out of just over seven million—67 per cent) expressed their views. The outcome was a majority (2.4 million against two million votes) for a retention of the existing system. It is impossible to provide any detailed analysis of the sociology of the referendum results, but it is significant that the opposition did well in the Kathmandu valley and the Tarai, with particularly good results in the more urbanised areas, and that areas with relatively high literacy rates (a crude indicator of the level of economic and social development) were more strongly in favour of a change of political regime. The ethnic minorities in the hill areas (Tamangs, Magars, Gurungs, Kiratis, Sherpas, etc.)—in whom some place considerable hopes for Nepal's future development on the basis of their relative freedom from the 'fatalism' said to cripple the 'struggle for modernisation' (eg. Bista 1991)—were reported to have voted largely for the Panchayat system.[18] But, given the restrictions effectively imposed on local politics for two decades under the partyless Panchayat system, and the efforts of local beneficiaries of that system to influence the outcome, the result provided a clear signal that opposition to the existing system was very substantial, particularly in the more 'developed' areas and among the urban classes.

Meanwhile, the formation of a commission to consider reforms to the constitution was also announced in May 1980. The results of its deliberations were presented in November and in December 1980 the king announced the third amendment to the Nepalese constitution. Ironically, as has been pointed out by Shaha, it was precisely twenty years earlier that King Mahendra had taken over all powers after dissolving the first ever elected parliament, dismissing the popular government of the day and imprisoning the prime minister and members of his cabinet; it was also on the same date eighteen years previously that King Mahendra had promulgated the current constitution.[19] The reforms introduced in the new constitution included renewed official commitment to decentralisation,[20] but failed to remove the ban on political parties or politically-motivated organisations, and trades unions were still effectively outlawed.

Political parties, while not officially recognised, now became increasingly active. There were general elections in 1981 and, as a result of limited reforms which allowed partial direct election to the national assembly, several political activists on the left became members of parliament.[21] However, the Nepali Congress as a whole boycotted these

[18] Ibid.: 70.
[19] Ibid.: 98.
[20] Bienen *et al*, 1990: 69.
[21] Shaha, op.cit.: 11.

elections, as did the major factions of the Communist Party. According to official sources, over 60 per cent of voters took part despite the boycott; but an independent analyst has suggested that the proportion was probably closer to 40 to 45 per cent[22] and that in many cases—notably in Kathmandu itself—votes were cast 'against the powers that be and symbolised widespread popular protest against the manner in which so-called political reforms were being carried out'.[23]

Growing dissatisfaction with the existing regime created increasing unity within the opposition movement. In May 1985, the Nepali Congress launched a campaign of civil disobedience, starting with a general strike; at the same time, the communists initiated a 'fill the jails' campaign. The state responded with mass arrests. The *satyagraha* movement appeared to be gaining ground when, in June 1985, a series of bombings across the country as well as in front of the palace in Kathmandu led to a number of deaths. Responsibility was claimed by the Janabadi Morcha (People's Front), based in India, who stated that they had planted the bombs to proclaim the start of their campaign to topple the monarchy, install a democratic republic and abolish private property.[24] The civil disobedience campaign was called off. There were mass arrests (an estimated 1,750 according to Amnesty International) and numerous reported cases of human rights violations.[25] In August a special anti-subversion act—the Destructive Crimes (Special Control and Punishment) Act—was rushed through parliament.

But while the opposition struggled to change the existing political system, the government and the palace were committed to the idea that political stability under the status quo was the key to economic and social development. Clearly (from the results of the referendum) there were still many, particularly in rural areas, who shared this view. During 1985, the king again emphasised his concern to bring about a decentralisation of administrative power and development responsibilities, down to the village or town panchayat level. Towards the end of the year, he also publicly pledged to provide for the 'basic needs' of the Nepalese people by the year 2000, and promised a celebration of the Silver Jubilee of the partyless Panchayat system.

During the second half of the decade the unofficial extra-parliamentary opposition continued to gain ground, although support remained patchy across the country as a whole and was still concentrated in the urban areas. National elections were held in 1986 and were again boycotted by the major factions of the Nepali Congress and the Communist Party. However, nine leftists (including five declared Marxist-

[22] Ibid.: 110.
[23] Ibid.: 112.
[24] Ibid.: 150.
[25] cf. Seddon, 1986b: 53.

Leninists), all of whom were openly in favour of the restoration of multiparty democracy, were elected to the national assembly, as were a further eight non-leftists with known democratic leanings. But under the partyless Panchayat system all candidates were supposed to pledge their general support for the programmes of the government, said to have been formulated under the active guidance and leadership of the king. This might explain why 'none of the candidates during their election campaign deemed it fit to address the national and international issues of public importance, like the steady decline in agricultural production and economy, the growing trade and balance-of-payment deficits and the aggravation of ecological and environmental conditions....'[26]

This is all the more striking in view of the continuing economic problems of the 1980s and the government's attempt to balance the requirements of an IMF-sponsored stabilisation programme (initiated in 1985) and structural adjustment package (adopted in 1987), with a Basic Needs programme initiated in 1986-87.[27] According to the World Bank, 'adjustment in Nepal has not included the kind of cuts in public services or increases in the prices of staples which are often associated with adverse impacts on the poor under structural adjustment in other countries'.[28] But the consumer price index, which had more than doubled in the 1970s, doubled again during the 1980s, with an annual rate of inflation between 1980 and 1987 of over 10 per cent (for the previous two decades inflation had averaged between five and seven per cent). The urban poor in the Tarai and in the hills suffered particularly, as a result of their heavy reliance on purchased foodgrain,[29] as did the rural poor who were obliged to purchase foodgrain to supplement their inadequate domestic production. Borrowing to cover consumption expenditure led to increased indebtedness among both rural and urban poor. The 'struggle for basic needs in Nepal' was proving as hard at the end of the 1980s as it had at the end of the previous decade.

In fact, during the two decades from 1970 to 1989, per capita growth in GDP averaged only about 0.75 per cent.[30] Growth in agriculture was particularly slow: between 1975 and 1988 foodgrain production increased by about 20 per cent, while population increased by about 40 per cent. As the World Bank put it, 'Nepal has gone from being a food exporter to a net importer, and cash crops remain of minor importance—accounting for only about 15 per cent of crop production. Yields of almost all key crops have been declining, with the limited increases in output accounted for mainly by expansion of cropped area

[26] Shaha, op.cit.: 141.
[27] HMG, 1986; HMG, 1989; World Bank, 1990.
[28] World Bank, 1991: 29.
[29] Ibid.: 205.
[30] Ibid.: 26.

into more marginal lands'.[31] If industry, by contrast, experienced a significant rate of growth, particularly in the second half of the decade (5.5 per cent) and manufacturing did especially well (5.7 per cent), with important consequences for the growth in formal sector employment (up 14 per cent on average in the first half of the 1980s), the effect of this was negligible, given the very small part played by the industrial formal sector in national GDP (4-5 per cent at the end of the 1970s) or in employment (some 1 per cent of the total labour force).

The introduction in 1986-87 of a structural adjustment programme under the auspices of the IMF and the World Bank was certainly followed by a significant increase in GDP growth, both in agriculture and in industry, and while the balance of trade deficit increased, the balance of payments registered a record surplus. Inflation, however, continued to rise: the average growth rate in consumer prices between 1980 and 1987 was 10.3 per cent a year, while in 1986-87 they grew by over 13 per cent, and in 1987-88 by around 11 per cent. The effects on household budgets, particularly among the urban poor and lower income middle classes, were appreciable.

During 1988 and 1989, the government lost support and credibility. In June 1988 a motion of no confidence tabled by 53 of the 140 members of the national assembly spoke of the deepening problems facing the economy and of the need to guarantee the 'basic needs' of the Nepalese population. The government's critics argued that the economic crisis could be resolved only if the political system was reformed and multiparty politics reinstated. There was even talk of another (fourth) amendment to the constitution, designed to make certain concessions to the unofficial opposition; and in November the king met the leader of the outlawed Nepali Congress, Ganesh Man Singh, to discuss possible political reforms.

Inflation began to drop during 1988-89, and for a short while it appeared that economic conditions might improve. But in March 1989 the trade and transit treaty with India expired; major differences between the governments of the two countries prevented the signing of a new treaty and a trade dispute rapidly turned into a conflict which was to last until September. As a result of a partial trade embargo by India, Nepal was effectively deprived of some 80 per cent of the goods normally imported by land, and rationing was introduced less than two weeks after the borders were closed. Prices soared, basic goods became extremely hard to come by, hoarding was widespread and a black market developed. In April, students seized on the trade dispute and worsening economic conditions to protest against the government; thousands marched in Kathmandu and there were clashes with the police, who used tear gas and riot sticks to break up the demonstrations. The university

[31] Ibid.: 27.

was closed, and a 'holiday' was declared for all primary and secondary schools in the capital. In May, the general secretary of the Nepali Congress declared that the country's economic crisis could give the party its best chance of forcing reform and regaining power: 'without the development of democracy, economic development is not possible'.[32] In September, the Nepali Congress planned to hold a week-long celebration throughout the country in honour of the first elected prime minister, B.P. Koirala, to draw attention to the failings of the government and the partyless Panchayat system. Virtually every district in Nepal was involved, but before the event had really got under way, more than 900 party members were arrested; official sources confirmed that the police were holding several hundred persons for 'undesirable activities', including allegedly 'misleading the masses over price rises and shortages'.[33]

Throughout the rest of the year, the Nepali Congress and the Communist party organised systematically for a major campaign against the government. The political system appeared, to an ever-widening section of the population, to imprison dynamic forces for change, and the pressure to transform it was becoming unbearable.

Entering the 1990s

In January 1990, plans were announced at the Nepali Congress Conference in Kathmandu for the launch of a Movement for the Restoration of Multi-Party Democracy, to take place in February. The United Left Front (ULF) joined with the Nepali Congress in organising the campaign, supported by five other, more radical, communist party factions which had organised themselves as the United National People's Front but refrained from joining the coalition officially.

The movement's original objectives were simply to end the ban on political parties and restore multiparty democracy. But it unleashed a mass movement of unprecedented size and scope, in which years of dissent and unrest were finally and comprehensively expressed. The 'programme' became broader and more radical, with some elements even calling for the ending of the monarchy and the establishment of a democratic republic. Women were involved as well as men, especially in the Kathmandu valley towns and in the eastern Tarai, where women factory workers were particularly active.[34] Clashes with the security forces led to numerous arrests, with the number of injured and dead steadily mounting. Protests from professional groups, intellectuals and human-rights activists, as well as expressions of concern from foreign representatives in Nepal regarding state violence in response to the demonstrations, increased the pressure on the government.

[32] *The Guardian*, 20 May, 1989.
[33] *Far Eastern Economic Review*, 21 September, 1989.
[34] Mikesell, 1991: 17.

On 6 April 1990, King Birendra's announcement (see Hoftun in this volume) failed to prevent a massive demonstration (involving an estimated 200,000 people) in Kathmandu for an end to the ban on political parties, which resulted in serious clashes with the security forces. This huge demonstration was started by a rally of some 10,000 women in Patan. Some 50 people were killed and many more injured in these incidents. After a curfew had been imposed, torchlight demonstrations were held along the roadsides by villagers on the outskirts of the capital.

Within a few days, the ban on political parties was officially lifted, the word 'partyless' was suspended from the constitution and the existing institutions of government (including the National Assembly) dissolved. Just over a week later an interim coalition government was formed. Political reforms had undoubtedly been initiated as a direct result of the mass movement, but many in the movement felt that the leadership had been too ready to compromise and to allow the conservative forces defending the existing regime to regain the initiative. Arguably, they had been surprised by the speed with which the palace and the government appeared to concede the specific objective of the movement—the lifting of the ban on political parties; on the other hand, it is also almost certainly the case that the opposition leadership, even that of the various communist party groups of the ULF, had itself become somewhat concerned at the very radical demands of some tendencies within the mass movement. As one commentator on the left has argued, 'the small concession of suspension of the word 'partyless' from the constitution, won by the People's Movement, was enough to allow the leaders to assert that democracy had been won. According to this claim, their next move was to demobilise the masses and domesticate the movement. After nearly two months of struggle and sacrifice, the people were asked not to make demands, to be patient, and to let their leaders take care of things in order to 'preserve' democracy, as if the most minimal concession by the palace had created democracy. Yet the movement had only started to become successful once it had gained its own spontaneity and the initiative had passed out of the hands of the leaders'.[35]

This analysis is to some extent supported by the evident preparedness of the 'recognised' political opposition, including the leadership of the ULF, to withdraw their demand for an interim constitution and accept participation in an interim government operating under the old regime. Various articles of the constitution relating to the partyless Panchayat system were suspended, but the constitution remained in force, leaving the king with his powers only minimally diminished. At the same time, the organisational structures which had developed over

[35] Ibid.: 7.

the previous months were by no means entirely dismantled and the enormous growth in political consciousness associated with the mass mobilisation of the democracy movement during early 1990 was by no means entirely dissipated. The interim government and its actions would be carefully monitored, and judged.

During its year in office, the interim government faced increasing economic difficulties.[36] Nepal remained one of the world's poorest countries (115th in per capita GNP out of 120 countries, according to the 1989 World Development Report), with an extremely low rate of economic growth, and the heaviest reliance on agriculture of any country in the world (57 per cent of GDP and 93 per cent of the labour force). The attempts by the World Bank and other donor agencies to promote a structural adjustment programme during the second half of the 1980s and the dispute with India and trade embargo during 1989 had increased the strains within the economy. The economic impact of the trade dispute has been estimated as a reduction by 1.5 per cent of GDP. At the same time inflation, already running at over 10 per cent a year during the 1980s, soared: the prime minister had promised that prices would come down by 35 per cent; but they rose by nearly 30 per cent during 1990.

The government was also plagued by scandals; one of the major criticisms of the old system was its susceptibility to corruption, but several ministers in the interim government were charged during the year with corrupt practices and illegal activities. The legitimacy of the administration was progressively undermined as evidence of inefficiency and malpractice mounted. Divisions within the cabinet, always considerable, became sharper, and there was growing concern among many who had been active in the democracy movement that their demands for radical reform were being ignored in favour of a compromise with the palace and other conservative forces. The United Left Front had initially insisted on an interim constitution and the formation of a constitutional assembly; in the event, however, the constitution was drawn up by a drafting committee nominated by the ministers of the interim government, casting some doubt on its commitment to radical reform. Meanwhile, the political scene grew increasingly confused as political parties proliferated and reports of clashes between the supporters of different parties also grew in number. At the grass roots, as in the government, the strength of the democracy movement seemed in danger of being dissipated.

In September, after many delays, a draft constitution was completed; in November, after some hesitation, it was accepted by the king.

---

[36] For a pungent assessment of these problems, see the 'White Paper on the State of the Economy in Nepal' produced by finance minister Pandey in May 1990—cf. Shaha 1990: 93-126.

National elections were held in May 1991, and were contested by 1,126 candidates representing 20 political parties, and 219 independents. The turn-out was generally high, suggesting a heightened political consciousness and widespread commitment to the new democratic process throughout the country. The Nepali Congress gained an overall majority (with 110 seats), while the United Marxist-Leninist Communist Party (formed when the two major factions of the Nepal Communist Party agreed to merge in January 1991) was returned as the second largest group in the new National Assembly (with 69 seats). Supporters of the old 'partyless Panchayat' system, who had formed their own party (the National Democratic Party) to fight the elections, were generally unsuccessful—their party gained only four seats in all.

The failure of the Congress to gain a more substantial victory (and particularly the personal defeat of the prime minister at the hands of the general secretary of the Communist party) was significant, as was the success of the communists in Kathmandu and other major towns: in the capital they won four out of five seats. The communists offered to work with the Congress Party to form a coalition government, but by the end of May the Nepali Congress general secretary, G. P. Koirala, was leading a new Nepali Congress government and the president of the Nepal Communist Party (United Marxist-Leninist) was official leader of the opposition. It is likely that, over the next few years, the relative strength of the communists in the urban areas and the Tarai will prove increasingly important in influencing government economic and social policy.

The Congress government committed itself publicly to establishing 'a new order' in Nepal, in which democracy and development were to go hand in hand. In a speech delivered at the cabinet's swearing-in ceremony, the prime minister declared that Nepal was entering 'a new era of full-fledged democracy', but he also warned of 'a very grave and deteriorating economic condition'.

In October 1991 the National Planning Commission of HMG Nepal produced an important document providing the guidelines for the next Five Year Plan (1992-1997), in which it was argued that 'development is not just a mechanistic function of capital and technology. It is a social and political process of mobilising and organising people to the desired goals. This will be possible only when people themselves are associated in the decision-making process...and, more importantly, in benefit-sharing (with regard to development activities)'.[37]

Development is identified here as a social and political as much as an economic process; and democracy is seen both as a precondition for successful economic development and as an aspect of social development. Democracy is equated with the ability of different sections of

[37] HMG Nepal, 1991: 8.

Nepalese society to express their different interests and, for the first time in thirty years, to debate openly, and from different perspectives, the economic, social and political direction of Nepal's future: in this way, democracy becomes an integral part of the strategy for development. This is clearly the view of the majority of those currently advising the government on economic affairs. It also appears to be, broadly, the view of the government itself.

But how far can the rhetoric be translated into reality? Is the Nepalese state capable of radical reform and transformation to become an effective agency for change, and what will be its role in promoting development? Also, how far will ordinary individuals and local communities be able to take the initiative and, through their own activities and through democratically elected local, district and national government, be able themselves to promote economic and social development? What, realistically, are the prospects for development, or democracy, in Nepal during the 1990s, and beyond?

Strategies for Development
History teaches us that the transformation of societies is a complex process—what Lenin referred to as 'combined and uneven development'. Theories of development, however, although essentially empirical generalisations derived from the comparative analysis of specific historical experiences, tend to construct models that are simplified and often crudely distorted versions of historical experience. Their capacity to provide detailed guides to the empirical analysis of particular cases is therefore strictly limited; they may allow us to explain the past, but they rarely enable us to foresee the future; still less do they provide blueprints for intervention.

In the case of Nepal, however, as indeed in many other cases in the 'developing world', relatively simplistic models based on specific theories of development have often determined the character of interventions by government and other agencies, while even the more detailed academic studies of Nepalese economy and society have frequently been cast explicitly within a framework provided by a specific development theory.[38]

Theories of economic and political development all too rarely incorporate crises or sudden events in their image of how change takes place. But the use of the term 'crisis' implies a dramatic situation, often an entirely new concatenation of circumstances, which marks a turning point. It can be argued that the events of early 1990, although evidently rooted in the past (as I have tried to demonstrate) constituted a crisis, and a turning point. In such a situation there are inevitably few guidelines for those who would foresee the future and predict the likely development of events. What follows is an attempt, based on the avail-

[38] Recent examples include Blaikie *et al*, 1980; Bista 1991.

able evidence, to identify the broad direction of what may be to come.

Government Strategy

The elected government of Nepal is now accountable to parliament, and it is to be anticipated that as a result there will be broader participation than hitherto in the process of policy formulation and also a closer scrutiny and evaluation of proposed policies and overall strategy. So far, the government has had little time to demonstrate its intentions, but there are important indications already of a powerful commitment to a distinctive strategy for development in which a greater role will be accorded to the 'grassroots'.

In May 1990 the finance minister, D.R. Pandey, had already signalled the need for a change of approach. In his 'White Paper on the State of the Economy in Nepal' he observed, 'Nepal has over the past years conducted its structural adjustment programme with foreign assistance. The programme's chief objectives of consolidating the economy remain relevant even after political changes. However, the government will hold a somewhat different perspective on the basic principles of the current structural adjustment programmes. Efforts need to be made to arrange for assistance from the donor community for programmes designed to raise the living standards of the common people by extending the benefits of development to them, as social justice demands, by incorporating the sectoral programmes into the larger economic policy and by keeping the rate of development high. The new government will have to concentrate on improving programmes in the agricultural, irrigation and forestry sectors, with a view to alleviating poverty'.[39]

Certainly, the seriousness of Nepal's environmental, economic and social crisis is recognised by the Congress government. It is now formally recognised, by international and other foreign development agencies, that it is publicly committed to give a high priority to rural development (and within that, to poverty alleviation and resource management), to decentralise the state apparatus, to give greater power to local (district) elected government and to promote popular participation at the grass roots.[40] In June 1991, the UNDP summarised, from a number of sources, a statement of the general goals, strategies and priorities of the new government of Nepal (UNDP 1991):

programmes to alleviate poverty to receive the highest priority. The requirements of women, children and economically and socially disadvantaged citizens will be paramount in determining the design of Nepal's development programmes;

[39] Shaha, 1990: 122-3.
[40] cf. FAO, 1991: 3, 108.

special attention to be given to improving people's access to safe drinking water, basic education and family planning so as to improve the quality of life;

a concerted effort to be made to launch programmes that generate income among the rural poor;

the promotion of forestry and environmental protection to feature prominently in HMGN's plans, both as a matter of conserving and responsibly exploiting the environment, and as a means of providing inccme generation opportunities for the poor;

emphasis to be given to expanding the nation's production base. Productive sectors such as agriculture and industry will receive high priority in order to promote rural and urban income generation;

the five macro-economic components of the Structural Adjustment Programme: macro-economic stability, improved revenue collection and resource mobilisation, increased investment efficiency, more efficient public sector enterprises, and the promotion of the private sector will receive strong support and form important elements of Nepal's economic policy.

A new willingness to consider radical approaches to economic and social development is evident in the 'approach paper' produced by the National Planning Commission in October 1991 and designed to provide the conceptual framework for the Eighth Five Year Plan (for 1992-1997), due to be published early in 1992. And, while declarations of intent are by no means the same thing as practice tried and tested, they provide an important indication of what might become government policy over the next five years. Given the relationship between the National Planning Commission and the government, it is almost certain that the conceptual framework of the next five year plan is already broadly established by this 'approach paper'.

Crucially, according to the 'approach paper', 'the government strongly believes that the pace of development can be accelerated only with the active involvement of people in the development process.'[41] The emphasis in future will be on developing the grassroots activity required to ensure that development is sustainable at the local level as well as generally throughout the country. It will promote at the earliest opportunity a programme of effective devolution of power (and financial responsibility) which will make the district the major focus for the state's activities in development. The emergence after local elections in spring 1992 of two tiers of local government—at the village development committee level and at the level of the district committee—will provide the framework for a democratic and responsive local state capable of providing the technical and material support required for

[41] HMG, 1991: 30.

effective local development.

According to the document, the next five year plan will accord higher priority to rural development and emphasise the importance of sustainable agriculture and natural resource management in rural development. The 'approach paper' also argues that 'the economic enhancement of the villages, with increased delivery of social, economic and market services and increased access to drinking water and alternative forms of energy, is essential for their transformation into sustainable villages in the near future, which is one of the principal objectives of the Plan'.[42] Thus, active local participation and sustainable development are the two 'keys' to the government's basic economic strategy.

It is recognised that there is room for non-government initiatives for economic and social development. A task force was created under the interim government (in September 1990) with the specific objective of drawing up guidelines for the NGO sector; and one of the first initiatives of the new government in 1991 was to establish its own group to review the proposals made and to advise government accordingly. The National Planning Commission 'approach paper' states that 'the government will create the necessary policy and implementation environment...conducive for the participation of the private sector, the community and the NGOs'.[43] The active encouragement of local NGOs is already official government policy, although the definition of an NGO remains a matter of debate and there is a tendency to confuse NGOs with 'the private sector'. It is also explicitly recognised that 'a number of national and international NGOs are already playing an important developmental role in Nepal. In order to increase their effectiveness, the government will define specific areas and sectors in which NGOs could contribute more effectively'.[44]

These indications suggest a new willingness on the part of government, and of those advising the government, to consider seriously a new approach to development in which the role of 'civil society' is significantly greater and in which the state plays more of a facilitating role. Given a commitment to more open democratic politics and a system of elected local and national government, there is now a very real hope that the tide is flowing strongly towards a renewal of 'community based' local development as the foundation for national economic and social development.

It is likely that these development agencies will, broadly, adopt approaches and strategies which conform to these general priorities. For example, in 1991 the FAO produced a crucial strategy document for the

[42] Ibid.: 11.
[43] Ibid.: 8.
[44] Ibid.: 9.

programming of assistance to Nepal's agriculture, forestry and natural resources development (AFNRD), in which four major 'strategic programmes' are identified: policy analysis and planning; developing sustainable farming systems; management of natural resources and environment; and poverty alleviation and food security. In this document the major 'strategic programmes' are all clearly informed by current government policy and priorities. In 1990 the World Bank produced its key strategy document for 'relieving poverty in a resource-scarce economy', which places great emphasis on poverty alleviation, but also develops a general strategy in conformity, broadly, with the government's stated objectives, priorities and approach.

The majority of foreign NGOs are also moving towards a similar recognition of the government's priorities for development and its commitment to decentralisation and 'popular participation' through local groups and non-government organisations as a key element in the official development strategy. The Lutheran World Federation/World Service, for example, (with its overall goals of ensuring peace and justice, overcoming poverty and hunger, and protecting the endangered environment), is now committed in its 'programme strategy and medium term plan' to a strategy based on integrated rural development projects with a primary concern for improving the economic and social welfare of disadvantaged communities in backward regions of Nepal, through projects which rely crucially on active local community participation for sustainable development.[45] Other NGOs are adopting a broadly similar approach.

There has also been growing recognition of the need for foreign development agencies to coordinate their approach and activities to a greater degree and also to support the government's strategy. At least at the level of development strategy, there is evidence of a new commitment on the part of all the major institutions responsible for defining and implementing development in Nepal to work together to construct a coherent framework for sustainable development based on active popular participation. For the first time in thirty years, the tide is flowing in the right direction.

The Strategy of the International Agencies
It is important to assess the view of the major international development agencies regarding Nepal's prospects and the appropriate strategy for development, for these agencies have a major impact on what is both conceivable and what is feasible for any government in Nepal. In the late 1980s, the IMF and the World Bank have already supported certain kinds of policies in the name of 'stabilisation' and 'adjustment' designed ostensibly to improve Nepal's chances for development; but the Bank has also supported many elements of the government's Basic

[45] cf. Seddon *et al*, 1992.

Needs Programme of 1987. The role of the Bank, in particular, is likely to be of major importance in the future.

A sober assessment of the problems facing Nepal at the beginning of the 1990s has been provided by the Bank, in its recent country review (1990; 1991), which sets out some of what it identifies as the key problems. It observes that poverty in Nepal remains chronic: by the most conservative definition, between seven and eight million of Nepal's total population (around 19 million) live in absolute poverty. Most of these are poor peasants and sub-marginal farmers, although an increasing number depend on off-farm incomes derived from a variety of sources in the informal sector of the economy. For the Bank the solution, in the long run, is productivity growth coupled with population control. Meanwhile there will remain a large number of absolute poor, and it is therefore accepted as legitimate to consider a sustained programme of support to the poor, some of it production-oriented and some of it welfare-oriented.[46] For the Bank, the major task is to combine structural economic reforms with the fulfilment of basic needs.

For the Bank, the fact that the people of Nepal remain in 'a state of poverty' is basically rooted in the insufficiency of the resource base vis a vis excessive population; hence the title of the report, *Relieving Poverty in a Resource-Scarce Economy*. The limited gains made in terms of GDP growth, it notes, have been eroded by population increase; the population doubled since 1960 and is projected to double again over the next twenty-five years. Within ten years it is anticipated that the labour force will be growing at about 0.4 million persons a year—twice the average rate experienced in the 1980s. In the long run, it is argued, economic growth would have to be based on the expansion of services, energy and industry; but even under the most optimistic assumptions, the formal sector will be unable to absorb more than about 15 to 20 per cent of the labour force by 2010, and in the medium term agricultural intensification and agriculturally-led growth in the informal sector are considered to be the key preconditions for economic growth and improved incomes.

It is recognised, however, that the agricultural land base is rapidly approaching saturation, and that increased productivity would require 'a more subtle blend of agricultural interventions than has been tried to date'.[47] It is felt that the expansion of the informal sector holds out some hope, although it could only follow growth led by the other sectors, especially agriculture, and wages there remain close to a subsistence minimum.

[46] This focus on the alleviation of poverty derives not just from an analysis of the crisis facing Nepal, but from a more general reconsideration of the Bank's approach to the problems of the least developed countries—cf. its World Development Report for 1990—World Bank, 1990b.

[47] World Bank, 1991: xii.

The Bank argues that, in the rural areas in particular, 'the poor could fare better...by freeing up the political and social environment at the village level to allow more self-reliant activity; and by eliminating some of the more exploitative aspects of labour and construction contracting arrangements. Also the current tenancy system provides disincentives both to maximising output, to equitably sharing the costs of inputs, and to allowing security of tenure'.[48]

The report concludes that there is no easy poverty alleviation strategy for Nepal, although it estimates that significant gains could be made through a combination of measures—mostly involving increased labour absorption in agriculture coupled with productivity gains in low-input farming systems, informal sector growth and some redistributive measures (if tightly focused). As regards the package of policy measures recommended, these include measures with clear political implications: tenancy reform, improvements in labour contracting arrangements, decentralisation of government, administration and technical services, and encouragement of non-government organisations (both national and local). Even the Bank, with its strict focus on 'economic' issues, has evidently begun to recognise the need for a more far-reaching reconsideration of the basis for economic and social development in Nepal, and to envisage institutional changes involving a considerable devolution of power to local government and non-government organisations (including local communities). At the same time, it recognises the need for the state to play its part in development, and argues that 'the government now has an opportunity to play a more aggressive role'.[49]

The Bank's recognition that specific 'policy measures' (implying, in effect, political reforms) are required for effective economic and social development is all the more significant given the fact that the review was produced on the basis of a mission carried out in November 1989, nearly six months before the political crisis of April 1990 and a year and a half before the election of the new government in May 1991. Its support for a new approach to economic and social development under the new political conditions will be of major importance, given the weight of the donor community in influencing Nepal's own orientation towards development, and the crucial role of the Bank in the international donor community's deliberations regarding development strategy.

One major area where the government and the World Bank may differ is the issue of population growth. The Bank is emphatic that population growth is a major constraint on Nepal's economic and social development and must be a priority for state intervention. Thus, 'the most fundamental factor contributing to poverty in Nepal has been the

[48] Ibid.: 117.
[49] Ibid.: xv.

rapid increase in population.... The two most critical consequences of this population explosion are unsustainable labour force growth, and saturation of the agricultural land base.... Availability of agricultural land has declined from 0.6 Ha. per person in 1954 to 0.24 Ha per person in 1990.... As a consequence of this pressure cultivation has been expanded up hill slopes and on to poorer land on plateaus and ridges. Marginal productivity is thus falling, and the land base itself is deteriorating—as soils are depleted, and erosion accelerates with encroachment onto more fragile slopelands'.[50]

The Bank envisages a major commitment to curbing population growth through improvements in primary health care and the expansion of family planning. It criticises the 'approach paper' of the National Planning Commission for not adopting a similar position: 'one area of concern is the relatively low priority accorded the population growth issue in the paper. While it is acknowledged that this is important, the document does not give the impression that policy-makers have accepted the fact that curbing population growth is the *central* element of any effort to raise incomes'.[51]

The World Bank's preoccupation with population growth as the central issue goes back a long way; at the end of the 1970s, it had already concluded that 'Nepal's demographic situation is amongst the worst in the world and is deteriorating rapidly. Even though demographic pressures already strain the capacity of the land to provide minimally adequate supplies of food, all reasonable projections point at an inevitable and steadily worsening situation through the turn of the century and beyond'.[52] Certainly, the government of Nepal was also convinced in the 1970s that population growth was the key problem. In September 1972, the king argued that 'in the context of economic development, if we fail to maintain some equilibrium between population growth and production, especially in the agricultural sector, it is certain that all our efforts at development will be nullified. At the same time, it will also bring about ever deepening problems of poverty, destitution, denudation of forests, forced occupation of forest land, soil erosion, in brief the problems of environmental pollution. It is in the light of such a realisation that we should make a consistent effort, while we still have the time, to expand the family planning programme both in the city and in the villages'.[53] And at the end of the decade, in a document outlining the fundamentals of the Sixth Plan (for 1981-86), the National Planning Commission emphasised the crucial importance of family planning and birth control: 'in the last analysis, all our efforts at

[50] World Bank, 1990: 23-4.
[51] World Bank, 1991: 93-4.
[52] World Bank, 1979: 35.
[53] Cited in Seddon, 1987: 260.

multiplying job opportunities and increasing income levels will be simply wasted, no matter how well conceived the programmes of that nature are and how brilliantly executed, if effective steps are not taken to rein in the runaway population growth.

Failure in this direction will create an economic and social situation fearful to contemplate. It follows, therefore, that the population control programme should be pursued with greater intensity and wider effect than now'.[54]

However, as I have argued at length elsewhere, the fact that 'population growth is outstripping production' can be turned the other way around—it is clear in Nepal that 'production is failing to meet the needs of the Nepalese population as it grows'.[55] To draw the conclusion that population growth is largely responsible for all the other problems of development in Nepal is a gross oversimplification and ignores the crucial fact that demographic change, like material deprivation or poverty, is a social product, conditioned and determined in the last analysis by the economic and social structures of the state in question. The fact that population growth is 'outstripping' production does not mean that population growth should necessarily be seen as the crucial variable, or that the priority for state action should be to develop population control programmes. While it is undoubtedly important that primary health care programmes and programmes aimed at improving adult education and functional literacy (such as those promoting non-formal education classes for women, which have proved so successful in many areas) should include a component relating to family planning, in addition to others, and that efforts should be made to improve access to contraception, it is extremely debatable whether this should be identified as the priority.

Arguably the whole question of increasing production and employ-ment and of raising incomes through sustainable development is far more crucial. There is abundant evidence from other developing coun-tries to suggest that improved security of livelihood and income together with reduced morbidity and mortality (particularly infant mortality) play a far more strategic role in reducing the birth rate and the average size of families in the long run than state managed programmes for population control. It is to be hoped that the new government of Nepal and others concerned with the determinants of economic and social development will not simply take for granted the view of the World Bank and other agencies regarding the priority of controlling population growth.

Although the Bank focuses on the relationship between poverty and population growth in its analysis, it also refers to the 'resource-scarce

---

[54] Cited in ibid.
[55] Ibid.: passim.

economy' of Nepal, and considers measures for the improvement of agriculture and physical resource management. As regards agriculture, it is argued that in the Tarai the priority is the development of irrigated agriculture through the spread of small-scale irrigation (especially shallow tubewells) in the hills; while small-scale irrigation is also important, the emphasis is on reforestation and community forestry projects which will improve the availability of fodder and hence of organic fertiliser, and on the development of low input systems with stable yields. Thus, 'the recent shift to a farming systems research and extension system should be strongly supported. To benefit the poor in particular, the new research outreach programme should (a) place the focus of research on low input systems with stable yields, (b) promote more work on livestock, which are an integral part of poor farmers' farming systems, (c) encourage more research on horticulture as part of the overall cropping system, particularly in accessible areas where production of fruits and vegetables could provide considerable income'. It is also stressed that 'in order to produce information useful to poor farmers, extension and research staff will have to be trained to communicate with poor farmers in general, and particularly with female and low caste farmers'.[56]

If the Bank is in favour of a change in the approach to agricultural development, it is more wary about the issue of control over resources. One way of increasing productivity might well be to improve security of tenure and access to land for farming; this would imply a land reform, with an emphasis on redistribution in the Tarai and on greater collective control over 'common resources' in the hill areas. The Bank certainly considers reforms to the tenure system but argues that 'a redistributive land reform does not seem to be currently a prospect in Nepal'[57] and suggests a number of politically feasible, 'second best' measures, focused mainly on the Tarai. These include completion and termination of the 1964 reform; legalisation of alternative tenancy arrangements (other than full life-time security of tenure); and improvement of procedures for registering and recording land transactions. But land reform is clearly a subject of continuing debate. The government's 1987 Basic Needs Programme included a reference to the need for agrarian reforms, and the White Paper on land tenure produced in 1987-88, although it received little publicity, did discuss current land tenure problems in detail. With a new democratically-elected government in power, land reform may once again be a politically realistic proposition; it is to be hoped so.

The discussion of land reform by the Bank focuses on access to land for agricultural purposes. What the Bank has little to say about is legis-

[56] World Bank, 1990: 63.
[57] World Bank, 1990a: 36.

lation relating to the transfer of common property resources to local collectivities which make use of them. The subject of physical resource management is one that now attracts increasing attention in Nepal. On the issue of physical resource management the Bank argues especially (apart from the need to curb population growth) for greater user management of resources (especially forests).

The emphasis in government documents on greater 'grassroots' involvement in development activities for the creation of sustainable agriculture and physical resource management is echoed in (or echoes) the World Bank's recognition of the strategic importance of involving 'users' groups' (local communities) in the management of their own resources. Slowly, through the 1970s and 1980s, 'the experience in forest management has led to the realisation that for the preservation and addition to local resources, the responsibility must fall on the people themselves'.[58] The significance of this gradual recognition by both government and external agencies of the intimate relationship between 'self-management' at the 'grassroots' and effective sustainable development cannot be overestimated.

The Bank does not explicitly consider in detail the political and administrative framework for economic and social development, but clearly shows itself open to the idea of new initiatives in this regard. Users' groups, self-management, community forestry, are all regarded positively; more explicitly, it is argued that two important reforms now taking place have, potentially, very considerable implications for Nepal's future development: 'the first is greater self-reliance, participation in development initiatives, and organisation among rural people. The second is decentralisation of administrative responsibilities to district and local level, along with the establishment of local representative councils (pursuant to the Decentralisation Act of 1982)'.[59] The Bank is sceptical, however, of the experience to date of experiments in popular participation and decentralisation. It points out that initiatives to encourage local community mobilisation both for self help and to articulate collective demands have so far been limited so that they do not challenge the existing political and economic order—the distribution of real political power—although it recognises that 'the transfer of political power to local levels can potentially increase responsiveness'.[60] Under the new political regime, however, there is at least the potential for a significant redistribution of power. Whether that takes place will depend to some extent on the commitment of political parties and movements supposedly representing the interests of disadvantaged workers and peasants, who have hitherto failed to achieve

[58] Lohani, 1978: 146.
[59] World Bank, 1991: 108.
[60] Ibid.: 109.

effective representation in the rural areas, and their capacity to mobilise their supporters to ensure that local government is responsive to their needs. It will also depend on continuing commitment at the national level to policies which promote self-reliance and genuine broad-based local economic and social development.

Finally, the World Bank envisages (as indeed does the government) a greater role for non-government organisations of all kinds in development activities at the 'grassroots'. It suggests that 'the principal benefit of NGOs may be that they can operate free of the political and social constraints which limit the capacity of government programs to help the poor', but at the same time it recognises that 'caution should be exercised, because to the extent that existing economic interests are threatened by organising the poor, it seems unlikely that NGOs will be allowed to operate freely'.[61] Here again, what will eventually determine the capacity of NGOs to work with local communities to promote collective action for sustainable development is the changing balance of power within those communities and the ability of hitherto disadvantaged social groups to express and realise their needs and interests. On the other hand, because NGOs promote collective action for sustainable development, and support the actions of disadvantaged groups to improve their own position within local communities, the NGOs themselves help to change the balance of power in favour of such groups.

Another major multilateral agency, whose influence on the strategy for economic and social development adopted by the government over the next five years is likely to be considerable, is the United Nations Food and Agriculture Organisation (FAO). In November 1991 the FAO undertook a major review of Nepal's agriculture, forestry and natural resource development (AFNRD) possibilities and proposed an overall strategy for future development in these crucial areas. The significance of this review and strategy statement is potentially great, for a number of reasons: '(f)irst, the timing of the review immediately before the formulation of the Eighth National Development Plan allows (the government of Nepal) to consider it as a contribution to the overall strategic framework for planning AFNRD. Secondly, recent changes in the political direction of Nepal have led to a redefinition of development goals and modalities. These have coincided with a significant reappraisal of approaches to aid and technical assistance by UN International Agencies, especially UNDP, the major source of funds for FAO's operations in Nepal. Finally, there has been a growing concern within FAO to reformulate its assistance programme in a more integrated and comprehensive manner which would emphasise its global concern for sus-

[61] Ibid.

tainable agriculture and rural development (SARD)'.[62]

The FAO review recognises at the outset certain major concerns of the Nepalese government, 'arising from its strong commitment to democratic values'. Those that are of particular relevance to the Review are the high priority given to rural development, the accepted need for decentralisation and people's participation, and the basic goals of poverty alleviation and resource conservation'.[63] It concludes that any strategic programme 'should be based on the democratic priorities of decentralisation and participation'.[64]

The proposed strategy is formulated in terms of four Strategic Programmes: policy analysis and planning; developing sustainable farming systems; management of natural resources and environment; poverty alleviation and food security. The strategy is designed 'to achieve the overall goals of poverty alleviation, the sustained development of the production potential and the conservation of the natural resource base within a participatory and decentralised control system.... The main implementation principles...which are needed to overcome some of the conditions of administrative malaise inherited from the previous political system (are): participation, decentralisation, multidisciplinary team approach, quality of delivery, incentives, sustainability'.[65] As regards the first of these, which relates most directly to the democratic involvement of the local population in development activities, the review notes that the idea of 'popular participation' has been a stated concern of Nepal's development planning and administration for a number of years but that this has had little impact in practice. It accepts, however, that 'the current government has a much clearer commitment to democracy (government for and by the people) which provides a much greater impetus to articulating participation into real and practical actions. Participation is not just a side condition as a political value attached to AFNRD. It is a mode or vehicle for development intervention'.[66]

If the government and the major development agencies alike identify a new approach to development in Nepal, in which the active participation of individuals and communities at the grassroots has a crucial role to play in promoting, through their self-help and collective expression of their interests and needs, the broad-based economic and social development of Nepal—and if they see democratic participation as a mode of development intervention, as a means to development—clearly a great deal depends on the extent to which such a broad-based democratic participation can be built and sustained in the years to come. What are the

[62] FAO, 1991: 87.
[63] Ibid.: 3.
[64] Ibid.: 87.
[65] Ibid.: 97.
[66] Ibid.

prospects for the maintenance and extension of popular democracy at the grassroots and at all levels?

Prospects for Popular Democracy

Most theories of development suggest, not that popular democracy is a prerequisite for effective economic and social development, as the new conventional wisdom suggests for Nepal, but rather that it is economic and social development that provides the basis for effective democracy; that without development, democracy is not possible. Some even argue that no 'real' democracy is possible in a given society without that society having reached certain levels of economic development: no liberal (or bourgeois) democracy without capitalism; no proletarian (or socialist) democracy without socialism. Prior to that, some form of 'guidance' from above is required.

In many developing countries, Nepal included, radical as well as conservative political theorists have joined with radical as well as conservative politicians in arguing that, at an 'early stage' of political and social development, a multi-party system in particular promotes division when what is required is 'unity'; and that only when a certain economic and social development has taken place, and only when the class structure of a more developed economy and society has emerged, can a more open, pluralist system produce general benefits. Meanwhile, a one-party or no-party state provides the only effective political framework for economic and social development.

Although the history of the political movement for democracy in Nepal goes back to the 1920s at least, and the various democratic parties played a crucial political role in developing a systematic opposition to the Rana regime which was finally overthrown in 1951, it was only in the late 1950s that democratic party politics became a real possibility.

In 1957, when King Mahendra proclaimed that general elections would be held on 18 February 1959, he did so in response to popular pressure and in order to provide a stable democratic government for Nepal. He stated clearly in 1958 that he blamed political instability for the lack of development in the country during the seven years that followed the overthrow of the Ranas and the reinstatement of the monarchy, and he proposed a new political framework. His 1958 proclamation proposed the early establishment of a commission to draw up a constitution providing for a bicameral legislature, a nominated advisory assembly and a council of ministers, including representatives of political parties as well as independent nominees. The first general elections were held in spring 1959 under a new constitution which established a parliamentary system of government, and the Nepali Congress—which stood for democratic socialism—won 73 out of the 109 seats in the lower house. The first—socialist—government was formed in May 1959

However, when King Mahendra exercised his emergency powers less than two years later (in December 1960) to dissolve both houses of parliament, ban all political parties and imprison the prime minister and other members of the government, he claimed that he was obliged to do so in order to preserve the country's unity, integrity and sovereignty. Two years later he introduced what he claimed was a 'more suitable' and 'authentic' political regime, that of the partyless Panchayat system. He claimed that the political parties and multipartyism had proved disruptive and prone to factionalism, and indicated his belief that a multiparty system would not provide the basis for national integration and development.

Throughout the next thirty years, under the Panchayat system, political parties continued to be active, despite their unofficial status. While many of the smaller parties remained essentially groupings around particular prominent leaders, several—notably the Nepali Congress and the major factions of the Communist Party—established themselves as mass parties with a substantial popular following. Their support remained heavily concentrated in the urban areas and in the densely populated and politically volatile Tarai; in the hills and the mountain areas, the mass of the population remained more conservative, preferring either to remain uninvolved in politics or to support the existing political regime. This tendency for there to be a distinction between hills and Tarai, between rural and urban, and between less developed and more developed areas and regions within Nepal in terms both of political involvement and political orientation has significantly affected the structure and dynamic of politics in Nepal; it has also coloured many studies of Nepalese politics and the potential for progressive change.

In earlier analyses, I (together with colleagues) tended to be pessimistic about the prospects for political transformation in Nepal, largely because of our focus on the rural areas and our conception of Nepal as a society in which precapitalist relations of production predominated (as a result of its structural underdevelopment). In *Nepal in Crisis* we argued, on the basis of fieldwork during 1974-75 in the rural areas of west central Nepal supplemented by a reading of the relevant available literature, that 'the very nature of production in Nepal and of the social relations associated with the predominant forms that production takes inhibits the development of organised political movements capable of articulating mass demands'.[67] We explained that we could see 'no reason to believe that the peasantry of Nepal will discover a collective political expression of its needs which reaches beyond mere populist rhetoric in time to save millions of people from

[67] Blaikie *et al*, 1980: 45.

impoverishment, malnutrition, fruitless migration and early death'.[68] Our consideration of the dynamics of change in the urban areas tended to see 'growth and stagnation' rather than the basis for economic, social and political transformation. The general thrust of the analysis was what might be termed 'radical pessimism'.

In subsequent work, however, we emphasised that 'since our original fieldwork we have been increasingly concerned to examine not only what have been, are and will in the future be the forces operating to generate and maintain the process of underdevelopment, but also 'what is to be done', and by whom, to undermine or reverse this process. It is essential to recognise that the lower classes, like other classes in Nepalese society, are not simply passive...they have a crucial part to play in making their own history and that of Nepal, and it may already be possible to identify the directions and forms which their action will take'.[69]

This led to a greater focus on 'the struggle for basic needs in Nepal'[70] and to a consideration, based on fieldwork during 1978 in west central Nepal, of the various forms taken by the struggle by the exploited and oppressed classes of Nepal, both in the rural and in the urban areas. While we were able to reveal the extent to which submarginal peasants and landless labourers struggled to express their needs and defend their interests in the context of exploitation and oppression throughout the rural areas, and were thus active agents in their own history, our analysis tended to see the major impetus for change deriving from the struggle of the various disadvantaged social classes in the urban areas, for 'what class struggle there is in Nepal is largely concentrated in the Tarai and in the towns. In the Tarai, where over ninety per cent of industrial production is located, the industrial workforce is concentrated under capitalist relations of production, and the workers, although forbidden to join trade unions, have managed a greater degree of organisation'.[71]

In an analysis of the urban labour force, it was argued that 'for signs of more systematic efforts to defend and promote the interests of working people we must look to the upper stratum of lower paid workers...(and) to those so ambiguously termed 'the self-employed'.[72] It was argued that, in Nepal as in many underdeveloped countries, 'such organisations as exist...ostensibly for the advancement of the interests of working people tend to be dominated by those in relatively secure and better paid jobs, whose class position is, in certain important respects, different from that of the mass of the working population.

---

[68] Ibid.: 284.
[69] Seddon *et al*, 1979: 4.
[70] Blaikie *et al*, 1979.
[71] Seddon *et al*, 1979: 19.
[72] Seddon, 1979: 163.

This is not surprising, given their comparatively stronger economic and political situation, their greater freedom of action and lesser pre-occupation with the daily problems of subsistence and security. Some of the so-called self-employed share these characteristics and have, in addition, a degree of economic independence which permits certain freedoms'.[73] The study identified an upper stratum of skilled and qualified white collar workers able to exert some pressure to improve conditions, and concluded that, 'whether in the public or the private sector it is this latter section of the urban labour force that appears the most vocal and the best organised; also the most explicitly dissatisfied with their immediate condition. We would suggest that it is from this quarter, and from among the small businessmen that is likely to develop one important base for political opposition to the status quo'.[74]

The essay concluded with the following comment: 'We have not here examined in any detail, for lack of adequate data, the characteristics of the higher level bureaucrats and state employees, university teachers and 'professionals' in private enterprise; but it is highly probable that, despite their relatively privileged position, they too will, in the short and even medium term, apply increasing pressure on the government and aristocratic ruling class to adopt more radical economic and political measures, if only to prevent the collapse of the Nepalese economy and state'.[75]

In the decade after these studies were undertaken, the growing pressure for economic and political reform became more evident. The capacity of the existing regime to promote effective economic and social development was increasingly seen as inadequate. By the mid-1980s some external agencies, such as the World Bank, were pushing for 'structural adjustment' and economic liberalisation, while other agencies combined with internal 'progressive' forces to exert considerable pressure for the retention of a commitment to 'basic needs'. In their different ways they were responding to the deepening economic crisis and the 'failure' to establish a more dynamic framework for development in Nepal. The major force for political change was the organised political movements which drew their support mainly from the urban working class and the middle classes, but which in the Tarai also appear to have gained support among workers in the informal sector and among small businessmen.

Growing optimism on my own part about the potential for collective action in the urban areas under the auspices of the major democratic movements (the social democrats and socialists within the Nepali Congress and the socialists and communists in other parties) was

[73] Ibid.
[74] Ibid.: 177.
[75] Ibid.

demonstrated in an essay on the nature of the working class in Nepal. Here, while it was recognised that 'it is not surprising that few studies of the political economy of Nepal have focused on the industrial working class and its economic, social and political role', it was also argued that 'even if the Nepalese industrial working class is small in size and recent in formation, its historical role is by no means insignificant'.[76] However, many analyses have underestimated the extent to which Nepalese economy and society have evolved over the past thirty years. In particular they underestimate the political significance of the demographic changes in rural areas and the associated process of urban growth. The urban population, which constituted only some 1.3 million in 1985, will have grown to 7.8 million by 2010; the population of the Tarai is expected to increase from some 7 million in 1985 to 14.2 million in 2010. While many parts of the Tarai remain isolated and remote, there is an increasing 'urbanisation' of the rural areas, with population density growing rapidly and many of those living in the countryside dependent in some way on the urban economy.

In my analysis of the political significance of the Nepalese working class, I suggested that, in any future political mobilisation of opposition to the status quo exemplified by the present political regime and the government, 'workers' support will be of critical importance, and it will be gained by providing a real hope of improving conditions at work and more generally in the economy, as well as by encouraging greater participation in democratic politics at all levels'.[77] During the second half of the 1980s, as I have tried to demonstrate, the outlawed political parties and movements were very effective in involving workers in the growing opposition movement. The potential for a broad-based alliance involving workers and peasants as well as the middle classes was demonstrably growing.

In September 1988, in response to a review of *Nepal—A State of Poverty,* I wrote, 'those who would contribute to the progressive transformation of Nepalese economy and society must recognise both the dynamic inherent in the Nepalese masses and the objective constraints they face. For this reason it is my belief that a broad popular front, in which different and even conflicting interests might be able to organise and express themselves openly, would constitute the initial and most effective basis for fundamental transformation at this time'.[78] I had in mind a broad alliance, including the Nepali Congress and Communist Party supporters, rallying around issues of democracy and human rights, as a first stage in a process of more far-reaching change leading towards a genuine popular democracy. Such an alliance would be able to

---

[76] Seddon, 1986: 22.
[77] Ibid.: 23.
[78] Seddon, 1988: 1.

mobilise a mass movement for political change, drawn from virtually all sections of Nepalese society, including landless labourers and submarginal peasants in the rural areas.

In the event, it would seem, such an alliance was indeed able to encourage a mass movement, which during the first two years of the decade was able to transform the political regime. The partyless Panchayat has been replaced by a multiparty system and a new democratically-elected government is in place. It remains the case, however, that in Nepal today politics is predominantly an urban affair, although it is true that many rural areas are now more significantly politicised than before (particularly in the Tarai); what will determine the future development of Nepal, however, will be the extent to which democratic politics develops in the rural areas and the ways in which the new conventional wisdom of popular participation by local communities in sustainable development will be translated into effective practice.

Very substantial questions and problems remain, which require resolution if the rhetoric of 'democracy and development' is to be translated into effective reality. For example, there is still considerable uncertainty regarding the detail of how powers will actually be devolved to the district level, and some concern that decentralisation will, yet again (for this is not the first attempt to promote decentralisation of administration in Nepal), fail to achieve what have always been its stated objectives: to increase local participation in planning and implementing development strategies, to mobilise local resources for development, and to increase the accountability of officials to citizens.[79] There is always the possibility that 'decentralisation's significant role for local political institutions increases the politicisation of projects and makes it difficult to reach the poorest strata'.[80] But all the evidence suggests that this time the reform will be relatively far-reaching and supported both by financial decentralisation and a new system of local government in which the voice of the 'poorest strata' should be able to make itself heard. The prospect of a relatively autonomous and powerful democratically elected local government working in close collaboration with a decentralised system of administration and technical services is indeed a positive one.

Perhaps more crucially, the concept of 'community development' itself has always been problematic; certainly the idea of the village panchayat in Nepal as a single 'community' has been immensely problematic over the past thirty years. At the end of the 1970s, one Nepalese commentator observed that 'in a village society where there are economic as well as cultural contradictions, the word 'people' becomes meaningless unless local institutions are able to resolve the prevailing

[79] Bienen *et al*, 1990: 72.
[80] Ibid.: 73.

class and cultural stratification in a politically conscious manner'.[81] As
I wrote, before the demise of the partyless Panchayat system, 'the
conception of the panchayat as village 'community' ignores economic,
social and cultural divisions, while 'Panchayat democracy' allows them
no overt political expression. The panchayat or village is now officially
regarded as an appropriate basis for various forms of community
development. But as long as economic and social differences and
inequality at the local level cannot be formally recognised and
legitimately expressed, then it is doubtful whether 'the people' will be
able to participate effectively in their own economic and social
development'.[82] What has changed?

The recognition and expression of difference and inequality is now
possible through the democratic process associated with the election of
candidates presenting clear alternative programmes and policies at the
local level. The new 'openness' should enable and indeed oblige both
constituents and candidates for local government office to face the real
problems of how best to resolve these differences and inequalities in the
interests of the community as a whole or, if not possible, in the interests of the majority. It is clear that there are strengths in this new system, particularly as far as landless and submarginal peasants, and other
disadvantaged groups who now have a chance to express their own
interests, are concerned; but there are also weaknesses. Already, it has
been argued by some of the foreign NGOs involved in grassroots rural
development activities and working closely with local communities,
that divisions between political factions all too often serve to open up
deeper divisions within local communities and make certain kinds of
collective or collaborative activities more difficult. Thus, 'Village
Development Committees, a key tool for the participation of local
people in the planning and implementation of programmes, have
become embroiled in party politics, and much energy that was
previously directed at development schemes has been redirected to
political campaigns'.[83] Furthermore, it has been suggested, 'a political
problem potentially more serious than the domination of one faction
over others is the domination of the entire system—especially at village
and ward levels—by the richest farmers'.[84]

These concerns are very real, but even where politics may be seen as
being detrimental to collective 'community' development activity in the
immediate aftermath of the momentous political changes that have
clearly permeated even the remotest of villages, it is felt that 'the long-
term prospects for development are looking brighter as a result of the

[81] Lohani, op.cit.: 146.
[82] Seddon, 1987: 272.
[83] Lutheran World Federation, 1991: 5.
[84] Bienen et al, 1990: 73.

political changes. Already there is evidence that people are more free to speak out against injustices, demand their rights and take the initiative into their own hands'.[85] The problem of exploitation and oppression within local power structures remains, of course, but at least the political framework now exists for the expression of the collective interests of socially disadvantaged groups and classes and for their direct representation in local government through democratic elections. It will now be the responsibility of those political parties presenting themselves as the champions of such disadvantaged groups to develop their activities and organisation at the grass roots.

But if politics in the form of popular democracy is to take root, in the rural areas in particular, and to meet the needs of the disadvantaged who constitute the mass of the Nepalese people, it must become less 'ideological' and more pragmatic; less driven by factional differences and more rooted in the everyday realities of economic and social practice in the Nepalese countryside and urban centres. At the same time, development activities and interventions must become more 'political', more aware, that is, of the different and often mutually opposed interests that exist within local communities and within Nepalese society more generally, and more openly prepared to confront the existence of such conflicting interests in the 'practice of development'.

There is, I would argue, no necessary relationship between 'development' and 'democracy'—and indeed both take various forms in different historical circumstances—but they are closely interdependent in many ways. In Nepal in the 1990s it appears that, for the first time in many decades, there is a chance for a positive relationship to develop in which collective expressions of need can be translated through various forms of local organisation and collective endeavour, with real support from above and outside, to produce the basis for sustainable development. The problems and the difficulties remain enormous—the economic crisis has not been resolved; but the political framework has been established, if only in a precarious and fragile form. There is also, for the first time, a surprising degree of agreement on the broad strategy for development. If indeed there is a tide in the affairs of men, it may just prove to be flowing in the right direction.

In such a situation, as I have argued elsewhere, 'where, despite the deepening crisis and the emergence of new progressive forces, the conservative vested interests within the state bureaucracy and in the wider political economy remain extremely powerful, the role of outsiders—whether academics or aid agencies—must be to provide sharper and more critical analysis of the complex and changing situation, and to provide effective support and encouragement for those most evidently committed to devise and implement measures—at all levels—that are

[85] Lutheran World Federation, op.cit.: 5.

both realistic and yet progressive in terms of their capacity to defend and promote the well-being of the rural and urban masses whose social and material deprivation remains so considerable'.[86]

Postscript

Ironically, toward the end of April 1992, the week after the first draft of this essay was completed, reports from Kathmandu suggested that 'two years after the democratic revolution paved the way for a popularly elected government in the mountain kingdom of Nepal, a wave of popular discontent is threatening to derail the country's infant democracy'.[87] Earlier in the month, street demonstrations mounted by leftwing activists had led to clashes with the police which left at least twelve people dead and many more injured. This evidently fuelled growing dissatisfaction with the Nepali Congress government. The anger at the violence with which the demonstrations were contained was underpinned by discontent over rising prices which had doubled food costs and trebled electricity rates. After the shootings, anti-government demonstrations became more frequent in Kathmandu.

Earlier in this essay, I argued that the relative strength of the communists in urban areas and in the Tarai would prove increasingly important over the next few years in influencing the government's economic and social policies. My prediction over-estimated the time that it would take for the communists, and other parties defeated in the national elections, to mount an assault on the government and try to extend their popular support. In April 1992 the various leftist groups demanded the resignation of the prime minister by the end of the month and declared their intention to call a strike on 3 May if he did not comply. However, senior Congress leaders argued that their government could survive the crisis, although they admitted that they faced a serious challenge. If, as was anticipated by some, the Nepali Congress had been beaten by the Left in the municipal elections in May, it would really have been under pressure—either to form some kind of coalition with the communists, or to increase the level of repression. In the event, the local election results vindicated the Congress leaders' confidence: the Congress took 77 per cent of seats in 56 out of 75 district councils.

For the time being, it would appear that the government has sufficient support to maintain its general course. All those who are committed to the establishment of a genuine popular democracy for development in Nepal must hope that the progressive forces in government and in opposition, and in the country at large, will be able to maintain a commitment to peaceful, democratic change and continue to exert strong pressure through legitimate channels to ensure that the long

[86] Seddon, 1987: 274.
[87] *The Guardian*, 27 April, 1992.

march towards democracy and development in Nepal proceeds in good order.

REFERENCES

ARTEP, *A Challenge to Nepal: growth and employment.* Bangkok, 1974.

Bienen, H., Kapur, D., Parks, J. and Riedinger, J., 'Decentralisation in Nepal', *World Development,* 18, 1, 61-75, (1990).

Bista, D. B., *Fatalism and Development: Nepal's Struggle for Modernisation.* Calcutta, 1991.

Blaikie, P.M., Cameron, J, Feldman, D.P., Fournier, A. and Seddon, D., *The Effects of Roads in West Central Nepal.* A report to ESCOR. Overseas Development Group, Norwich, 1976.

Blaikie, P.M., Cameron J. and Seddon D., *The Struggle for Basic Needs in Nepal.* Paris, 1979.

Blaikie P.M., Cameron J. & Seddon D., *Nepal in Crisis: growth and stagnation at the periphery.* London, 1980.

Bonk, T., *Nepal: Struggle for Democracy.* Bangkok, 1991.

FAO., *Perspective Study of Agricultural Development for Nepal,* Rome, 1974.

FAO., *Nepal Programme Review and Development Mission. Interim Draft. Volume 1. Main Report.* Kathmandu, November, 1991.

Gaige, F., *Regionalism and National Unity in Nepal.* Berkeley, 1975.

HMG, Nepal, *Basic Needs Fulfilment in Nepal by the Year 2001.* Basic Needs Task Force, National Planning Commission, unpublished paper, 1986.

HMG, Nepal, *Programme for Fulfilment of Basic Needs (1985-2000).* National Planning Commission, Kathmandu, 1984.

HMG, Nepal, *Approach to the Eighth Five Year Plan, 1992-1997.* National Planning Commission, Kathmandu, October, 1991.

Hutt, M., 'The blowing of the April wind: writers and democracy in Nepal', *Index on Censorship,* 19, 8: 5-9 (1990).

IFAD., *Final Report of the IFAD Special Programming Mission to Nepal.* Rome, 1979.

Lohani, 'Industrial policy: the problem child of history and planning in Nepal', in *Nepal in Perspective,* edited by Rana and Malla, Kathmandu, 1978.

Lutheran World Federation/World Service, *Annual Report, 1990.* Kathmandu, 1991.

Mikesell, S., 'The politics of mass demobilisation in Nepal', unpublished paper, 1991.

Pant, Y.P. & Jain, S.C., *Rural Problems and Rural Development in Nepal.* New Delhi, 1980.

Rana, P.S., *Rana Nepal: an insider's view.* Kathmandu, 1978.

Seddon, D., 'The urban labour force', in *Peasants and Workers in Nepal*, (ed.) D. Seddon with P.M. Blaikie & J. Cameron, Warminster, 1979.

Seddon, D., 'Manufacturing unease: Nepal's labour movement', *Inside Asia*, 7: 22-23 (February - March, 1986).

Seddon, D. 1986b. 'Held without Trial', *Inside Asia*, 10, November-December, 52-3.

Seddon, D., *Nepal—A State of Poverty*. New Delhi, 1987.

Seddon, D., 'A Rejoinder (to Sudhindra Sharma)', *APROSC Newsletter*, 65, September, 1988, 1, 5.

Seddon, D., Blaikie, P.M. and Cameron, J., *Peasants and Workers in Nepal*. Warminster, 1979.

Seddon, D., Hvam, S., Achariya, R. and Thapa, D., *Lutheran World Service Nepal Programme. Review Mission Report*. Norwich, 1992.

Shaha, R., *Three Decades and Two Kings (1960-1990): eclipse of Nepal's partyless monarchic rule*. Kathmandu, 1990.

Shaha, R., *Politics in Nepal, 1980-1990: referendum, stalemate and triumph of people power*. New Delhi, 1991.

Wolf, S., Whelpton, J., Gaenszle, M. & Burghart, R., 'Private newspapers, political parties and public life in Nepal', *European Bulletin of Himalayan Research*, 1, 3-15 (1991).

World Bank, *Economic Situation and Prospects of Nepal*. IDA, Washington, 1973.

World Bank, *Nepal, Development Performance and Prospects: World Bank Country Study*. South Asia Regional Office, Washington, 1979.

World Bank, *Nepal: Relieving Poverty in a Resource-Scarce Economy*. A joint World Bank/UNDP Study. Report 8635-NEP. Country Department 1, Asia Region, Washington, 1990.

World Bank, 1990b. *World Development Report*, Washington, 1990.

World Bank, *Nepal: Poverty and Incomes. A World Bank Country Study*. Washington, 1991.

NOTES ON AUTHORS

Dr. Richard Burghart is Professor of Ethnology at the University of Heidelberg. His publications on Nepal include 'The disappearance and reappearance of Janakpur' in *Kailash*, 6, 4 (1978) and 'Formation of the concept of nation state in Nepal' in *Journal of Asian Studies*, 44, 1, (1984). He died in 1994.

Lieutenant Colonel N. A. Collett was Commanding Officer, 6th Queen Elizabeth's Own Gurkha Rifles.

Mr. Martin Hoftun was studying for a Ph.D in Nepalese politics and history at Wadham College, Oxford until his tragic death in a aircrash near Kathmandu on 31 July, 1992. With Bill Raeper, who died in the same accident, Hoftun wrote *Spring Awakening: An Account of the 1990 Revolution in Nepal* (Delhi, 1992).

Dr. Michael Hutt is Lecturer in Nepali at the School of Oriental and African Studies in the University of London, and convenor of the Himalayan Research Forum there. His publications include *Himalayan Voices: an Introduction to Modern Nepali Literature* (Berkeley, 1991).

Dr. Alan Macfarlane is Professor of Anthropological Science in the University of Cambridge and a Fellow of King's College, Cambridge. His publications include *Resources and Population: a Study of the Gurungs of Nepal* (Cambridge, 1976), *The Origins of English Individualism,* (1978) and *The Culture of Capitalism* (1987).

Dr. David Seddon is Professor of Development Studies at the School of Development Studies in the University of East Anglia. His publications include *Peasants and Workers in Nepal* (Warminster 1979); *The Struggle for Basic Needs in Nepal* (Paris 1979); *Nepal - a State of Poverty* (New Delhi, 1987); and (with Piers Blaikie and James Cameron) *Nepal in Crisis - Growth and Stagnation at the Periphery* (London, 1980).

Dr. John Whelpton, now teaching in Hong Kong, has specialised in the 19th and 20th-century history of Nepal. His publications include *Jang Bahadur in Europe* (Kathmandu, 1983) and *Kings Soldiers and Priests: Nepalese Politics and the Rise of Jang Bahadur Rana, 1830-1857* (New Delhi, 1991).